DATE DUE

SEP 2 6 2002	
OCT - 6 2003	

BRODART.   Cat. No. 23-221

Shyness

Shyness is a pervasive feature of contemporary life. International surveys confirm that large numbers of people consider themselves as shy and a significant proportion suffer from acute anxiety in everyday social situations. This volume aims to provide an overview of significant contemporary psychological research into shyness, bringing together perspectives from developmental psychology, social psychology and clinical psychology.

Key topics covered include:

- the relationship between inhibition in infancy and later shyness;
- the psychophysiology of shyness and blushing;
- the impact of shyness on interpersonal relationships;
- coping strategies.

Written by some of the leading international authorities in the field, this book offers a wealth of original research material, and a survey of the most important contemporary approaches to the topic. It represents essential reading for any researcher or scholar in psychology.

W. Ray Crozier is Reader in Psychology at Cardiff University School of Social Sciences, and is a chartered psychologist and a Fellow of the British Psychological Society. His previous publications include *Individual Learners*, and the edited collections *Shyness and Embarrassment: Perspectives from Social Psychology* and *Decision-Making* (with R. Ranyard and O. Svenson).

Routledge Progress in Psychology

Shyness
Development, consolidation and change

**Edited by
W. Ray Crozier**

London and New York

First published 2000
by Routledge
11 New Fetter Lane, London EC4P 4EE

Simultaneously published in the USA and Canada
by Routledge
29 West 35th Street, New York, NY 10001

Reprinted 2001

Routledge is an imprint of the Taylor & Francis Group

Typeset in Garamond by Rosemount Typing Services, Thornhill
Printed and bound in Great Britain by TJI Digital, Padstow, Cornwall

British Library Cataloguing in Publication Data
A catalogue record for this book is available from the British Library

Library of Congress Cataloging in Publication Data
Shyness : development, consolidation, and change / edited by W. Ray Crozier.
    p. cm.
  Includes bibliographical references and index.
  1. Bashfulness. 2. Bashfulness in children. I. Crozier, W. Ray, 1945-
BF575.B3 S575 2001
155.2'32–dc21

00-062749

ISBN 0–415–22432–2

Contents

Figures

Tables

Contributors

Jens B. Asendorpf (PhD, University of Giessen, Germany) was research associate at the Max Planck Institute for Psychological Research in Munich from 1982 to 1994, and since 1994 has been full professor at the Department of Psychology, Humboldt University, Berlin. His current research focuses on the transaction between personality and social relationships in both childhood and adulthood, personality types, and the implicit assessment of self-concept through cognitive methods.

Anders G. Broberg (PhD, Göteborg University, Sweden) is currently associate professor at the Department of Psychology, Göteborg University and research psychologist at the Child and Adolescent Psychiatry Centre at the Queen Silvia Children's Hospital in Göteborg. His research interests are in developmental psychopathology with a special emphasis on stress and resilience. Temperament and attachment are two areas of interest from that perspective.

Katherine E. Buckley (MA, Wake Forest University) is a doctoral student in social psychology in Wake Forest University.

Bernardo J. Carducci (PhD, Kansas State University) is professor of psychology and director of the Shyness Research Institute at Indiana University Southeast in New Albany, Indiana. His research focuses on the manner in which shy individuals describe their experience of shyness, its consequences, and their adaptive responses to it.

W. Ray Crozier (PhD, Keele University, England) is reader in psychology in the School of Social Sciences, Cardiff University. His research interests include shyness and its relation to embarrassment, blushing, and the social psychology of creative development.

Peter Farvolden (PhD, Waterloo, C.Psych) is a clinical psychologist and research co-ordinator at the Anxiety Disorders Clinic at the Hamilton Health Sciences Corporation, McMaster Site. His research interests include the behavioural and cognitive behavioural treatment of anxiety and anxiety-related disorders, neurobiology and neuropsychology of anxiety and anxiety-related disorders, subtypes of social phobia, Obsessive-Compulsive Disorder (OCD) spectrum disorders, and hypnosis.

Lynne Henderson (PhD, Pacific Graduate School of Psychology) is a visiting scholar in the Department of Psychology, Stanford University and co-director of the Shyness Institute, Portola Valley, California. Her research interests include the treatment of shyness and self-conceptualisations in successful adaptation.

Jerome Kagan (PhD, Yale University) is the Daniel and Amy Starch professor of psychology at Harvard University. His research interests include temperamental differences in development and emotional and cognitive development in infants and young children.

Margaret Kerr (PhD, Cornell University) is currently an associate professor and co-director of the Center for Developmental Research at Örebro University (Sweden). Her research focuses on risk and protective conditions in childhood and adolescent development, and their life-course implications.

Michael E. Lamb (PhD, Yale University) is currently head of the section on social and emotional development in the Intramural Research Program at the National Institute of Child Health and Human Development in Bethesda, Maryland, where he conducts research on early social development in diverse cultural contexts, the origins and implications of individual differences in child temperament, and the elicitation and evaluation of children's testimony about alleged experiences of abuse.

Mark R. Leary (PhD, University of Florida) is professor of psychology at Wake Forest University. His research centres on social motivation and emotion, particularly in the context of people's concerns with how they are perceived and evaluated by others.

Catherine Mancini (MD, McMaster, FRCP (C)) is a psychiatrist, co-director of the Anxiety Disorders Clinic at the Hamilton Health Sciences Corporation, McMaster Site and an assistant professor in the Department of Psychiatry and Behavioural Neurosciences at McMaster University in Hamilton, Ontario, Canada. Her research interests include the treatment of anxiety disorders across the lifespan, anxiety disorders in children and adolescents, the development of social anxiety and social phobia, subtypes of social phobia, the neurobiology and neuropsychology of anxiety and anxiety-related disorders, the obsessive-compulsive disorder (OCD) spectrum disorders, and treatment resistance in anxiety and anxiety-related disorders.

Jonathan M. Oakman (PhD, Waterloo, C.Psych) is a clinical psychologist and assistant professor in the Psychology Department of the University of Waterloo. He is also affiliated to the Anxiety Disorders Clinic at the Hamilton Health Sciences Corporation, McMaster Site. His research interests include social anxiety, developmental aspects of social anxiety and social phobia, neurobiology of personality and social anxiety, and the behavioural and cognitive behavioural treatment of anxiety and anxiety related disorders.

Clare M. Pollock (PhD, University of London) is currently senior lecturer in the School of Psychology at Curtin University of Technology in Perth, Western Australia. Her research interests are human factors, safety and human-computer interaction.

Lynne D. Roberts (BSc Hons, Curtin University) is a PhD student at the School of Psychology at Curtin University of Technology in Perth, Western Australia. She is currently senior research officer with the Health Department of Western Australia. Her main research interest is the social use of computer-mediated communication.

Louis A. Schmidt (PhD, University of Maryland, College Park) is assistant professor of psychology at McMaster University. His research interests include the neural basis of socio-emotional development with a particular interest in individual differences in shyness.

Axel Schölmerich (PhD, University of Osnabrück, venia legendi, University of Mainz) is professor of developmental psychology at the Ruhr-University in Bochum, Germany. His research interests focus on mechanisms and processes of early emotional regulation and development, from both biopsychological and cultural perspectives.

Leigh M. Smith (MA, University of Western Australia) is head of the School of Psychology at Curtin University of Technology in Perth, Western Australia. His principal interests are in the areas of methodology and measurement. He is currently involved in research on individual and community responses to disasters with an emphasis on resilience and recovery.

Joan Stevenson-Hinde (PhD, Brown University; ScD (Cambridge University)) is senior research fellow in Cambridge University. Her research interests are in behavioural inhibition in young children and anxiety in families, within the framework of both temperament and attachment theory.

Susan L. Tasker (BSc, McMaster University) is a graduate student in psychology at McMaster University. Her research interests are in the areas of infant temperament and pre- and early post-natal stress on early brain development.

Michael Van Ameringen (MD, McMaster University, FRCP (C)) is a psychiatrist, co-director of the Anxiety Disorders Clinic at the Hamilton Health Sciences Corporation, McMaster Site in Hamilton and an assistant professor in the Department of Psychiatry and Behavioural Neurosciences at McMaster University in Hamilton, Ontario, Canada. His research interests include the treatment of anxiety disorders, neurobiology and neuropsychology of anxiety and anxiety-related disorders, developmental aspects of social anxiety and social phobia, subtypes in social phobia, and treatment resistance in anxiety and anxiety-related disorders, Obsessive-Compulsive Disorder (OCD) spectrum disorders, habit disorders, and anxiety disorders in children and adolescents.

Adrian Wells (PhD, Aston University, England) is reader in clinical psychology at the University of Manchester and also works as consultant clinical psychologist in Central Manchester NHS Trust. He has worked extensively in the field of cognitive theory and therapy of anxiety disorders and was a member of the Oxford Cognitive Therapy group. His current interests are cognitive theory and treatment of social anxiety and generalised anxiety disorder, and the development and application of metacognitive theory to understanding emotional disorders.

Philip G. Zimbardo (PhD, Yale University) is professor of psychology at Stanford University and co-director of the Shyness Institute, Portola Valley, California. His research interests include shyness, the effects of temporal perspective on behaviour, cognition and emotion.

Foreword

Philip G. Zimbardo and Lynne Henderson

The more we study shyness in various research paradigms, the more we teach courses on shyness, the more shy clients we treat in our Shyness Clinic, the more we discover how fascinating shyness is. Indeed, we believe that shyness represents one of the most central and intriguing dimensions of the human condition. It highlights the most vulnerable core of all people who desperately want acceptance, respect, and love from others while continually fearing rejection and negation of self. But by avoiding others or adopting the lowest of behaviour profiles, they create self-fulfilling prophecies of a hostile, critical, rejecting world. The egocentric preoccupation of shyness leads actors to see themselves as being at stage centre. They also long for attention. Yet as shyness leaves them intensely fearful of being noticed by hosts of critical reviewers, shy actors watch the play from the anonymity of the wings. The central dialectic of shyness is engagement versus detachment, of living embedded/saturated in the life-enriching web of social community as opposed to living a diluted existence that is risk-free and safe as invisible observers of the stream of life flowing by.

Shyness is fascinating because of the range of people it encompasses in its behavioural continuum. At one end, there is the naturally cautious reserve in novel situations, typical of most children and animal species, and wise angels, who do not rush into novel situations before discreetly checking them out. At the other end, shyness spirals downwards to isolation, loneliness, and a self-loathing that results in depression, stress, loneliness, and even paranoia, as evident in the recent case of the homicidal 'Unabomber', pathologically shy mathematics professor, Ted Kaczinsky.

Shyness is fascinating because of the many factors that go into its construction: shyness may be erected on a biological/genetic foundation, supported by cultural scaffolding, elaborated by social architecture in families, schools, and playgrounds, and detailed by personal experiences that add negative affective colouring and biased cognitive framing. Shyness thus implicates the total panoply of human functioning (genetic, physiological, affective, cognitive, conative, developmental, personality, and social). It can start, develop, and stop at any point in the life cycle, is nearly universal, tends to be free of gender bias, but full of ethnic specificity and cultural variability.

We find it fascinating because the traditional persona of the self-effacing, withdrawn shy introvert may yield to masks worn by socially skilled shy extroverts or even dominating social bullies whose bravado conceals the insecurities of an inner child with a bruised sense of self-esteem. The social anxiety of shyness is triggered by a host of situations and target individuals and its consequences are equally varied. While some shy people report positive aspects of being shy, the majority of shy people complain of an array of negative consequences that are undesirable and wish they could be changed.

Fascinating also because shyness, which initially seems the exception to the apparent norm of pervasive sociability, is, in fact, the normative condition in our society and most others. When we consider all those who report being currently dispositionally shy, previously so, and add in the situationally shy, what remains is at most 5–10 per cent of most populations who are the true blue, not now, not ever, non-shys. Indeed, we believe that there may be only one degree of separation between any person and someone who is or was shy.

Even more intriguing is new research indicating that shyness is on the rise in the United States, steadily increasing over the past decade to assume epidemic proportions. That research has traced the expanding universe of shyness from the standard of 40 per cent of reported shyness in the 1970s and 1980s up to 50 per cent and beyond currently. So where once shyness could be considered a form of individual pathology, now it may well be better construed as an index of societal pathology, a signal that forces are at work in our society fuelling this sudden rise in the experience of shyness. Some of those forces may come from the growing addiction to technologies that entertain and inform us at the cost of isolating us and making us socially passive, as well as from socially deficient family structures, and socially defunct neighbourhood structures that foster anomie rather than amity. These are some of the vectors in a public health model of shyness as a social disease currently spreading its web across our society.

This new book on shyness promises to be a major contribution to our understanding of the complex interplay between biology, temperament, individual differences, social and cognitive processes. And from some of these new understandings of the dynamics of shyness in children and adults come innovative ideas about treatment modalities for reducing and overcoming the negative impact that shyness has on so many among us. Editor Ray Crozier has lined up a remarkable cast of the foremost experts in this new field of 'shyness workers' who share with us their theories, hypotheses, research evidence, treatment conceptions and outcomes. The basic thematic structure of this volume is also intriguing as it moves us from considering the origins in the development of shyness to the interim process of 'consolidation' where negative spiralling of misperception, misattributions, anxiety, shame, self blame, and asocial responding often operates to exacerbate the pain of shyness. In our terms, what emerges is a silent, dark prison of shyness.

The final chapters then hold the promise of liberating these extremely shy individuals from that self-imposed prison through various therapeutic interventions. We hope these new ideas will serve as a catalyst to the next generation of shyness workers to come up with even more formidable research paradigms and thus further increase our understanding of this fascinating human drama.

This volume contributes to the growing body of literature on shyness, social anxiety, and social phobia. Although it is primarily intended for the academic community the style is accessible and it has much to offer to the lay reader. Reading it will reveal that psychologists have much to say of value about this fascinating human drama.

Acknowledgements

I am grateful to Sandra, John and Beth Crozier for their support and encouragement while I was preparing this volume. I first met several of the contributors to the volume when, on behalf of the Welsh Branch of the British Psychological Society in conjunction with the School of Education, Cardiff University, I organized the International Conference on Shyness and Self-consciousness that was held in Cardiff in July 1997. For their help with the organization of the conference I thank Jonathan Cheek, John Crozier, Libbe Kooistra, Neil Selwyn, Pat Sheehan and Barry Torrington (Chair) and members of the Welsh Branch Committee. The conference confirmed that there was exciting research into shyness being carried out from a range of perspectives and the intense international media interest showed that shyness is widely regarded as a fundamental and intriguing aspect of social experience. In 1999 I wrote to eminent psychologists working in the field inviting them to contribute to this collection of original chapters. Just about everybody I approached was in a position to accept the invitation and I am grateful to the contributors for agreeing to participate. I am grateful to Philip Zimbardo, who presented the keynote talk at the conference and who has made such a significant contribution to shyness research, for kindly agreeing to write the foreword jointly with Lynne Henderson.

1 Shyness and social relationships

Continuity and change

W. Ray Crozier

Perspectives and definitions

Perspectives on shyness

Psychological surveys find that substantial numbers of people regard themselves as shy (Zimbardo *et al.*, 1975; Carducci, this volume, Chapter 11). However, it is only recently that shyness has attracted sustained research interest. The paucity of research in the past owes much to the domination of the study of individual differences in social behaviour by theories that prioritized the personality traits of extraversion and neuroticism, neither of which captures what is commonly understood by shyness. The neglect was perhaps more apparent than real, in that many of the concerns expressed by shy people were addressed in the psychological literature but were labelled in diverse ways, for example as reticence, social skills deficits or, more recently, social phobia. Nevertheless, willingness on the part of psychologists to embrace the ordinary language term shyness, notwithstanding the ambiguities involved in this, has stimulated interest in social anxiety. Because consideration of shyness and social anxiety is to be found in different branches of psychology, much of this research is published in separate journals and consequently is scattered. One of the goals of this volume is to bring together key representatives of diverse approaches to shyness.

Adopting a wider perspective, a growth of interest in shyness was contingent on paradigm shifts in psychology or, if this is to overstate the case, at least the foregrounding of hitherto peripheral theoretical positions. One such shift was away from behaviourist explanations to a focus on cognitive processes. This moved from an emphasis on construing social difficulties in terms of deficits in skill towards recognition of the importance of the individual's self-concept and his or her preoccupations and self-appraisals. Chapter 12 in this volume, by Wells, illustrates particularly well the cognitive approach but its influence is felt throughout the book.

A second shift is from the primacy of environmental explanations characteristic of behaviourism to the employment of biological, indeed evolutionary explanations. Along with this has come a revival of interest in the concept of *temperament*. There are numerous definitions of temperament but core elements are captured by Rutter (1987: 447) when he writes of 'differences that appear early in life, show substantial stability over time, represent predictable modes of response, and possibly have fairly direct neurobiological correlates'. This concept has made a major impact on research into shyness, particularly Kagan's theory of the temperament of inhibition. Kagan (this volume, Chapter 2) provides an overview of recent developments in the theory but its influence is evident in several chapters, most notably the contributions by Schmidt and Tasker (Chapter 3), Schölmerich, Broberg, and Lamb (Chapter 4), Kerr (Chapter 5) and Stevenson-Hinde (Chapter 6).

Shyness and related concepts

It is always open to researchers to define terms as they wish provided they supply details of how the terms are operationalized. However, progress in a field is hindered if there is a proliferation of definitions or if the same term is used in different ways or different terms are used in equivalent fashion. Research into shyness has suffered in this way; shyness is not a precise term. It refers to feeling awkward or uncertain in social situations. It is associated with self-consciousness, excessive monitoring of behaviour and over-rehearsal of potential utterances. The shy person feels anxious and often (though not invariably) appears anxious to others. Shyness takes the form of hesitation in making spontaneous utterances, reluctance to express opinions and making responses to the overtures of others that reduce the likelihood of further interaction. We illustrate these tendencies with excerpts from three written responses to a questionnaire distributed to a sample of university students asking them to describe in their own words an occasion on which they felt shy.

> At my engagement party there were many friends and relatives. We [my fiancé and I] were the centre of attention which made me feel uneasy and rather self-conscious. The main moments of shyness was [sic] when we were opening presents and cutting the cake. Everyone's eyes were on us and cameras were flashing. I was feeling a bit shaky, hot and cold and my face having a permanent blush. The pressure of everyone's eyes penetrating, as if in to my body, was overpowering at specific moments. I felt that I had to impress everyone and I kept on trying to visualize how I looked, how I was presenting myself ... . It was difficult because I am shy in front of people especially when I am the centre of attention.

> I felt inadequate. I believed I was too young to say anything that would have been of the remotest interest to these people. I felt awkward as if out

of place even though we were all there together as we belonged to the same Tennis Club. When anyone did ask me something I would be so concerned about how to reply that I could feel myself heating up and turning red. I tried to find something else to do so I could break away from the group ... . I don't think it has been resolved as I still feel inferior around such a group of adults – I don't get embarrassed or feel shy with an individual from this group but once the 'gang' is assembled I feel intimidated.

I'm afraid that I'm the kind of person who is almost permanently shy! Lacking confidence, I sometimes find it an ordeal to step outside the front door every morning ... . I try not to draw attention to myself, and am apt to fall silent in trying situations (for me a 'trying situation' can be (e.g.) sitting with friends then being joined by someone I don't know – this is enough to make me withdraw). I have many times 'opted-out' of situations – although I usually regret this later, for example I frequently turn down invitations to socialize considering these an ordeal rather than a pleasure.

People typically draw upon such beliefs, somatic symptoms and behaviour in attributing shyness to themselves although research shows that there are individual differences in the weight that they attach to any of these (Pilkonis, 1977a; Cheek and Watson, 1989; Carducci, this volume, Chapter 11). The origins of these components of shyness, how they relate to each other and their implications for social interactions and interpersonal relationships are questions that currently preoccupy researchers.

Psychological approaches vary in the relative emphasis they give to these components. Thus Leary (1986: 29) argues that 'shyness' should be restricted to a particular syndrome, the concurrent experience of anxiety and inhibited behaviour (hesitation, awkwardness). According to this usage social anxiety is therefore not synonymous with shyness but is a broader concept. On the other hand, attribution theorists such as Zimbardo (see below) and trait researchers (e.g. Cheek and Krasnoperova, 1999) argue that the cognitive component is central to understanding shyness and that for some shy people at least, somatic symptoms or problems with behaviour play a minor role in their shyness.

The issue of definition is complicated by the attention paid by developmental psychologists to concepts that seem to have considerable overlap with shyness, namely *behavioural inhibition* and *social withdrawal*. Measurements of overt behaviour are important in the research associated with each of these concepts for determining, say, whether a child is inhibited or not or is withdrawn or not.

Inhibition, in the research undertaken by Kagan's group at Harvard or Stevenson-Hinde's group at Madingley, is assessed in the context of the child's behaviour in a set of specially arranged episodes. These involve encounters with unfamiliar adults and novel toys or activities. Inhibition is defined in terms of fretting, crying, making distress calls, withdrawal and absence of spontaneous interaction with the researcher across the set of episodes, and also in terms of reactions to specific episodes. Of course, the studies are interested in making predictions about children's 'real life' social behaviour outside the laboratory. Their shyness is assessed in terms of ratings provided by parents or teachers or systematic observations of behaviour in natural settings. It is not necessary to take into account how these situations look to the child. Indeed this would not be possible in studies undertaken with small infants. However, if we wish to consider the relationship between inhibition and shyness in later childhood or beyond, then the subjective dimension has to be taken into account, since shyness after the early years has a strong social-evaluative element. This is true of the nature of the situations that elicit it as well as of personal descriptions of the experience of shyness, responses to items on self-report questionnaires, and so on.

Social withdrawal can take various forms. Rubin and Asendorpf (1993) distinguish it from social isolation and from sociometric measures of *neglect* (children who receive few peer nominations, positive or negative) or *rejection* (children who receive negative nominations, e.g. are disliked). Rubin and Asendorpf regard shyness and inhibition as distinct forms of withdrawal: '*Shyness* is one form of social withdrawal that is motivated by social evaluative concerns, primarily in novel settings. Inhibition is a form of withdrawal characterized by social aloneness or withdrawal in novel settings' (Rubin and Asendorpf, 1993: 14). Yet there are problems with these definitions. People who describe themselves as shy or who obtain high scores on a trait measure of shyness might not be withdrawn in behaviour. Carducci (this volume, Chapter 11) identifies 'extraverted' and sociable coping strategies that can be adopted by shy people. Also there is ambivalence in shyness that is not captured by the notion of being withdrawn.

Withdrawn behaviour is often attributed to shyness. To pick up on the example of the convicted serial murderer mentioned in the Foreword by Zimbardo and Henderson, Kaczinsky was described by those who knew him as shy, withdrawn, and a loner (Ferguson, 1997). However, it might be that withdrawn behaviour is the extreme of the dimensions of introversion or low sociability and characterizes someone who is aloof and self-contained with solitary interests, rather than someone who is shy in the sense of lacking confidence or being anxious about interacting with people. We return below to consider evidence for the distinction between shyness and introversion.

The most consistent differences in observed behaviour between shy and less shy individuals are obtained on measures of verbal performance, specifically the timing and frequency of speech acts. In comparison with their less shy peers, shy adults take longer to produce their first utterance in conversation with an unfamiliar person, are slower to break a silence in conversation and speak for a smaller proportion of the time (Pilkonis, 1977b; Cheek and Buss, 1981; Bruch *et al.*, 1989). Similar trends emerge from studies of children. For example, Kagan (1994: 133) reported that 7-year-old children who had initially been identified as inhibited when they were 21 months old took significantly longer than non-inhibited children to produce their spontaneous comments during a test session. Although hesitation or reticence can be classified as instances of withdrawn behaviour, this usage can result in confusion. They might also be interpreted in strategic terms, for example, as a self-presentation ploy (Leary and Buckley, this volume, Chapter 9) or as the observable consequence of a 'safety behaviour (Wells, this volume, Chapter 12).

Research into the clinical condition of social phobia is also relevant to the definition of shyness. The relationship between shyness and social phobia is controversial. Beidel and Turner (1999: 205) offer a summary of similarities and differences. They claim that the constructs have a number of features in common. Both involve elevated levels of physiological reactivity. Both are characterized by negative cognitions including fear of being negatively evaluated by others, self-deprecating thoughts and self-blaming attributions for social difficulties. Self-focused attention is salient in both. Beidel and Turner argue that social phobia differs from shyness in that it has a lower prevalence in the population, it has a more chronic course, more pervasive functional impairment, and a later age of onset.

Notwithstanding this analysis, shyness and social phobia are different kinds of concepts. Someone can experience shyness or face serious difficulties in social life without this coming to the attention of anyone else. On the other hand, social phobia is a diagnostic category influenced by factors such as the availability of medical services and the ability of physicians to make the diagnosis. It is a quasi-legal term (particularly in insurance-funded medical systems or where compensation claims are concerned). Social phobia would seem to have the advantage over a 'fuzzy' concept like shyness of being based on a precise set of defining criteria, as set out, for example, in the diagnostic and statistical manuals (DSM) of the American Psychiatric Association. In practice, however, criteria change in the light of research and clinical experience. Thus, the criteria for social phobia have altered in successive editions of the DSM. Current controversies are over the distinction between generalized and specific social phobia and the relationship between social phobia and avoidant personality disorder. Social phobia has been characterized as a persistent fear of situations where people might be subject to scrutiny by others; they fear that their behaviour will lead to embarrassment or humiliation. This causes a significant amount of distress because they recognize that the fear is excessive. Avoidant personality disorder has been defined in terms of hypersensitivity to social rejection, low self-esteem, social withdrawal, and reticence. Each of these categories has some overlap with shyness as this has been construed in social psychological or personality research (see Oakman, Farvolden, Van Ameringen and Mancini, this volume, Chapter 13).

Furthermore, diagnostic systems have been criticized on a number of grounds (e.g. Pilgrim, 2000). They are empirical and are not based on theoretical principles or understanding of the psychophysiological basis of the conditions they identify. They fail to do justice to the complexity of psychological problems by imposing a distinction between those who have a condition and those who do not. The criteria can seem arbitrary, for example, in specification of the duration of a problem before the diagnosis can be made.

It is important to recognize the complexity (and richness) of the phenomena associated with the concept of shyness. Despite the ability of most people to get through each day in a complex social world, to carry out routine transactions, and form relationships that are more or less satisfactory, scientific approaches to understanding these phenomena show how complicated they are. In parallel fashion, language capabilities are acquired effortlessly by most people, but understanding how this is achieved challenges the finest minds. Faced with the complexity of the phenomena and the difficulty of reaching consensual definitions, psychologists have to be particularly careful in their use of terminology and, as scientists, they are obliged to specify their terms, procedures and measurements. These steps will permit the application of techniques such as meta-analysis that can bring order to a diversity of studies.

Shyness should, I believe, be construed in behaviour systems terms (Stevenson-Hinde and Shouldice, 1993). A systems approach emphasizes the patterning or organization of behaviours. 'In the study of behaviour as well as neuroscience the investigator must typically deal with interlocking networks of organisational processes, rather than being satisfied with simple linear conceptualisations' (Fentress, 1991: 78, cited by Stevenson-Hinde, this volume, Chapter 6).

To consider a hypothetical case, an adult might be reluctant to attend a social function because he will not know many people there and he thinks he will not know what to say to anyone. He attends because he is obliged to do so, and he remains in the background or keeps close to his partner, the one person he is confident with. If he has to be engaged in conversation, he says little. If he cannot avoid speaking, he makes brief utterances or adopts a very neutral position on the topic of conversation. Alternatively, he might 'warm up' and contribute in a lively fashion until, say, his work superior joins the group; even though the latter says nothing, her presence is enough to silence the shy person. A pattern like this is familiar to any shy person or to any researcher. It can be understood in terms of a motivational system, where one set of behaviours can be substituted for another depending on circumstances. The notion of withdrawal fails to do justice to this aspect. Nor should a shy person's ability to interact confidently with familiar others be seen as aberrant; this is also part of the system, and demonstrates that the conditions for shy reactions are not present.

Shyness seems best understood in terms of systems designed to cope with threat. Research is beginning to identify brain structures and processes underlying these systems (Kagan, Chapter 2; Schmidt and Tasker, Chapter 3; Oakman *et al.*, Chapter 13, all this volume). While acknowledging the impressive evidence gathered in these endeavours, my own position is that shyness also involves self-consciousness, which is associated with shame and embarrassment. I suggest that blushing (see Chapter 10) is an output of a 'shame system'. Gilbert and McGuire (1998) have attempted to understand shame within an evolutionary framework and Schore (1998) has studied its physiology. Future research should aim to identify the links between shyness, wariness and fearfulness on the one hand, and shyness, shame and self-consciousness on the other. A related distinction between fearful and self-conscious shyness has achieved some support (see Schmidt and Tasker, Chapter 3; Kerr, Chapter 5: Oakman *et al.*, Chapter 13). Oakman and his co-authors suggest that this distinction might have implications for treatment, with interventions based on exposure to feared situations being more effective for the fearful form, and cognitive interventions (see below) more suitable for the self-conscious form.

Issues

The chapters in this volume fall into three topic areas roughly corresponding to the elements in the subtitle of the volume, 'development, consolidation, and change'. The first group of chapters is concerned with the origins of individual differences in shyness and its development through childhood. The second group examines the influence of shyness upon social interaction processes and personal relationships. The notion of 'consolidation' is intended to refer to an important feature of shyness: shy people tend to adopt behaviours or strategies that are intended to help them cope with social situations, but which are counter-productive in the long term. This tendency extends to how they perceive social situations and their contribution to them. Shy people are quick to identify potential threats in situations, hold unrealistic expectations about them and underestimate their own social skills. The third group of chapters also relates to these issues, as they discuss how people cope with shyness and the therapeutic interventions that are available to help them overcome their social difficulties.

I now introduce each group of chapters in turn, highlighting emerging themes: the temporal stability of inhibition; the impact of shyness on longer-term relationships; cognitive approaches to interventions. Reference is made to a strength of current enquiries evident in several chapters, namely an interest in the identification of the neuroanatomical basis of individual differences in inhibition and shyness.

Origins and development of shyness

Shyness has been identified as a basic temperament (e.g. Buss and Plomin, 1984) and is similar to categories of the 'slow to warm up' child (Chess and

Thomas, 1986) and the 'inhibited' child (Caspi, 2000). Research demonstrates that these temperaments are stable over extended periods of time. However, the most substantial body of research has been into inhibition. Although this is conceived by Kagan as broader than shyness in that it represents a reaction to a range of unfamiliar situations or objects, it is similar to shyness in important respects. The child's upset at meeting a stranger, his or her hesitation in making spontaneous utterances to an adult, and a tendency to stay at the edge of activities with other children without joining in, have all been shown to be characteristic of inhibited children. This research programme (Kagan, this volume, Chapter 2, provides an overview of recent developments) has had a profound influence on studies of shyness. Its efforts to identify the biological basis of the temperament have generated considerable research. Longitudinal studies of childhood inhibition and shyness have been undertaken by research teams involving Broberg in Sweden, Lamb in the United States, and Schölmerich in Germany (see Chapter 4); Fox and Schmidt in the United States (see Schmidt and Tasker, Chapter 3); Kerr in Sweden (Chapter 5); and Stevenson-Hinde in England (Chapter 6).

The temporal stability of shyness

One longstanding issue is the temporal stability of inhibition and shyness. Interpreting evidence on the stability of temperament is not straightforward. The basic data are estimates of the shared variance between measurements taken at time 1 and at time 2.[1] There are numerous factors that can affect the proportion of shared and non-shared variance in the data, over and above the inevitable measurement error. There are factors that inflate correlations between measures, for example, bias within raters. If the same informant provides the ratings on separate occasions there is a risk that raters will be influenced by their recollection of the earlier rating or by their own intuitive 'theory' of the child's personality, with the result that they attribute more consistency than is warranted. Where different raters of the same child are involved they may confer or they may share intuitive theories about the nature of shyness; the result is that errors in ratings are correlated.

There are factors that reduce the values of correlations, for example changes in the growing child's social environment. Clearly the demands made upon an infant are different from the demands upon a pre-school child or a school child. Encounters with unfamiliar adults are relatively rare for the youngest participants in these research studies but more frequent for older children (although Asendorpf and Meier, 1993 have evidence to show that such encounters are relatively infrequent at any age). When children begin school they enter a larger and more complex social world and are in the company of large numbers of children as well as of adults. Furthermore, these adults will be evaluating them, expressing praise or criticism and comparing them with their peers. These changes are relevant to the issue of the appropriateness of measurements taken at different ages and the nature of the assessments of inhibition has to change in order to take this into account. Asendorpf (1993: 287) argues that the influence of inhibition on behaviour is strongest when people enter novel settings, therefore its effects should be most pronounced at life transition points, for example, starting university (Asendorpf, this volume, Chapter 7). This implies that the temporal stability of measurements depends on the ages at which they are taken.

There are changes within the child, perhaps in temperament itself, related to maturation of the nervous system. The relationship between behavioural and physiological measures can be complex and it takes different forms at different ages. Emotional reactivity becomes less evident as children grow older and become used to meeting unfamiliar people. Children become more likely to respond differentially to varying degrees of familiarity. They are also socialized into suppressing signs of heightened emotion and become more influenced by display rules for emotion.

There are developments in the children's thinking about the social world and about the self. Both cognitive development and changes in the environment may be associated with the distinction between early-appearing fearful shyness and later-appearing self-conscious shyness first made by Buss (1980, 1986). It remains to be seen whether these two forms of shyness characterize different children. For example, inhibited children might develop the fearful form whereas a cohort of children who were not previously inhibited might be predisposed to develop the self-conscious form. This would take place when they are about 4 to 5 years of age following necessary cognitive developments. This process would produce distinct groups of children. Alternatively, inhibited children might be predisposed to develop the self-conscious form so that the underlying temperament is expressed in different ways at different ages. One of the problems in addressing this question empirically is the dearth of measures of the two forms of shyness. However, some research suggests that this might be overcome. Asendorpf (1989) has managed to tease out the separate influences of unfamiliarity and social-evaluative concerns. Kerr (this volume, Chapter 5) has utilized ratings made at different ages to provide measures of early- and later-appearing shyness.

What is the evidence for stability? The origins of childhood shyness and fearfulness can be detected in the infant's first months. Kagan (this volume, Chapter 2) reports that inhibition in the second year and shyness at 4 years can be predicted by measurements of reactivity – a pattern of motor activity and crying – taken at 4 months of age. There is evidence of temporal stability in reactivity, although this is more compelling for low reactive children than for high reactive children. Only a minority of the high reactive children were consistently inhibited at subsequent assessments although scarcely any of them became uninhibited. High reactive children were more likely to have acquired symptoms of anxiety at 7½ years. In a separate cohort inhibition in the second year correlated with an assessment of social anxiety at 13 years.

Schölmerich, Broberg and Lamb (Chapter 4) report findings from a study of a sample of children who were assessed on a number of occasions between the ages of 3 months and 13 months. Measurements based on maternal reports, observations of mother–child interactions and physiological recordings showed increasing stability and coherence over the first year. Schölmerich *et al.* conclude that during the first year 'behavioural inhibition and shyness gradually emerge from a broader background of negative emotionality'.

Theories of inhibition make predictions about physiological measures and these have been examined for evidence of temporal stability. Kagan has argued for the involvement of the amygdala and its projections: 'infants born with a low threshold in the amygdala and its projections should behave like high reactive infants and display vigorous limb movements and distress to unfamiliar stimuli' (Chapter 2). He has derived predictions about mean heart rate and heart rate variability and other peripheral measures of sympathetic nervous system reactivity. His own research has shown that inhibited children have a higher and more stable heart rate than uninhibited children. However, this difference was not identified among the older children in his own laboratory and has not been consistently found in other laboratories (e.g. Marshall and Stevenson-Hinde, 1998). In the study reported in Chapter 4, Schölmerich *et al.* also failed to find correlations between an observational assessment of inhibition and measures of heart rate, vagal tone or levels of cortisol.

Fox and his associates (e.g. Schmidt and Tasker, this volume, Chapter 3) propose a relationship between frontal hemisphere asymmetry and negative emotionality and shyness. Research based on EEG measures has shown that reactive and inhibited children have a tendency to greater activation in the right compared to the left frontal area. Schölmerich *et al.* (Chapter 4) provide an overview of findings from EEG studies which indicate an association between negative emotionality and greater activity in the right frontal hemisphere. Schmidt and Tasker approach the question of the stability of measurements in two ways. First, they report research that examined the very short-term stability (over a period of 90 seconds) of frontal EEG activity. They formed groups of infants who varied in their asymmetry scores (right versus left frontal power) and in the variability of scores. It was found that infants who had a *stable* pattern of greater right frontal hemisphere activity were more distressed in a novel situation than were infants in the other groups. Second, they have investigated the relationship between inhibition and EEG asymmetry measures in a longitudinal study that followed children from 9 to 24 months. Those who exhibited a stable pattern were more likely to be assessed as inhibited at 24 months.

There is evidence (reviewed by Kerr, this volume, Chapter 5) that childhood shyness affects important life transitions in adulthood (e.g. timing of marriage or entry into a stable career). However, she points out that little is known in detail about the long-term effects of shyness, because the evidence has not been collected. Nor, she argues, has research taken into account different forms of shyness. Her prediction is that self-conscious shyness will have more effect on later adjustment than the early form despite existing evidence that stable inhibition is associated with a higher incidence of anxiety disorders (Hirshfeld *et al.*, 1992). Kerr bases this argument largely on the unavoidable and insidious nature of self-evaluative concerns: 'Self-conscious shyness is all about having unavoidable bad feelings about one's interactions with others and the way others think about one's self. ... People with these tendencies should, almost by definition, be dissatisfied with the quality of their interactions with others.' Her chapter presents findings that broadly support the hypothesis that shyness that first appears in adolescence is more likely to be associated with measures of the frequency and quality of interactions than shyness that appears earlier. However, Kerr points out that conclusions have to be qualified by gender differences. There were links among women between early-appearing shyness and measures of psychological well-being and the quality of relationships with partners.

Questions of the temporal stability of inhibition and of the relationships between behavioural and psychophysiological measures at different ages have attracted a considerable amount of empirical research in recent years. The picture that has emerged is not altogether straightforward, but the results are certainly promising, particularly if the difficulties inherent in undertaking this kind of research are taken into account. There are psychophysiological differences between inhibited (or shy) individuals and those who are less inhibited. Children who are shy at one age tend to be shy at another age, and there is evidence that early shyness is predictive of social difficulties in later life.

Trait shyness and personal relationships

As shy children grow older, their shyness can become a core aspect of their personality and of their self-concept; they think of themselves as 'shy'. They also cope with their shyness in ways that effectively prevent them from overcoming it. Therefore we should expect to find not only that shy people feel awkward and ill at ease in social encounters but that these unsatisfying interactions, together with a tendency to attribute their difficulties to their own shortcomings, should have longer-term effects. Testing hypotheses about the social impact of shyness demands the construction of appropriate (and psychometrically sound) measures and these have been developed within a trait conception of personality.

Self-consciousness and self-presentation

The initial impetus to psychological research into shyness in adulthood was provided by the Stanford Shyness Survey (Zimbardo et al., 1975) and this revealed very clearly that shyness was a core aspect of many people's self-concept. The approach taken in the survey was direct (and deceptively simple), asking participants whether or not they considered themselves to be shy and eliciting from them what they regarded as the characteristic thoughts and feelings associated with shyness and its consequences for their social interactions. This approach represented a social psychological perspective to shyness, relating it to self-perception and attribution processes. The research indicated inter alia that shyness was a response to specific kinds of social situations, and reported that it could be a serious personal problem for many individuals. Carducci (this volume, Chapter 11) provides an account of some recent research based on the survey.

One of its principal findings was that intense mental activity accompanied shyness. This included self-consciousness and fear of negative evaluation by others. These aspects have received further attention from two influential models of social anxiety. The first, set out by Buss (1980), regards shyness, shame, audience anxiety and embarrassment as distinctive forms of social anxiety and assigns a central role in these forms to self-attention processes. The second, elaborated by Schlenker and Leary (1982), relates anxiety to self-presentation processes. Its premise, that social anxiety is produced by a combination of the motivation to create a desired impression in others and doubts that one is able to do so, has had a significant influence on shyness research. The self-presentation approach is represented here in the chapter by Leary and Buckley (Chapter 9). Its emphasis on the individual's concerns about being evaluated by others has also been linked to processes of development, for example in Asendorpf's (1989) theory of shyness, and has influenced clinical applications, as in Leary's self-presentation model of social phobia (Leary and Kowalski, 1995). It also offers a plausible account of the approach–avoidance conflict that has been identified as central to shyness (Crozier, 1990).

The self-presentational model has been applied to blushing. This is a puzzling phenomenon at both psychological and psychophysiological levels of explanation. People tend to blush when they are embarrassed, and Buss (1980: 129) regards blushing as the 'hallmark of embarrassment'. However, people do not always blush when embarrassed and they sometimes blush when they experience shame or when they are shy (as illustrated in the recollections of shyness quoted above). Crozier (this volume, Chapter 10) reviews theories that regard the blush as an expression of embarrassment and as a reaction to being the centre of unwanted attention. Analysis of instances of blushing implies that the cause of blushing is more to do with unwanted exposure than with conspicuousness. Specifically, people blush whenever an event exposes, or threatens to expose, something about themselves that they do not wish to be disclosed. A number of embarrassing incidents that were recalled by participants in two studies followed this pattern.

Self-focused attention and self-presentation concerns are elicited by specific events or predicaments. Nevertheless, theories of social anxiety have endorsed a trait perspective, proposing that social anxiety (and shyness as a specific form of this) is a stable attribute of persons, a predisposition to react to at least certain kinds of situations with psychological discomfort. This trait can be measured and predictions about shyness can be tested. We now consider the trait approach to shyness.

Shyness as a trait

That the trait approach achieved some ascendancy in the study of personality owed much to the seminal conceptual contributions of Allport (e.g. 1937) and major programmes of empirical research undertaken by Cattell, Eysenck and others in the 1950s and 1960s. This approach to personality suffered reverses following the influential critique made by Mischel (1968). Mischel argued that the fundamental assumption of the trait approach, that there is consistency in an individual's behaviour across situations, had not been empirically supported. The trait perspective has now regained much of its ascendancy, in part due to convincing counter-arguments by theorists, in part due to the success of the 'Big Five' theory in bringing order to the field, and in part due to fresh willingness on the part of psychologists to consider biological explanations. This has revived interest in temperament and the role of genetic–environmental interactions in influencing personality.

My own professional interest in shyness arose in the context of the trait approach and I was initially concerned with two issues. The first was why, given the pervasiveness of shyness, it had not been more prominent in factor analytical personality research. The second was whether shyness was a unitary trait. I took a historical approach to addressing the first question and found that the earliest applications of factor analysis in the domain of personality had regularly identified a shyness factor. For example, Mosier (1937) isolated a factor in responses to the Thurstone Neurotic Inventory that he labelled *Self-consciousness in face to face situations*. The items 'Are you troubled with shyness?', 'Do you keep in the background on social occasions?' and 'Do you have difficulty in starting conversation with a stranger?' had high loadings on this factor but negligible loadings (smaller than 0.20) on an orthogonal factor labelled *Lack of self-confidence*. Shyness factors were identified in subsequent research, for example Comrey (1965) and Cattell (1973).

Shyness seemed to occupy an ambiguous position in Hans Eysenck's seminal theory of personality; sometimes it was assigned to introversion, sometimes to neuroticism. Eysenck offered a resolution of this by arguing for two forms of shyness. The first is introverted shyness, where the individual 'does not care for people, would rather be alone, but if need be can effectively take part in social situations' (Eysenck, 1956: 121). The second is neurotic shyness, where the individual is 'troubled about being self-conscious, experiencing feelings of loneliness, troubled with feelings of inferiority and self-conscious with superiors, worrying over humiliating experiences' (Eysenck and Eysenck, 1969: 27). Factor analysis subsequently established that shyness items and sociability items load on separate factors (Cheek and

Buss, 1981), providing support for Eysenck's claim that shyness and lack of sociability represent distinct traits.

There is debate about the extent of overlap between these traits (Bruch *et al.*, 1989) but it does seem useful to maintain the distinction. For example, Schmidt and Tasker (this volume, Chapter 3) review psychophysiological evidence that suggests that inter-individual variation in these traits is associated with differences on autonomic and cortical measures (heart rate and frontal EEG activity measures). They offer an explanation of this pattern of findings in terms of a model of individual differences in reactivity to threat that involves an interaction among environmental factors, the frontal cortex, and the HPA (hypothalamic–pituitary–adrenocortical) and serotonergic systems. This willingness of shyness researchers to combine physiological measures, observations, and self-report data is characteristic of current approaches.

Debate continues over whether shyness is a unitary trait or whether it can be divided into two, three, or more sub-types (Cheek and Krasnoperova, 1999). When different measures of shyness are administered, they turn out to be intercorrelated to a substantial degree and seem to be measuring a common factor (Briggs and Smith, 1986). On the other hand, Cheek and Krasnoperova (1999) have demonstrated that alternative forms of analysis show that it is meaningful to distinguish between forms of shyness.

Research has examined the correlates of shyness measures and has tested hypotheses about the impact of shyness. The successful application of measures such as the Cheek and Buss scale (1981) shows the value of conceptualizing shyness as a unitary trait. This research has tended to concentrate on the study of face-to-face interactions, typically between individuals who do not know each other very well. The social interactions are typically observed and participants are also asked to report on their experiences. However, it is also important to consider the broader social impact of shyness. Several of the chapters in this volume investigate the links between shyness and longer-term social relationships, whether this is the influence of these relationships on shyness or the impact of shyness upon the quality of relationships.

Shyness and personal relationships

A child's relationship with his or her primary caregivers has long been thought to exert a powerful influence on personality development. The psychoanalyst John Bowlby drew upon ethological and psychoanalytical concepts in devising attachment theory, and this theory has instigated a substantial body of empirical research. The research owes much to the effectiveness of the 'strange situation' as a measure of different categories of attachment (Ainsworth et al., 1978). Stevenson-Hinde (Chapter 6) identifies an interaction between attachment and the temperamental category of behavioural inhibition, concluding that the predicted correlation between inhibition and physiological measures is found only among those children with secure attachment status. She interprets this in terms of the ability of securely attached children to 'express their emotions in a relaxed and open manner, without the need to develop any particular strategy'.

As noted above, Kerr (Chapter 5) discusses the effect of early- and later-appearing shyness on the quality of social relationships assessed at the age of 37 years. Shyness that develops in adolescence (at least among males) is associated with having fewer friends, fewer emotional ties to others, poorer partnership relationships and less frequent and less satisfying sexual relationships. Asendorpf (Chapter 7) examines the effect of shyness upon students' adjustment to university. He presents findings from the Berlin Relationship Study, a longitudinal investigation of students' personality and social relationships throughout their career at university (the findings show that shyness influences relationships; the converse does not hold). The social relationships of the 25 per cent of the sample who were most shy were compared on a regular basis with those falling below the median in shyness scores. The shy students had more problems initiating new relationships, including romantic attachments, and they were more likely to rely upon pre-university friendships. What is distinctive about the shy students is the slow speed at which their new friendships and social networks were formed rather than the overall size of their networks. Thus it took shy students up to one year to attain the size of network reached by non-shy students in three months. In addition, shy students were more likely to suffer from chronic loneliness.

A cliché about shy adolescents in a technological age is that they withdraw from interpersonal relationships and become preoccupied with solitary pursuits such as computer games. In recent years the Internet has provided opportunities for shy people to interact at a distance, to communicate with others without the need for face-to-face meetings. Roberts, Smith and Pollock (Chapter 8) examine the influence of shyness on use of these opportunities. Shy participants in their study reported that they were less shy when they were interacting 'on-line' by means of a text-based virtual environment. There are also suggestions in the results that, for many but not all participants, this trend carried over to actual social encounters. The study implies the benefits of further research into this growing medium of communication. Overall, the findings support the conception of shyness as motivation to be sociable combined with lack of self-confidence in the ability to do so. Shy individuals do make use of the Internet to interact with others, and this shows that they are motivated to be sociable. They also report increased confidence in their ability to interact. The findings indicate the key role of self-consciousness in shyness; as one participant remarks, 'obviously on the computer one is in no danger of being ridiculed or made fun of – the others can't see you so there is no real danger of rejection'.

Leary and Buckley (Chapter 9) review evidence that shy people have less satisfactory relationships and their needs for acceptance by others are unfulfilled. The chapter discusses three factors in this. Shyness limits opportunities to develop satisfying relationships; shy people behave in ways that discourage the growth of such relationships; they convey impressions that fail to attract others' attention and interest. The problem faced by the shy is that the origins of their anxiety are to be found in their desire to be accepted and valued by others but their anxiety leads to behaviours which make it less likely that they will be accepted. The only resolution of this dilemma is to change the other 'term' in the self-presentation 'equation': to increase confidence that desired impressions can be conveyed. The final chapters in this volume consider how this might be attempted.

Coping and change

Helping people deal with their anxiety has always been a goal of clinical interventions, whether these are based on psychodynamic conceptions or cognitive–behavioural approaches. This is also true of social anxiety. A syndrome of social phobia has been recognized as a diagnostic category since its inclusion in the third edition of the Diagnostic and Statistical Manual (DSM-III) of the American Psychiatric Association published in 1980. There have been two general approaches to intervention for social phobia, pharmacological treatments and psychotherapeutic procedures.

A substantial literature has reported findings of studies of pharmacological interventions (Hood and Nutt, in press). Many of these have taken the form of controlled investigations including double-blind placebo-controlled research designs. Variations of this design include testing more than one drug treatment against a placebo condition, or comparing cognitive–behavioural therapy with a drug treatment and a placebo condition. The most common pharmaceutical interventions for social phobia have used medications that have been developed for and are established in the treatment of depression and anxiety disorders. Attention has focused on the MAOIs (Mono-Amine Oxidase Inhibitors) and the SSRIs (Selective Serotonin Reuptake Inhibitors). The most promising of these have been the SSRIs (Van Ameringen *et al.*, 1999). However, the relative success of these interventions raises several questions that are discussed by Oakman *et al.* (this volume, Chapter 13). Little is known about how these treatments are effective or why they work for some individuals but not for others. Oakman and his co-authors argue that it is important to consider shyness and generalized social phobia as 'multi-component constructs' and they explore the relationships between dominance and affiliative behaviour, neurochemical functioning and pharmacological interventions. Their approach draws upon the Interpersonal Circumplex model in an ambitious attempt to relate its dimensions of dominance versus submission and warmth versus coldness to the activity of the neurotransmitters serotonin and dopamine. They compare this model with findings from research into the administration of drugs that selectively affect neurotransmitters in both animal and human subjects. Finally, they discuss the implications of this approach for the treatment of social phobia.

The systematic investigation of the influence on social phobia of the administration of drugs that are known to have effects on neurotransmitters such as norepinephrine and serotonin is of obvious clinical benefit. It also has theoretical relevance since some theories of shyness have suggested a key role for individual differences in levels of neurotransmitters (e.g. Kagan, 1994; this volume, Chapter 2). Nevertheless there remains a huge gap in understanding between establishing the effectiveness of pharmacological interventions (particularly if they are not universally effective) and explaining how these neurotransmitters or variation in their levels affect social anxiety or behaviour. As Cooper, Bloom and Roth (1991: 4) point out, 'at the molecular level, an explanation of the action of a drug is often possible; at the cellular level, an explanation is sometimes possible; but at a behavioural level, our ignorance is abysmal'.

Psychological treatments for social phobia are currently dominated by cognitive–behavioural approaches. These reflect a shift from behaviourist approaches such as systematic desensitization, social skills training and flooding techniques, to an emphasis on producing systematic changes in cognitions. Rather than being regarded as an acquired habit, anxiety is seen as the result of aberrations in thinking, and therefore therapy should be directed at correcting or challenging the bias and distortions allegedly to be found in the assumptions and beliefs of anxious people. Cognitive processes in social phobia can be investigated using methods that have been developed in the laboratory. These include priming methods, the Stroop paradigm and performance of tasks that make varying demands on the working memory system by requiring different amounts of central executive and storage processes (Clark, 1999).

One of the most influential of recent cognitive therapeutic models was originally produced by Clark and Wells (1995) and is discussed in this volume by Wells (Chapter 12). At the core of the model is a set of processes occurring during exposure to feared situations. These include the individual's appraisal of a social situation as dangerous, the processing of the self as a social object, cognitive and somatic symptoms, and the initiation of 'safety behaviours'. The analysis of safety behaviours has been very influential and seems to make sense of many aspects of the behavioural component of shyness and social anxiety. The individual takes some action that he or she believes will fend off the feared event. When this event eventually fails to happen this outcome is attributed to the action that was taken, the 'safety behaviour'. Because of its apparent success this action will tend to be repeated whenever a threat is detected. For example, an individual might have a fear of blushing and will take steps to try to reduce body temperature or apply cosmetics to mask the blush. These behaviours can be irrational or superstitious, in that they may be unconnected to the outcome. They can even bring about the feared outcome when the behaviour of shy people draws attention to themselves. They also prevent the individual from coming to terms with the need to identify and cope with the causes of the anxiety.

Carducci (Chapter 11) is also concerned with how people cope with their anxiety. He presents a content analysis of shy people's written responses to an open-ended question asking them what they did to deal with their shyness. Responses suggested that, rather than passively enduring their difficulties, shy individuals were active in implementing coping strategies. However, as in the case of safety behaviours, these strategies were largely limited in their effectiveness, and often counter-productive. They could also create further problems for the individual, for example when alcohol or other drugs are used in an attempt to cope with social situations.

Concluding remarks

Despite the apparent simplicity of the concept and its pervasiveness in everyday life, scientific investigation of shyness shows it to be a complex topic. Research has been devoted to the concepts of behavioural inhibition and social phobia which are distinct from shyness in important respects but which also have a considerable degree of overlap. Discomfort in social situations, particularly novel ones or those where the individual feels that he or she is being evaluated by others, is associated with self-consciousness and with a tendency to adopt coping behaviours that are often ineffective and counter-productive. The volume brings together perspectives into these experiences from developmental psychology, social psychology and clinical psychology. Some chapters tackle theoretical issues, others present original findings. Several issues are examined across chapters: factors that influence the development of shyness; the psychophysiology of shyness; its stability across the life span; the impact of shyness on long-term social relationships, whether at university or via the Internet; how people cope with and can be helped to overcome their shyness.

Notes

1 Kagan prefers to conceptualize inhibition as a category to which any individual does or does not belong. Similarly, lack of inhibition is regarded as a separate category. Thus many children will not belong to either category. In this case, stability is the extent to which children who are in one category at time 1 remain in the same category at time 2.

References

Ainsworth, M.D.A., Blehar, M.C., Waters, E. and Wall, S. (1978) *Patterns of Attachment*, Hillsdale, NJ: Erlbaum.

Allport, G.W. (1937) *Personality: A Psychological Interpretation*, New York: Holt.

Asendorpf, J.B. (1989) 'Shyness as a final common pathway for two different kinds of inhibition', *Journal of Personality and Social Psychology*, 57: 481–92.

Asendorpf, J.B. (1993) 'Beyond temperament: a two-factorial coping model of the development of inhibition during childhood', in K.H. Rubin and J.B. Asendorpf (eds) *Social Withdrawal, Inhibition, and Shyness* (pp. 265–89), Hillsdale, NJ: Erlbaum.

Asendorpf, J.B. and Meier, G.H. (1993) 'Personality effects on children's speech in everyday life: sociability-mediated exposure and shyness-mediated reactivity to social situations', *Journal of Personality and Social Psychology*, 64: 1072–83.

Beidel, D.C. and Turner, S.M. (1999) 'The natural course of shyness and related symptoms', in L.A. Schmidt and J. Schulkin (eds) *Extreme Fear, Shyness, and Social Phobia: Origins, Biological Mechanisms, and Clinical Outcomes* (pp. 203–23), New York: Oxford University Press.

Briggs, S.R. and Smith, T.G. (1986) 'The measurement of shyness', in W.H. Jones, J.M. Cheek and S.R. Briggs (eds) *Shyness: Perspectives on Research and Treatment* (pp. 47–60), New York: Plenum Press.

Bruch, M.A., Gorsky, J.M., Collins, T.M. and Berger, P.A. (1989) 'Shyness and sociability reexamined: a multicomponent analysis', *Journal of Personality and Social Psychology*, 57: 904–15.

Buss, A.H. (1980) *Self-consciousness and Social Anxiety*, San Francisco: Freeman.

Buss, A.H. (1986) 'A theory of shyness', in W.H. Jones, J.M. Cheek and S.R. Briggs (eds) *Shyness: Perspectives on Research and Treatment* (pp. 39–46), New York: Plenum.

Buss, A.H. and Plomin, R. (1984) *Temperament: Early Developing Personality Traits*, Hillsdale, NJ: Erlbaum.

Caspi, A. (2000) 'The child is father of the man: personality continuities from childhood to adulthood', *Journal of Personality and Social Psychology*, 78: 158–72.

Cattell, R.B. (1973) *Personality and Mood by Questionnaire*, San Francisco: Jossey-Bass.

Cheek, J.M. and Buss, A.H. (1981) 'Shyness and sociability', *Journal of Personality and Social Psychology*, 41: 330–9.

Cheek, J.M. and Krasnoperova, E.N. (1999) 'Varieties of shyness in adolescence and adulthood', in L.A. Schmidt and J. Schulkin (eds) *Extreme Fear, Shyness, and Social Phobia: Origins, Biological Mechanisms, and Clinical Outcomes* (pp. 224–50), New York: Oxford University Press.

Cheek, J.M. and Watson, A.K. (1989) 'The definition of shyness: psychological imperialism or construct validity?', *Journal of Social Behavior and Personality*, 4: 85–95.

Chess, S. and Thomas, A. (1986) *Temperament in Clinical Practice*, New York: Guilford.

Clark, D.M. (1999) 'Anxiety disorders: why they persist and how to treat them', *Behaviour Research and Therapy*, 37: S5–S27.

Clark, D.M., and Wells, A. (1995) 'A cognitive model of social phobia', in R. Heimberg, M. Liebowitz, D.A. Hope and F.R. Schneier (eds) *Social phobia: Diagnosis, Assessment and Treatment* (pp. 69–93), New York: Guilford Press.

Comrey, A.L. (1965) 'Scales for measuring compulsion, hostility, neuroticism, and shyness', *Psychological Reports*, 16: 697–700.

Cooper, J.R., Bloom, F.E. and Roth, R.H. (1991) *The Biochemical Basis of Neuropharmacology*, 6th edition, New York: Oxford University Press.

Crozier, W.R. (1990) 'Social psychological perspectives on shyness, embarrassment, and shame', in W.R. Crozier (ed.) *Shyness and Embarrassment: Perspectives from Social Psychology* (pp. 19–58), Cambridge: Cambridge University Press.

Eysenck, H.J. (1956) 'The questionnaire measurement of neuroticism and extraversion', *Revista de Psicologia*, 50: 113–40.

Eysenck, H.J. and Eysenck, S.B.G. (1969) *Personality Structure and Measurement*, London: Routledge and Kegan Paul.

Fentress, J.C. (1991) 'Analytical ethology and synthetic neuroscience', in P. Bateson (ed.) *Development and Integration of Behaviour* (pp. 7–120), Cambridge: Cambridge University Press.

Ferguson, P. (1997) 'A loner from youth', *CNN Interactive*. URL: http://cnn.com /SPECIALS/1997/unabomb/accused/early. Accessed 12 June 2000.

Gilbert, P. and McGuire, M.T. (1998) 'Shame, status, and social roles: psychobiology and evolution', in P. Gilbert and B. Andrews (eds) *Shame* (pp. 99–125), New York: Oxford University Press.

Hirshfeld, D.R., Rosenbaum, J.F., Biederman, J., Boulec, E.A., Faraone, S.V., Snidman, N., Reznick, J.S. and Kagan, J. (1992) 'Stable behavioral inhibition and its association with anxiety disorder', *Journal of the American Academy of Child and Adolescent Psychiatry*, 31: 103–11.

Hood, S.D. and Nutt, D.J. (in press) 'Psychopharmacological treatments: an overview', in W.R. Crozier and L.E. Alden (eds) *International Handbook of Social Anxiety*, Chichester, Sussex: Wiley.

Kagan, J. (1994) *Galen's Prophecy*, New York: Basic Books.

Leary, M.R. (1986) 'Affective and behavioral components of shyness: implications for theory, measurement, and research', in W.H. Jones, J.M. Cheek and S.R. Briggs (eds) *Shyness: Perspectives on Research and Treatment* (pp. 27–38), New York: Plenum.

Leary, M.R. and Kowalski, R.M. (1995) 'The self-presentation model of social phobia', in R. Heimberg, M. Liebowitz, D.A. Hope and F.R. Schneier (eds) *Social Phobia: Diagnosis, Assessment and Treatment* (pp. 94–112), New York: Guilford Press.

Marshall, P.J. and Stevenson-Hinde, J. (1998) 'Behavioral inhibition, heart period, and respiratory sinus arrhythmia in young children', *Developmental Psychobiology*, 33: 283–92.

Mischel, W. (1968) *Personality and Assessment*, New York: Wiley.

Mosier, C. I. (1937) 'A factor analysis of certain neurotic symptoms', *Psychometrika*, 2: 263–86.

Pilgrim, D. (2000) 'Psychiatric diagnosis: more questions than answers', *The Psychologist*, 13: 302–5.

Pilkonis, P.A. (1977a) 'Shyness, public and private, and its relationship to other measures of social behavior', *Journal of Personality*, 45: 585–95.

Pilkonis, P. A. (1977b) 'The behavioral consequences of shyness', *Journal of Personality*, 45: 596–611.

Rubin, K.H. and Asendorpf, J. (eds) (1993) *Social Withdrawal, Inhibition, and Shyness in Childhood*, Hillsdale, NJ: Erlbaum.

Rutter, M. (1987) 'Temperament, personality and personality disorder', *British Journal of Medical Psychology*, 60: 1–16.

Schore, A.N. (1998) 'Early shame experiences and infant brain development', in P. Gilbert and B. Andrews (eds), *Shame* (pp. 57–77), New York: Oxford University Press.

Schlenker, B.R. and Leary, M.R. (1982) 'Social anxiety and self-presentation: a conceptualization and model', *Psychological Bulletin*, 92: 641–69.

Stevenson-Hinde, J. and Shouldice, A. (1993) 'Wariness to strangers: a behavior systems perspective revisited', in K.H. Rubin and J. Asendorpf (eds) *Social Withdrawal, Inhibition, and Shyness in Childhood* (pp. 101–16), Hillsdale, N.J.: Erlbaum.

Van Ameringen, M., Mancini, C., Oakman, J.M. and Farvolden, P. (1999) 'Selective serotonin reuptake inhibitors in the treatment of social phobia: the emerging gold standard', *CNS Drugs*, 11: 307–15.

Zimbardo, P.G., Pilkonis, P.A. and Norwood, R. (1975) 'Shackles of shyness', *Psychology Today*, UK edition, 1 (6): 24–7.

2 Inhibited and uninhibited temperaments

Recent developments

Jerome Kagan

The study of temperamental contributions to the development of the child has enjoyed a great deal of popularity over the last 20 years due, in part, to the writings of Thomas and Chess (1997). Most investigators regard the term temperament as referring to a number of moderately stable psychological profiles, under some genetic constraint, that emerge during infancy or early childhood. There is some debate, however, on the number of temperaments, how they should be measured, and whether they should be conceptualized as continua or as categories.

It is not possible to predict the number of temperaments that will be discovered because most investigators rely on questionnaires for evidence. The problem with this strategy is that a person's verbal products have special features that are not characteristic of the phenomena that the sentences are intended to describe. Most individuals impose an evaluative construction on their behaviour, as well as the behaviour of their children. Hence, individuals who value sociability are likely to be threatened by timidity and will deny their own shyness as well as shy behaviour in their children. Second, words have quasilogical relations with each other; antonymic and hyponymic relations are two examples. The terms 'sweet' and 'sour' are semantic opposites implying that both sensations could not exist simultaneously, even though the sweet and sour pork dishes on Chinese menus provoke both taste sensations. Because humans are sensitive to the logical consistency of their verbal answers to questions, those who admit to frequent worries are likely to report that they are less joyous than filmed observations would reveal because of the antonymic relation between the words worry and joy.

Third, most words and sentences refer to discrete categories of events rather than blends. There is no word in English that describes the feeling generated when one hopes for good news about a loved one but fears the worst. In addition, every sentence assumes a comparison. The parent who reads on a questionnaire, 'Does your child like to go to parties?', will compare that preference with others. If one parent compares going to parties with an activity the child dislikes while the second parent compares it with one the child also prefers, the former is more likely to endorse the item than the latter even though both children like parties to an equivalent degree.

Further, individuals differ in their understandings of the meanings of words. Individuals from different social class groups or cultural backgrounds typically extract different meanings from the same words. Fifth, investigators cannot ask subjects about qualities that are not observable (for example, the amount of alpha or beta power in the EEG); and are unable to use words that are not part of the folk vocabulary. There is a small group of children who are extremely irritable, rarely smile, have a high heart rate, high muscle tension, and greater EEG activation in the right frontal area. A scientist examining these data would have to invent a novel temperamental category to capture this combination of qualities. Parents do not have access to all of the information that defines this category and, therefore, could not rate their child on this temperamental category. These problems with self-report questionnaire data imply that scientists who rely on questionnaires have to restrict their categories to a small number of easily understood ideas. Thus, future research on temperament will have to include behavioural observations.

The decision to regard temperaments as dimensions or qualitative categories is also controversial. Thomas and Chess regarded the easy, difficult, and slow-to-warm-up children as categories although they treated the variation within each of the nine dimensions they posited as continuous. Rothbart and Bates (1998), who nominated infant reactivity regulation as a primary temperament, regard them as continuous dimensions. Although most psychologists prefer continua over categories because of the inferential statistics available to them, Meehl (1995) has written about the utility of considering some of the profiles as qualitative categories. The most important argument for categories is that nonlinear functions are common in the life sciences. Unique relations between variables emerge at transition points where a small number of subjects who possess either high or low levels on several variables emerge. These individuals are likely to be members of a category.

The concepts of inhibited and uninhibited behaviour to the unfamiliar

The behavioural profiles characterized by avoidance of or suppression of spontaneity to discrepancy or novelty, as well as the complementary type characterized by approach to discrepancy, are usually nominated as two important temperamental categories. These concepts have attracted scientific attention because the relevant behaviours are observable and easily quantified in children as well as animals, appear early in development, have implications for later social behaviour and, therefore, adaptation, and, finally, differentiate among animal species as well as among strains within a species. My colleagues Nancy Snidman, Mark McManis, Doreen Arcus, Cynthia

Garcia-Coll, Steven Reznick, and I have been studying two temperamental categories of children that we call inhibited and uninhibited to the unfamiliar. The corpus of data we have gathered over the last 20 years has led to a small set of conclusions.

The first important discovery was that the behaviour of 4-month-old infants presented with visual, auditory, and olfactory stimuli revealed variation in motor activity and crying which predicted the emergence of inhibited and uninhibited profiles after the first birthday. About 20 per cent of infants show a combination of vigorous motor activity and crying to these stimuli because, we believe, they have low thresholds of excitability in the amygdala and its projections. These infants are called high reactive. The complementary group displayed low levels of motor activity and minimal irritability to the same battery because they have higher thresholds in the amygdala and its projections and they comprise about 40 per cent of the sample. These infants are called low reactive.

Research with animals reveals that the amygdala is responsive to unfamiliar events and is a necessary structure for the acquisition of conditioned reactions using aversive events as unconditioned stimuli that imply a fear state in the animal. The basolateral area of the amygdala sends projections to the ventral striatum and excitation of this structure induces limb movement in animals. Second, the amygdala is the origin of the amygdalofugal pathway whose projections to the central grey and anterior cingulate modulate distress cries. Thus, infants born with a low threshold in the amygdala and its projections should behave like high reactive infants and display vigorous limb movements and distress to unfamiliar stimuli. By contrast, infants born with a neurochemistry that raises the threshold of the amygdala and its projections should behave like low reactive infants and display minimal motor activity and minimal crying to unfamiliar stimuli. Further, this argument implies that high reactive infants should develop into avoidant and fearful children while low reactive infants should develop into relatively fearless, sociable children.

We observed most of these children when they were 14 and 21 months old. The children who had been high reactive infants were more fearful in reaction to a variety of unfamiliar events compared with the low reactive infants. About one-third of high reactives were very avoidant or fearful in reaction to a variety of novel events and only 3 per cent were fearless, while one-third of low reactives were minimally fearful and only 4 per cent showed high levels of fear (Kagan, 1994).

When evaluated at 4½ years of age, high reactives were more subdued than low reactives in their interaction with an unfamiliar female examiner. Specifically, they displayed significantly fewer spontaneous comments and smiles while interacting with the examiner. About a month after the laboratory session with the examiner, the child and parent returned for a play session with two other unfamiliar children of the same age and gender. The three parents sat on a couch in a large playroom while the three children played with age-appropriate toys. About two-thirds of low reactives but less than 10 per cent of the high reactives were outgoing and sociable while playing with two other unfamiliar children. Forty per cent of the high reactives were shy compared with only 10 per cent of the low reactives.

A group of 164 of the original sample of 462 children were evaluated again when they were 7½ years old. Initially, the mothers were sent a questionnaire and asked to rate their child on a three-point scale for descriptions of age-appropriate behaviour. Twelve of the questions dealt with anxious symptoms (for example, 'My child becomes quiet and subdued in unfamiliar places', 'My child is afraid of thunder and lightning', 'My child is afraid of animals'). Children who were described as being anxious were regarded as potential members of a category of anxious children. The mothers of these potentially anxious children were interviewed on the telephone and asked to provide examples to support their descriptions. On the basis of these interviews, some children were eliminated from the potentially anxious group. The teachers of the remaining children were interviewed on the telephone. The teacher had no knowledge of the child's prior behaviour or the purpose of the interview. The teacher described and then ranked the child with respect to all children of the same gender in that classroom for shyness and fearfulness. The mother's questionnaire and subsequent interviews with the mother and the teacher were then discussed by a trio of investigators. If all three agreed that the evidence indicated the child met criteria for anxious symptoms, the child was categorized as anxious (42 children or 26 per cent of the group met that criterion). This group was compared with 107 control children from the rest of the sample who did not meet criteria for any symptom. The remaining 15 children had symptoms other than anxiety. All 164 children came to the laboratory and a variety of procedures was administered to each.

The children who had been high reactive infants were most likely to have acquired anxious symptoms (45 per cent of the high reactives compared with only 15 per cent of low reactives were classified as having anxious symptoms). The high reactive children with anxious symptoms were most likely to have screamed in terror during the 21-month laboratory assessment when a person dressed in a clown costume unexpectedly entered the room where they were playing.

However, only 18 per cent of all the high reactive infants showed consistently inhibited behaviour at 14 months, 21 months, 4½ years, and 7½ years, and not one high reactive infant was consistently uninhibited across all these evaluations. By contrast, 29 per cent of those who had been low reactive infants were consistently uninhibited, and only one low reactive child developed a consistently inhibited profile.

The higher prevalence of anxious symptoms among the children who had been high reactives is in accord with the fact that 61 per cent of children from an independent cohort selected as inhibited in the second year of life were judged to have social anxiety at 13 years of age, compared with 27 per cent of children who were classified as uninhibited in the second year. Almost 50 per cent of the latter group told a psychiatrist interviewing them that they never experienced any sign of social anxiety (Schwartz, Snidman and Kagan, 1999).

These children are now being evaluated at 10 years of age. At the time of this writing, we have observed 32 10-year-olds who had been high reactive and 31 who had been low reactive infants. We have gathered EEG data under resting conditions and discovered that significantly more high than low reactives had greater activation on the right, compared with the left, frontal area. This result is in accord with the work of Davidson (1994) and Fox et al. (1996). Further, the children who showed greater activation on the right frontal area were emotionally subdued for they made significantly fewer comments while interacting with the female examiner.

The high reactives also showed signs of a more reactive sympathetic nervous system for they were more likely to show cooling of the index fingers, attributable to sympathetic constriction of anastomoses, while they were being administered a series of digits to recall. Further, the children who had been high reactive infants displayed a biological feature that implies possession of a reactive amygdala. The feature in question is a relatively large Wave 5 component of the brain stem auditory-evoked potential which is generated by the inferior colliculus to a series of clicks. Research with animals reveals that amygdalar activity can influence the excitability of the inferior colliculus and enhance the magnitude of Wave 5. High reactives, as a group, had a significantly larger Wave 5 component than low reactives, implying greater amygdalar reactivity. However, some high reactives who had been fearful in the second year and had a large Wave 5 at 10 years were not particularly shy in the laboratory at 10 years of age and some told an interviewer that they were neither shy nor anxious. This fact means that there can be a dissociation between the biological processes that form part of the foundation of a temperamental category and the contemporary behavioural phenotype. This distinction is captured by the cliché, 'You can't judge a book by its cover'.

The fact that some aspects of brain physiology that form the foundation of an inhibited temperamental type do not remain linked to inhibited behaviour indefinitely is analogous to the idea of penetrance in genetics. These data remind us that experience can change an early behavioural profile of timidity and shyness, linked to the excitability of the amygdala, to a more normative profile without eliminating completely the excitability of limbic structures that represented the foundation of the infant behaviour.

In collaboration with Jerrold Rosenbaum and Joseph Biederman of Massachusetts General Hospital, we have seen children from 21 months to 7 years of age who had parents with panic disorder, panic disorder with depression, depression alone, or control parents with no psychiatric symptoms. About 25 per cent of the children of parents with panic or panic with depression were inhibited in the laboratory, compared with 12 per cent of controls. In addition, the children of panic parents had a large temperature asymmetry between the pair of index fingers while watching a series of film clips, implying a labile sympathetic nervous system. There were twice as many children with a panic parent compared with children of controls who had temperature asymmetry values greater than 0.5°C between the pair of index fingers. When we combined a subdued inhibited profile with the examiner with a large temperature asymmetry, one in ten children with a panic parent, but only one in 100 control children, combined an inhibited style of interaction with this index of sympathetic lability. If inhibition were regarded as analogous to a physical illness such as cancer, the difference in risk between one in ten and one in 100 would be regarded as a fact of clinical significance.

Conscience development in children

These data have implications for the emotions of guilt and anxiety because these effects are mediated by the same circuits that mediate high reactivity and inhibition. Spontaneous activity in muscles, heart, arteries, gut, and skin is transmitted from the body to the medulla, the amygdala, and from the amygdala to the ventromedial prefrontal cortex. When this sensory information pierces consciousness, it motivates the individual to interpret the change in body tone. A frequent first guess, especially among individuals living in western society, is that they violated one of their ethical standards. The list of possible moral errors is so long that few adolescents or adults will have trouble finding some ethical mistake to explain the unwelcome feeling and, as a consequence, will experience a moment of guilt. Some chronically depressed persons are likely to belong to a group that interprets the difference in body tone as due to a violation of a personal standard. This group was the target of Robert Burton's (1621) classic book, *Anatomy of Melancholy*, written almost 400 years ago.

Many inhibited children reported as adolescents that they were afraid of being criticized by others. If inhibited children experience more intense bodily feedback and impose on this perception an interpretation that implies that they are less virtuous, they should become more civil and law-abiding than others from the same social class or ethnic category. The work of Kochanska (1991) supports this claim.

The notion of constraint

Although relations between variables are always contingent, the tightness of any sequence can vary over a broad range of probabilities. Because physics and chemistry began their growth before psychology, the predicate 'determine' became the preferred way to describe the relation between some prior event and an outcome. When the probability of one event following a prior one is high, for example, greater than 0.8, it is reasonable to conclude that the earlier event influenced the latter one directly. When the probability is low, for example, less than 0.4, it is more likely that the prior event affected the consequent indirectly, only for extreme cases, or in combination with other factors. A significant correlation between psychological or biological variables that is less than 0.4 is most of the time attributable to a small proportion of subjects, usually about 20 per cent, who have extreme values. Under these conditions, it is more accurate to use the verb 'constrain' rather than 'determine' to describe the effect of a prior condition on a subsequent outcome. Recall that 18 per cent of the children who had been high reactive infants became fearful toddlers, shy 4-year-olds, and anxious 7-year-olds. However, not one high reactive infant developed the complementary profile. Because more than 80 per cent of high reactive infants did not become consistently inhibited, it is misleading to suggest that a high reactive temperament determines a stable, inhibited profile and more accurate to suggest that a high reactive temperament constrains the probability of becoming a consistently uninhibited child.

Epilogue

The enthusiasm for discovering the biological contributions to behaviour, which we appropriately celebrate, has been accompanied by a loss of interest in each person's psychological interpretation of their experiences, together with an indifference to the cultural influences on those interpretations. The probability that a high reactive infant will be inhibited at age 10 will depend on the history of exposure to discrepant events or challenges, as well as the child's decision to seek or to avoid environments that are less predictable. Some inhibited children recognize that they are vulnerable to uncertainty and, as a result, avoid such situations. A small group who do not have that insight are likely to choose activities and plan lives that contain more uncertainty than they are prepared to deal with effectively. These varied decisions are not easily traced to the child's biology. Temperamental dispositions are linked to emotions, but the exact nature of those links is modulated by each individual's history and the cultural context in which their life is actualized.

References

Burton, R. (1621) [1923] *Anatomy of Melancholy*, London: G. Bell.
Davidson, R.J. (1994) 'Asymmetric brain function, affective style, and psychopathology', *Development and Psychopathology*, 6: 741–58.
Fox, N.A., Schmidt, L.A., Calkins, S.D., Rubin, K.H. and Coplan, R.J. (1996) 'The role of frontal activation in the regulation and disregulation of social behavior during the preschool years', *Development and Psychopathology*, 8: 89–102.
Kagan, J. (1994) *Galen's Prophecy*, New York: Basic Books.

Kochanska, G. (1991) 'Socialization and temperament in the development of guilt and conscience', *Child Development*, 62: 1379–92.

Meehl, P.E. (1995) 'Bootstrap taxometrics', *American Psychologist*, 50: 266–75.

Rosenbaum, J.F., Biederman, J., Hirschfeld-Becker, D.R., Kagan, J., Snidman, N., Friedman, D., Nineberg, A., Gallery, D.J. and Faraone, S.V. (in preparation) *A Controlled Study of Behavioral Inhibition in Children of Parents with Panic Disorder and Depression*.

Rothbart, M.K. and Bates, J.E. (1998), 'Temperament', in N. Eisenberg (volume editor), W. Damon (editor-in-chief), *Handbook of Child Psychology*, Volume 3 (pp. 105–76), New York: Wiley.

Schwartz, C.E., Snidman, N., and Kagan, J. (1999) 'Adolescent social anxiety as an outcome of inhibited temperament in childhood', *Journal of the American Academy of Child and Adolescent Psychiatry*, 38: 1008–15.

Thomas, A. and Chess, S. (1977) *Temperament and Development*, New York: Brunner-Masel.

3   Childhood shyness

Determinants, development and 'depathology'

Louis A. Schmidt and Susan L. Tasker

Introduction

Although some degree of shyness is experienced by most children during development, a small percentage (10–15 per cent) of children are consistently anxious, quiet, and behaviourally inhibited during social situations, in particular unfamiliar social situations (see Kagan, Chapter 2, this volume). Many of these children are characterized by a distinct pattern of physiological responses during resting conditions and in response to social challenge (see Kagan, Reznick and Snidman, 1987, 1988; Schmidt, Fox, Sternberg, Gold, Smith and Schulkin, 1999; Schmidt, Fox, Schulkin and Gold, 1999; Schmidt, Polak and Spooner, in press, for reviews) and some of them may be at risk for anxiety and internalizing-related problems (e.g., depression, social withdrawal) during early development (see e.g., Hirshfeld *et al.*, 1992; Rubin, Stewart and Coplan, 1995) and adjustment problems in later years (Bell *et al.*, 1993; Caspi, Elder and Bem, 1988; Schmidt and Fox, 1995; Zimbardo, 1977).

Our research programme has been directed largely towards addressing three questions:

- What are the origins of shyness in children?
- Is there stability in infant behavioural and physiological predictors of childhood shyness?
- Are there different types of shyness?

The purpose of this chapter is to review ongoing studies and recent evidence generated from our laboratory that may shed light on these three questions. In addition, we have recently begun addressing a fourth question: Are there any advantages to being a shy child? Our interest in this question stems from our concerns about the recent movement within the medical community and society as a whole to view most aspects of shyness as pathological and needing to be treated medically. We describe an ongoing qualitative study being conducted in our laboratory which gathers parental beliefs about shyness, with the goal being to establish social knowledge related to the positive aspects of some features of childhood shyness.

What are the origins of shyness in children?

Although childhood shyness has many definitions (Rubin and Asendorpf, 1993), one area that researchers seem to agree upon is that there are many determinants of shyness in children and understanding the multiple causes of this phenomenon is complex. The current literature on the aetiology of childhood shyness, however, has been dominated by two main schools of thinking: one leaning more towards biological determinants, the other comprising environmental causes. An excellent example of this issue is represented by the work of Jerome Kagan and his colleagues and of Joan Stevenson-Hinde and her colleagues reviewed in Chapters 2 and 6, respectively, in this volume.

It is important to point out that still others disagree on the conceptualization of shyness. For example, some researchers view shyness as an enduring quality of personality (i.e., a trait; see, e.g., Cheek and Krasnoperova, 1999), while others conceptualize shyness more along the lines of a psychological process (i.e., an emotion; see, e.g., Crozier, Chapter 10 this volume). Although each of these conceptualizations has merit, it is beyond the scope of this chapter to elaborate on them further.

The focus of our research programme has been on understanding the biological basis of childhood shyness and identifying early infant predictors of shyness using a multi-measure, multi-method approach (see Schmidt and Fox, 1999; Schmidt and Schulkin, 1999). Much of this research programme was spawned by the work of Jerome Kagan and his colleagues at Harvard. Kagan (1994, 1999; Kagan and Snidman, 1991) argued that the origins of extreme shyness in children may be linked to early infant temperament. He and his colleagues (Kagan and Snidman, 1991) found that infants who exhibited a high degree of motor activity and distress to the presentation of novel auditory and visual stimuli at 4 months of age were more likely to display fear and wariness to unfamiliar social and non-social stimuli when they became toddlers compared with infants who were less reactive at 4 months. These findings have been independently replicated by Fox and his colleagues (Calkins, Fox and Marshall, 1996). Kagan (1994, 1999) further speculated that individual differences in infant reactivity to novelty may be linked to sensitivity in forebrain circuits involved in the processing and regulation of emotion. More specifically, Kagan argued that children who become easily distressed during the presentation of novel stimuli may have a lower threshold for arousal in the central nucleus of the amygdala. This hypothesis is based largely on findings from studies of animals in which the amygdala plays an important role in the regulation and maintenance of conditioned fear.

The amygdala (particularly the central nucleus) plays an important role in the autonomic and behavioural aspects of conditioned fear (LeDoux, Iwata, Cicchetti and Reis, 1988; see also LeDoux, 1996; Nader and LeDoux, 1999; Rosen and Schulkin, 1998; Schulkin, McEwen and Gold, 1994 for substantive reviews). Stimulation of the central nucleus by electrical current facilitates fear-potentiated startle responses (Rosen and Davis, 1988); lesioning the amygdala and the central nucleus disrupt conditioned fear (Gallagher, Graham and Holland, 1990; Hitchcock and Davis, 1986; Kapp, Frysinger, Gallagher and Haselton, 1979; LeDoux, Sakaguchi, Iwata and Reis, 1986); and electrically kindling the amygdala, but not the dorsal hippocampus, facilitates fear responses in rats (Rosen, Hamerman, Sitcoske, Glowa and Schulkin, 1996). The amygdala also appears to be involved in the attentional aspects related to the recognition of changes in negatively valenced environmental stimuli (Gallagher and Holland, 1994). As well, the amygdala is known to be more reactive in defensive rather than non-defensive cats (Adamec, 1991).

We (Schmidt and Fox, 1998) tested Kagan's hypothesis: infants who are highly reactive should have a lower threshold for arousal in forebrain areas. We used a fear-potentiated startle paradigm to test this prediction. We measured startle eyeblink responses at 9 months of age in a group of infants, some of whom exhibited a high degree of motor activity and distress to novel auditory and visual stimuli at age 4 months. Infants were presented with a 95 dB burst of white noise for 50 ms during a baseline condition and when a stranger approached. Startle electromyographic (EMG) responses were measured from two miniature electrodes placed around the infant's right eye. We chose to measure the startle response because the neural substrates of potentiated startle are well mapped (Davis, Hitchcock and Rosen, 1987; Hitchcock and Davis, 1986) and involve the forebrain areas implicated by Kagan (1994). Furthermore, the startle response is known to vary during emotional processing. For example, Lang and his colleagues (see Lang, Bradley and Cuthbert, 1990) consistently found that the startle eyeblink was exaggerated during the processing of highly arousing and negatively valenced affective stimuli and attenuated during the processing of highly engaging and positively valenced affective stimuli.

We (Schmidt and Fox, 1998) found that infants who exhibited a high degree of motor activity and distress to novel auditory and visual stimuli at age 4 months exhibited a significantly greater startle amplitude to an approaching stranger at 9 months compared with relatively less reactive infants at 4 months. The high reactive infants were also more likely to exhibit greater relative right frontal electroencephalogram (EEG) activity at 9 months (Calkins *et al.*, 1996) and to be reported by their mothers as contemporaneously shy at age 4 compared with other infants (Schmidt *et al.*, 1997). These findings were consistent with Kagan's prediction. Taken together, the behavioural and physiological data reviewed here suggest two things:

- some infants who go on to develop shyness may be characterized by a lower threshold for arousal in forebrain areas;
- given the appearance of these behavioural and physiological correlates in the first year of life before the infant has been exposed to many important socialization factors (e.g., peer influence), the notion that some infants may have a predisposition towards shyness may have legitimacy.

We are now beginning to move the clock back to earlier in post-natal life. We have most recently begun to examine the relations among salivary cortisol, frontal EEG, and temperament in 12-week-old human infants. To date, we have noted relations between overall frontal EEG responses and salivary cortisol reactivity (Tasker and Schmidt, unpublished observations). There is a tendency for overall frontal EEG activation to predict salivary cortisol reactivity in response to stress. Infants who exhibit high overall frontal EEG activation during baseline conditions are likely to display a greater increase in cortisol following stress. These findings suggest that the pattern of overall frontal EEG activity may be an early marker of dysregulation of the adrenocortical system and emotional processes. These findings are of significance for several reasons:

- there may be a link between the frontal lobe and forebrain areas involved in the regulation of emotion and hormonal stress response;
- these patterns of cortical and hormonal activity are present within the first three months of life before some environmental influences (e.g., peers) can shape the child's personality;
- these physiological and neuroendocrine measures can be reliably indexed in infants during the opening months of life.

Is there stability in infant behavioural and physiological predictors of childhood shyness?

Another question that has been primary to our research programme concerns the stability of infant behavioural and physiological predictors of shyness. As mounting research evidence attests, psychological processes are not immutable in children and change appears to be the rule rather than the exception. The brain is highly susceptible to environmental input during the early years of life and, therefore, personality processes by implication are susceptible to this influence. The fact that, as our research demonstrates, some of the infants classified as highly reactive in early infancy do not go on to develop shyness suggests that this category of child is open to change (Fox, Henderson, Rubin, Calkins and Schmidt, in press). One question then becomes: what are the factors that may be influential in affecting this change? We have begun to address this question.

To date, there have been comparatively few studies that have examined the stability of infant behavioural and physiological predictors that underlie childhood shyness. Kagan (1991) noted that there was a fair degree of discontinuity in behavioural inhibition during the first 7 years of life. However, these sets of observations were based on behavioural and physiological measures collected at or after the second year of life. The lack of attention directed towards the stability of infant predictors of childhood shyness has been due in large part to the scarcity of longitudinal studies in place that could answer such questions. That is, other than Kagan's group, there appear to be no studies in which the question of stability in infant measures can be reliably evaluated (but see Schölmerich, Broberg and Lamb, this volume, Chapter 4). We have attempted to make inroads into rectifying this apparent void in the literature in at least two ways:

- to examine the short-term stability of infant behavioural and physiological measures known to correlate with and which are predictive of childhood shyness;
- to examine the stability of behavioural and physiological measures within the infant temperament category that Kagan describes as predictive of behavioural inhibition and childhood shyness.

We have been examining the short-term stability of frontal EEG asymmetry. Our interest in frontal EEG measures stems from a number of studies of infants (see Fox, 1991, 1994 for reviews), children (Fox *et al.*, 1995; Fox, Schmidt, Calkins, Rubin and Coplan, 1996), and adults (see Davidson, 1993; Davidson and Rickman, 1999 for reviews) which have linked these measures to emotional regulatory processes and individual differences in personality. For example, infants and adults consistently exhibit a pattern of greater relative right frontal EEG activity during the processing of negatively valenced affective stimuli and a pattern of greater relative left frontal EEG activity during the processing of positively valenced affective stimuli. These patterns of frontal EEG asymmetry emerge regardless of the modality of the affective stimuli.

Still other work by Davidson and Fox (see Davidson, 1993; Fox, 1991 for reviews) has revealed that the pattern of resting frontal EEG activity indexed off the anterior portion of the scalp was linked to individual differences in personality and affective style. Individuals who exhibit a pattern of greater right, versus left, frontal EEG activity during baseline conditions are more likely to be characterized as anxious, easily distressed, and depressed. Furthermore, individuals who exhibit a stable pattern of greater relative right frontal EEG activity at baseline over a 3-week period are known to report more intense negative affect in response to negative affective stimuli. Together, these sets of findings suggest that the pattern of frontal EEG activity may reflect emotional regulatory processes and perhaps individual differences in affective style.

We (Schmidt, 2000) examined second-by-second stability for 90 seconds in the pattern of frontal EEG activity in relation to temperament and autonomic patterning in 9-month-old human infants. We computed a traditional frontal EEG asymmetry score using right frontal EEG power *minus* left frontal EEG power for each of the one-second epochs. Positive scores on this metric are thought to reflect greater relative left frontal EEG activity (Davidson and Tomarken, 1989). We then formed three groups of infants based upon the psychometric properties of the individual asymmetry scores. *Group 1* comprised infants whose mean value was negative across the individual asymmetry scores and whose variability was low; *Group 2* comprised infants whose mean value was positive across the individual asymmetry scores and whose variability was low; and *Group 3* comprised infants whose mean value was around zero across the individual asymmetry scores and whose variability was high. In other words, *Groups 1* and *2* exhibited a stable pattern of right and left frontal EEG activity, respectively, while infants in *Group 3* exhibited a pattern of frontal EEG activity that was highly variable and changeable. We were able to distinguish the three groups based on measures of maternal report of infant temperament and heart rate. *Group 1* infants were, overall, reported to be more easily distressed to novelty and exhibited a higher resting heart rate compared with infants in the other two asymmetry groups. These findings suggest that infants exhibiting a stable pattern of greater relative right frontal EEG activity are more likely to be temperamentally distressed to novelty as reported by their mothers at age 9 months. This temperamental distress to novelty is analogous to the temperamental reactions that Kagan (Kagan and Snidman, 1991) describes as being predictive of childhood shyness.

We (Schmidt and Fox, 2000) have also recently begun to examine the stability of behavioural and physiological measures within the infant temperament group that Kagan has found to be predictive of behavioural inhibition and shyness with the hope of understanding why some infants with a temperamental predisposition towards shyness do not go on to develop shyness and whether changes on these measures would provide clues as to how to answer this question. As mentioned in the first section, we have been following a group of infants who were selected for temperamental qualities known to predict behavioural inhibition in the second year of life and shyness in the pre-school years. Using a design similar to Kagan and his colleagues (Kagan and Snidman, 1991), we selected infants at 4 months of age based upon their pattern of behavioural and affective responses to the presentation of novel auditory and visual stimuli. Two groups of infants were classified:

- high reactive and easily distressed;
- low reactive and nondistressed.

Children in the former group are known to be behaviourally inhibited in the second year. We then proceeded to examine the stability of behaviour and frontal EEG asymmetry from 9 to 24 months. We noted two things:

- as predicted, a significant percentage of infants within the high reactive group exhibited a stable pattern of right frontal EEG activity from 9 to 24 months of age;
- those who exhibited this pattern across this time period were likely to be behaviourally inhibited at 24 months.

As well, we found that, within the high reactive temperament category, of the infants whose pattern of frontal EEG asymmetry changed from right to left from 9 to 24 months, a significant portion of them were uninhibited at 24 months of age, suggesting that behavioural changes were paralleled by changes in frontal EEG activity. Overall, these sets of data suggest that there is stability in infant behavioural and physiological predictors of childhood shyness, and these measures are open to change and the extent to which they change is paralleled by changes in personality.

Are there different types of shyness?

A third question that we have been exploring concerns the idea that there may be different types of shy children. The notion that there may be different types of shyness is not new (see, e.g., Cheek and Krasnoperova, 1999). This idea stems from empirical work derived from the adult personality literature nearly two decades ago (Cheek and Buss, 1981) as well as theoretical work by Buss (1986) almost 15 years ago. Cheek and Buss (1981) described at least two types of shyness in undergraduates: individuals who are shy and low in sociability and individuals who are shy and high in sociability. Interestingly, Cheek and Buss (1981) were able to distinguish these two subtypes on behavioural measures. The shy/high social undergraduates exhibited more overt behavioural anxiety during an unfamiliar social situation than the shy/low social undergraduates. We will say more about this later. Around the same time, Crozier (1981) argued that shyness was not a unitary construct and that individual differences in shyness emerged from differences in self-esteem. (This is an excellent example of the point alluded to earlier concerning the treatment of shyness as a trait or a process: for Cheek and Buss individual differences in shyness are embodied in personality traits, while for Crozier, individual differences in shyness are captured in emotional processes.)

Buss (1986) presented a theory in which he argued that there may be at least two types of shyness: an early developing fearful shyness that is linked to stranger fear and wariness (perhaps analogous to the children described by Kagan, this volume, Chapter 2), and a later developing self-conscious shyness that is linked to concerns with self-presentation. Little empirical research, however, has been done to substantiate Buss's theoretical model. Two studies that do exist in the literature have found support for Buss's claim in young adults. For example, Bruch, Giordano and Pearl (1986) noted differences between fearful and self-consciously shy undergraduates in background and current adjustment. Bruch *et al.* (1986) noted that fearfully shy adults exhibited significantly lower scores on a test measuring how to deal with hypothetical problematic social situations compared with their non-shy and self-consciously shy counterparts; the non-shy and self-consciously shy groups were not distinguishable. Schmidt and Robinson (1992) found differences in self-esteem between the two shyness subtypes; the fearfully shy group reported significantly lower self-esteem compared with the self-consciously and non-shy groups.

We have used an approach-avoidance paradigm analogous to Cheek and Buss (1981) to conceptualize different types of shyness. Asendorpf and Meier (1993) have used a similar approach to conceptualize different types of shyness in children. As mentioned earlier, Cheek and Buss (1981) examined the relation between shyness and sociability. They argued that people avoid social situations for different reasons. Some people avoid social situations because they experience fear and anxiety in such situations (i.e., they are shy); others avoid social situations because they prefer to be alone rather than with others (i.e., they are introverted). Cheek and Buss noted that if shyness is nothing more than low sociability, then the two traits should be highly related and to be high on one trait means to be low on the other. The extent to which they might be orthogonal was an empirical question. Cheek and Buss noted that the two traits were only modestly related and they were able to distinguish them on a behavioural level. High shy/high social undergraduates exhibited significantly more behavioural signs of anxiety compared with undergraduates reporting other combinations of shyness and sociability.

We (Schmidt, 1999; Schmidt and Fox, 1994) examined the extent to which shyness and sociability were distinguishable on autonomic and cortical measures. Using a design similar to that reported by Cheek and Buss (1981), we attempted to distinguish shyness and sociability on cortical and autonomic measures collected during baseline and during a social stressor. We chose these measures because the pattern of frontal EEG (e.g., Davidson and Rickman, 1999; Fox, 1991) and autonomic activity (Porges, 1991) might reflect emotional regulatory processes and affective style. We found that high shy/high social undergraduates exhibited a significantly faster and more stable heart rate compared with high shy/low social subjects in response to an anticipated unfamiliar social situation (Schmidt and Fox, 1994). We also noted that both the high shy/high social and the high shy/low social undergraduates exhibited a pattern of greater relative right frontal EEG activity during baseline. However, the two subtypes were distinguishable based upon the pattern of activity in the left, but not right, frontal area. High shy/high social subjects exhibited significantly greater activity in the left frontal EEG lead than high shy/low social subjects. These sets of findings taken together suggest that different types of shyness are distinguishable on a behavioural, cortical, and autonomic level.

What are the origins of different types of shyness? We have been developing a frontal activation–neuroendocrine model that may account for different types of shyness. This model includes a complex interaction among the environment, frontal cortex, and the hypothalamic-pituitary-adrenocortical (HPA) and serotonergic systems. We believe that the frontal cortex plays a regulatory role in mediating forebrain areas such as the amygdala and HPA system in maintaining fear triggered by genes that code for the transportation and regulation of serotonin. It may be at the level of the frontal cortex that individual differences in shyness emerge.

We speculate that genes that code for the transportation of serotonin may play an important role in the regulation of some components of the fear system which includes the frontal cortex, forebrain limbic area, and HPA system. Serotonin has been implicated as a major neurotransmitter involved in anxiety and withdrawal (Westenberg et al., 1996). Some shy individuals may possess a genetic polymorphyism that contributes to a reduced efficiency of the transportation of serotonin. Such a genetic polymorphyism has been noted in adults who score high on measures of neuroticism (Lesch et al., 1996). The action of this reduced serotonin expression may be particularly evident in the forebrain limbic and frontal cortex where there are dense concentrations of serotonin receptors. The reduction of serotonin may play an important role in processes regulating the amygdala and HPA system: serotonin may serve to inhibit (or regulate) the action of amygdaloid firing and activation of the HPA system. The reduction of serotonin may contribute to overactivation of the amygdala and the HPA system in some individuals. The overactive amygdala stimulates the HPA system and the release of increased cortisol. This increase in cortisol may contribute to the pattern of frontal EEG activity noted earlier between shyness subtypes. For example, it is possible that there is differential lateralization of cortisol receptors in the frontal cortex. The frontal cortex is rich in corticosteroid receptors and has been implicated in regulating the HPA system in animals (Diorio, Viau and Meaney, 1993). Cortisol (corticosterone in animals) is known to facilitate fear-related behaviours and responses in animals and humans, including heightened corticotropin-releasing homone (CRH) startle responses (Lee, Schulkin and Davis, 1994) and freezing behaviour (Takahashi and Rubin, 1994) in rats. Moreover, exogenous administration of synthetic cortisol is known to increase right frontal EEG activity (a marker of stress) and anxious mood in healthy human adults (Schmidt, Fox, Goldberg, Smith and Schulkin, 1999) and adults with agitated depression (i.e., comorbidity of depression and anxiety) are known to exhibit elevated endogenous cortisol levels (Gold, Goodwin and Chrousos, 1988).

The overactive amygdala and dysregulated HPA system perhaps lead to the increased activity noted on resting psychophysiological and neuroendocrine measures that index forebrain and frontal cortical functioning. (Interestingly, the startle response, autonomic, and frontal EEG measures are all known to be sensitive to the manipulation of cortisol and have been linked to emotion dysregulation.) With this in mind, it may not be a coincidence that some shy children are characterized by elevated basal cortisol levels, high and stable resting heart rate, exaggerated baseline startle, and greater relative resting right frontal EEG activity. Resting EEG and heart rate measures may be 'by-products' not causal agents of a dysregulated fear system. The left frontal area may have a more dense collection of cortisol receptors in high shy/high social people compared with high shy/low social people, hence the pattern of greater activity in the left than right frontal area for the former group. Thus, it is at the level of the frontal cortex that we observe individual differences in shyness. When the two shy subtypes encounter actual or perceived social stress, there is an increase in heart rate, cortisol, and frontal EEG activity. The two subtypes will differ, however, in the pattern of behaviour and left frontal EEG activity. The shy/social subtype will experience an approach–avoidance conflict and a greater increase in left frontal EEG activity; the shy/low social subtype will not experience the same conflict, as they do not have the same need to affiliate. Thus, this subtype will tend to avoid social situations and will not present with the same pattern of left frontal EEG activity, although they may evidence an increase in cortisol and heart rate.

Are there any advantages to being a shy child?

A fourth, and most recent, question that we are beginning to explore concerns the positive aspects of shyness. This question was sparked largely by the current medical community and cultural fervent views that hold that being shy is a disadvantage that needs to be treated in order to lead a full life. A recent article that appeared in the *New York Times,* entitled, 'A bold rush to sell drugs to the shy', is illustrative of today's push by the medical community to 'pathologize' shyness. The article relates several case studies in which people who had problems dating and/or securing jobs that involved working with people were miraculously cured of their shyness by popping a selective serotonin re-uptake inhibitor (SSRI) pill. We believe that the message being communicated by the medical and pharmaceutical communities may influence parents of shy children and people who are shy to view their shyness as detrimental and something that can be cured. We view many features of shyness as possibly advantageous. For example, adults and children who are shy are often non-impulsive and keen listeners.

We have recently begun a study to investigate qualitatively the positive aspects of being shy. We are currently engaged in the development and validation of a parent survey (see Appendix A) that indexes some of the perceived advantages of shyness. To date, a large group of parents have been interviewed over the phone and in our laboratory using items from this survey. The goal of this study is to establish scientific knowledge that has implications for parents and teachers in terms of how to understand their shy child at home and in the classroom, with the intent being towards the understanding and 'depathology' of shyness. The preliminary data, which are qualitative, are summarized in Table 3.1 and reflect general answers that have been summarized from those parents who reported having a shy child and those who did not. Overall, parents of both shy and non-shy children seem to agree in terms of the positive aspects of shyness. It is important to point out, however, that this is a preliminary, qualitative study and the testing instrument has not been subjected to rigorous scientific standards as yet.

Conclusion

Shyness is a phenomenon that a large percentage of the population has reported experiencing at some point in their life (Zimbardo, 1977) and, to this end, probably reflects a normal emotional response to social interaction. For a small percentage of people, however, the thought of mixing with people appears to be debilitating and an enduring part of personality that is associated with a number of adjustment problems throughout life. In this chapter, we examined the origins and stability of shyness as viewed from the perspective of a personality trait. We also discussed the positive aspects of some features of shyness. We believe there is a real danger elicited by today's medical community, in that people who are shy and parents and teachers of shy children may rely on incomplete evidence to medicate quickly in an attempt to treat what may well be adaptive features of shyness.

Table 3.1 Summary of qualitative responses endorsed by parents of shy and non-shy children on parental measure of the advantages and disadvantages of having a shy child* and being a shy child**

Advantages	*Disadvantages*
Always well-behaved*	Object of bullying*, **
Diligent*	Moody*
Dress conservatively*	Appear aloof**
Non-impulsive	Lack self-confidence**
Compliant*	
Kind	

Appendix A

Parent survey

1 How many people currently live in your household?

2 Who are they (e.g., children, parents, other relatives)?

3 What is the birth order of the child (if siblings)?

4 Who is the primary caregiver during the day?

5 How much does your child enjoy being with other children his/her age?
(not at all) 1   2   3   4   5   6   7   *(very much)*

6 How much does your child enjoy being with adults?
(not at all) 1   2   3   4   5   6   7   *(very much)*

7 How much does your child enjoy playing alone?
(not at all) 1   2   3   4   5   6   7   *(very much)*

8 How much does your child enjoy playing with other children?
(not at all) 1   2   3   4   5   6   7   *(very much)*

9 How long does it take for your child to warm up to new children his/her own age?

Immediately
Within first 15-30 minutes
Within the first two hours
By the next play session
After a few play sessions
Longer

10 Would you say it takes a similar amount of time for your child to warm up to adults?

11 Would *you* consider your child to be shy?
(not at all) 1   2   3   4   5   6   7   *(very much)*

12 Would *others* consider your child to be shy?
(not at all) 1   2   3   4   5   6   7   *(very much)*

13. Would you consider yourself to be shy?
(not at all) 1   2   3   4   5   6   7   *(very much)*

14. Would you consider your spouse to be shy?
(not at all) 1   2   3   4   5   6   7   *(very much)*

15 The following could be considered to be advantages to *having* a shy child:
    strongly disagree; disagree; neutral; agree; strongly agree:
    - (a) my child doesn't talk to strangers
    - (b) my child is well-behaved at home
    - (c) my child is well-behaved at school
    - (d) my child likes being with me and my spouse
    - (e) other adults think my child is a pleasure to be around
    - (f) I do not worry that my child will get involved with the 'wrong crowd'

16 The following could be considered to be advantages of *being* a shy child:
    strongly disagree; disagree; neutral; agree; strongly agree:
    - (a) child doesn't get picked on by other children
    - (b) teachers like child better than other kids
    - (c) child likes school more than other kids
    - (d) child is well-liked by others
    - (e) child does well in school
    - (f) child is comfortable when alone

17 The following could be considered to be drawbacks to either *having* a shy child or *being* a shy child:
    strongly disagree; disagree; neutral; agree; strongly agree:
    - (a) child has very few friends
    - (b) child doesn't get involved in sports, or other extra-curricular activities
    - (c) child often feels uncomfortable in group situations
    - (d) child dreads going to school
    - (e) child wants to spend all his/her time with parents
    - (f) child needs to have more attention paid to him/her by parents

18 Do you think there are any other important issues relevant to your child being shy/not shy?

19 What is your occupation?

20 Education level obtained

Acknowledgements

The writing of this chapter and some of the work reported herein was supported by grants from the National Science and Engineering Research Council (NSERC; no. 203710-99; no. 203710-00) and the Social Science and Humanities Research Council (SSHRC; no. 410-99-1206) of Canada awarded to the first author. We would like to thank Diane Santesso for her helpful comments on earlier versions of this chapter.

References

Adamec, R.E. (1991) 'Individual differences in temporal lobe sensory processing of threatening stimuli in the cat', *Physiology and Behavior*, 49: 445–64.

Asendorpf J.B. and Meier, G.H. (1993) 'Personality effects on children's speech in everyday life: sociability-mediated exposure and shyness-mediated reactivity to social situations', *Journal of Personality and Social Psychology*, 64: 1072–83.

Bell, I.R., Martino, G.M., Meredith, K.E., Schwartz, G.E., Siani, M.W. and Morrow, F.D. (1993) 'Vascular disease risk factors, urinary free cortisol, and health histories in older adults: shyness and gender interactions', *Biological Psychology*, 35: 37–49.

Bruch, M.A., Giordano, S. and Pearl, L. (1986), 'Differences between fearful and self-conscious shy subtypes in background and current adjustment', *Journal of Research in Personality*, 20: 172–86.

Buss, A.H. (1986) 'A theory of shyness', in W.H. Jones, J.M. Cheek and S.R. Briggs (eds) *Shyness: Perspectives on Research and Treatment* (pp. 39–46), New York: Plenum.

Calkins, S.D., Fox, N.A. and Marshall, T.R. (1996) 'Behavioral and physiological antecedents of inhibited and uninhibited behavior', *Child Development*, 67: 523–40.

Caspi, A., Elder, G.H. and Bem, D.J. (1988) 'Moving away from the world: lifecourse patterns of shy children', *Developmental Psychology*, 24: 824–31.

Cheek, J.M. and Buss, A.H. (1981) 'Shyness and sociability', *Journal of Personality and Social Psychology*, 41: 330–9.

Cheek, J.M. and Krasnoperova, E.N. (1999) 'Varieties of shyness in adolescence and adulthood', in L.A. Schmidt and J. Schulkin (eds) *Extreme Fear, Shyness, and Social Phobia: Origins, Biological Mechanisms, and Clinical Outcomes* (pp. 224–50), New York: Oxford University Press.

Crozier, W.R. (1981) 'Shyness and self-esteem', *British Journal of Social Psychology*, 20: 220–2.

Davidson, R.J. (1993) 'The neuropsychology of emotion and affective style', in M. Lewis and J.M. Haviland (eds), *Handbook of Emotion* (pp.143–54), New York: Guilford.

Davidson, R.J. and Rickman, M. (1999) 'Behavioral inhibition and the emotional circuitry of the brain: stability and plasticity during the early childhood years' in L.A. Schmidt and J. Schulkin (eds) *Extreme Fear, Shyness, and Social Phobia: Origins, Biological Mechanisms, and Clinical Outcomes* (pp. 67–87), New York: Oxford University Press.

Davidson, R.J. and Tomarken, A.J. (1989) 'Laterality and emotion: an electrophysiological approach', in F. Boller and J. Grafman (eds) *Handbook of Neuropsychology* (pp. 419–441), Amsterdam: Elsevier Science.

Davis, M., Hitchcock, J.M. and Rosen, J.B. (1987) 'Anxiety and the amygdala: pharmacological and anatomical analysis of the fear-potentiated startle paradigm', in G. Bower (ed.) *The Psychology of Learning and Motivation* (Vol. 21, pp. 263–305), San Diego, CA: Academic Press.

Diorio, D., Viau, V. and Meaney, M.J. (1993) 'The role of the medial prefrontal cortex (cingulate gyrus) in the regulation of hypothalamic–pituitary–adrenal responses to stress', *Journal of Neuroscience*, 13: 3839–47.

Fox, N.A. (1991) 'If it's not left, it's right: electroencephalogram asymmetry and the development of emotion', *American Psychologist*, 46: 863–87

Fox, N.A. (1994) 'Dynamic cerebral processes underlying emotion regulation', in N.A. Fox (ed.) *The Development of Emotion Regulation: Behavioral and Biological Considerations.* (Monographs of the Society for Research in Child Development, pp. 152–66), 59 (2–3, Serial No. 240).

Fox, N.A., Henderson, H.A., Rubin, K.H., Calkins, S.D. and Schmidt, L.A. (in press) 'Stability and instability of behavioral inhibition and exuberance: psychophysiological and behavioral factors influencing change and continuity across the first four years of life', *Child Development.*

Fox, N.A., Rubin, K.H., Calkins, S.D., Marshall, T.R., Coplan, R.J., Porges, S.W., Long, J.M. and Stewart, S. (1995) 'Frontal activation asymmetry and social competence at four years of age', *Child Development*, 66: 1770–84.

Fox, N.A., Schmidt, L.A., Calkins, S.D., Rubin, K.H. and Coplan, R.J. (1996) 'The role of frontal activation in the regulation and dysregulation of social behavior during the preschool years', *Development and Psychopathology*, 8: 89–102.

Gallagher, M., Graham, P.W.A. and Holland, P.C. (1990) 'The amygdala central nucleus and appetitive Pavlovian conditioning: lesions impair one class of conditioned behavior', *Journal of Neuroscience*, 10: 1906–11.

Gallagher, M. and Holland, P.C. (1994) 'The amygdala complex: multiple roles in associative learning and attention', *Proceedings of the National Academy of Sciences*, 91: 11771–6.

Gold, P.W., Goodwin, F.K. and Chrousos, G.P. (1988) 'Clinical and biochemical manifestations of depression', *New England Journal of Medicine*, 319: 348–53; 413–20.

Hirshfeld, D.R., Rosenbaum, J.F., Biederman, J., Bolduc, E.A., Faraone, S.V., Snidman, N., Reznick, J.S. and Kagan, J. (1992) 'Stable behavioral inhibition and its association with anxiety disorder', *Journal of the American Academy of Child and Adolescent Psychiatry*, 31: 103–11.

Hitchcock, J. and Davis, M. (1986) 'Lesion of the amygdala, but not the cerebellum or the red nucleus, block conditioned fear as measured with potentiated startle paradigm', *Behavioral Neuroscience*, 100: 11–22.

Kagan, J. (1991) 'Continuity and discontinuity in development', in S.E. Brauth, W.S. Hall and R.J. Dooling (eds) *Plasticity of Development* (pp. 11–26), Cambridge, MA: MIT Press.

Kagan, J. (1994) *Galen's Prophecy: Temperament in Human Nature*, New York: Basic Books.

Kagan, J. (1999) 'The concept of behavioral inhibition', in L.A. Schmidt and J. Schulkin (eds) *Extreme Fear, Shyness, and Social Phobia: Origins, Biological Mechanisms, and Clinical Outcomes* (pp. 3–13), New York: Oxford University Press.

Kagan, J., Reznick, J.S. and Snidman, N. (1987) 'The physiology and psychology of behavioral inhibition in children', *Child Development*, 58: 1459–73.

Kagan, J., Reznick, J.S. and Snidman, N. (1988) 'Biological basis of childhood shyness', *Science*, 240: 167–71.

Kagan, J. and Snidman, N. (1991) 'Infant predictors of inhibited and uninhibited profiles', *Psychological Science*, 2: 40–4.

Kapp, B.S., Frysinger, R.C., Gallagher, M. and Haselton, J.R. (1979) 'Amygdala central nucleus lesions: effects on heart rate conditioning in the rabbit', *Physiology and Behavior*, 23: 1109–17.

Lang, P.J., Bradley, M.M. and Cuthbert, B.N. (1990) 'Emotion, attention, and the startle reflex', *Psychological Review*, 97: 377–95.

LeDoux, J.E. (1996) *The Emotional Brain*, New York: Simon and Schuster.

LeDoux, J.E., Iwata, J., Cicchetti, P. and Reis, D.J. (1988) 'Different projections of the central amygdaloid nucleus mediate autonomic and behavioral correlates of conditioned fear', *Journal of Neuroscience*, 8: 2517–19.

LeDoux, J.E., Sakaguchi, A., Iwata, J. and Reis, D.J. (1986) 'Interruption of projections from the medial geniculate body to an archineostriatal field disrupts the classical conditioning of emotional responses to acoustic stimuli in the rat', *Neuroscience*, 17: 615–27.

Lee, Y., Schulkin, J. and Davis, M. (1994) 'Effect of corticosterone on the enhancement of the acoustic startle reflex by corticotropin releasing factor (CRF)', *Brain Research*, 666: 93–8.

Lesch, K.P., Bengel, D., Heils, A., Sabol, S.Z., Greenberg, B.D., Petri, S., Benjamin, J., Muller, C.R., Hamer, D.H. and Murphy, D.L. (1996) 'Association of anxiety-related traits with a polymorphism in the serotonin transporter gene regulatory region', *Science*, 274: 1527–31.

Nader, K. and LeDoux, J. (1999) 'The neural circuits that underlie fear', in L.A. Schmidt and J. Schulkin (eds) *Extreme Fear, Shyness, and Social Phobia: Origins, Biological Mechanisms, and Clinical Outcomes* (pp. 119–39), New York: Oxford University Press.

Porges, S.W. (1991) 'Vagal tone: an autonomic mediator of affect', in J. Garber and K.A. Dodge (eds) *The Development of Emotion Regulation and Dysregulation* (pp. 111–28), Cambridge: Cambridge University Press.

Rosen, J.B and Davis, M. (1988) 'Enhancement of acoustic startle by electrical stimulation of the amygdala', *Behavioral Neuroscience*, 102: 195–202.

Rosen, J.B., Hamerman, E., Sitcoske, M., Glowa, J.R. and Schulkin, J. (1996) 'Hyperexcitability: exaggerated fear-potentiated startle produced by partial amygdala kindling', *Behavioral Neuroscience*, 110: 43–50.

Rosen, J.B. and Schulkin, J. (1998) 'From normal fear to pathological anxiety', *Psychological Review*, 105: 325–50.

Rubin, K.H. and Asendorpf, J. (eds) (1993) *Social Withdrawal, Inhibition, and Shyness in Childhood*, Hillsdale, NJ: Erlbaum.

Rubin, K.H., Stewart, S.L. and Coplan, R.J. (1995) 'Social withdrawal in childhood: conceptual and empirical perspectives', in T. Ollendick and R. Prinz (eds) *Advances in Clinical Child Psychology* (Vol. 17, pp. 157–96), New York: Plenum Press.

Schmidt, L.A. (1999) 'Frontal brain electrical activity in shyness and sociability', *Psychological Science*, 10: 316–20.

Schmidt, L.A. (2000) 'Psychometric properties of resting frontal brain electrical activity (EEG) and temperament in 9-month-old human infants', Manuscript submitted for publication.

Schmidt, L.A. and Fox, N.A. (1994) 'Patterns of cortical electrophysiology and autonomic activity in adults' shyness and sociability', *Biological Psychology*, 38: 183–98.

Schmidt, L.A. and Fox, N.A. (1995) 'Individual differences in young adults' shyness and sociability: personality and health correlates', *Personality and Individual Differences*, 19: 455–62.

Schmidt, L.A. and Fox, N.A. (1998) 'Fear-potentiated startle responses in temperamentally different human infants', *Developmental Psychobiology*, 32: 113–20.

Schmidt, L.A. and Fox, N.A. (1999) 'Conceptual, biological, and behavioral distinctions among different categories of shy children', in L.A. Schmidt and J. Schulkin (eds) *Extreme Fear, Shyness, and Social Phobia: Origins, Biological Mechanisms, and Clinical Outcomes* (pp. 47–66), New York: Oxford University Press.

Schmidt, L.A. and Fox, N.A. (2000) 'Stability and change of frontal EEG asymmetry and behavior in temperamentally different human infants during the first two years of life', Manuscript submitted for publication.

Schmidt, L.A., Fox, N.A., Goldberg, M.C., Smith, C.C. and Schulkin, J. (1999) 'Effects of acute prednisone administration on memory, attention, and emotion in healthy human adults', *Psychoneuroendocrinology*, 24: 461–83.

Schmidt, L.A., Fox, N.A., Rubin, K.H., Sternberg, E.M., Gold, P.W., Smith, C. and Schulkin, J. (1997) 'Behavioral and neuroendocrine responses in shy children', *Developmental Psychobiology*, 30: 127–40.

Schmidt, L.A., Fox, N.A., Sternberg, E.M., Gold, P.W., Smith, C. and Schulkin, J. (1999) 'Adrenocortical reactivity and social competence in seven-year-olds', *Personality and Individual Differences*, 26: 977–85.

Schmidt, L.A., Fox, N.A., Schulkin, J. and Gold, P.W. (1999) 'Behavioral and psychophysiological correlates of self-presentation in temperamentally shy children', *Developmental Psychobiology*, 35: 119–35.

Schmidt, L.A., Polak, C.P. and Spooner, A.L. (in press) 'Biological and environmental contributions to childhood shyness: a diathesis-stress model', in W.R. Crozier and L.E. Alden (eds) *International Handbook of Social Anxiety: Research and Interventions Relating to the Self and Shyness*, Chichester, Sussex: John Wiley and Sons.

Schmidt, L.A. and Robinson, T.R., Jr. (1992) 'Low self-esteem in differentiating fearful and self-conscious forms of shyness', *Psychological Reports*, 70: 255–57.

Schmidt, L.A. and Schulkin, J. (eds) (1999) *Extreme Fear, Shyness, and Social Phobia: Origins, Biological Mechanisms, and Clinical Outcomes*, New York: Oxford University Press.

Schulkin, J., McEwen, B.S. and Gold, P.W. (1994) 'Allostasis, amygdala, and anticipatory angst', *Neuroscience and Biobehavioral Reviews*, 18: 385–96.

Takahashi, L.K. and Rubin, W.W. (1994) 'Corticosteroid induction of threat-induced behavioral inhibition in preweanling rats', *Behavioral Neuroscience*, 107: 860–8.

Tasker, S.L., and Schmidt, L.A. [Unpublished data].

Westenberg, H.G.M., Murphy, D.L. and Den Boer, J.A. (eds) (1996) *Advances in the Neurobiology of Anxiety Disorders*, New York: Wiley.

Zimbardo, P.G. (1977) *Shyness: What Is It, What to do About It*, New York: Symphony Press.

4 Precursors of inhibition and shyness in the first year of life

Axel Schölmerich, Anders G. Broberg and Michael E. Lamb

Viewed retrospectively, shyness appears to be a remarkably stable concept: many people who describe themselves as shy claim that they have been shy since childhood. Viewed prospectively, however, the stability appears less compelling. Even Kagan (1997: 35), whose typological orientation implies a high level of stability in the generalized tendency to approach or avoid novel stimuli, warns that 'further environmental conditions can modulate the behavioural profile; levels of motor attention and crying are not constant from day to day and daily experiences permit some children to learn to control their irritability and, later, their fear. It is even possible that experiences that reduce levels of uncertainty can alter the excitability of the limbic systems or change the density of receptors on neurons.'

Unfortunately, no existing data set allows us to follow a sufficiently large sample from early infancy into adulthood in order to determine how stable these tendencies really are. Kagan, Snidman and Arcus (1998) have reported impressive stability of the extreme groups they followed from 2 years of age into the school years, but the study design precluded quantification of stability coefficients for the broader population. Moreover, the stability of personality development may be more characteristic of certain types of individuals than of others (Asendorpf, 1990; Asendorpf and van Aken, 1991). In this chapter, we summarize what we have learned about stability and change during a short-term longitudinal study, which focused on the emerging features of behavioural inhibition during the first year of life.

We view shyness and inhibition as partially overlapping concepts. Inhibition is thought to be the more general concept, since it describes behavioural tendencies relevant for both social and non-social encounters, while shyness is only applicable to social situations (Jones, Briggs and Smith, 1986). Kagan, Reznick, Clarke, Snidman and Garcia Coll (1984) initially defined behavioural inhibition as a tendency to show reluctance, withdrawal, and fearfulness especially when encountering novel situations, objects or people. In their study of selected highly inhibited toddlers, Kagan, Reznick, Snidman, Gibbons and Johnson (1988) found that many of those became shy and isolated schoolchildren. It may be, however, that inhibition and shyness show different long-term developmental trajectories, since specific and different coping mechanisms could be effective in dealing with different situations. For example, Asendorpf (1990) found situation-specific effects on the development of inhibition during childhood in assessing reactions to strangers and familiar people in different settings, and he postulated that shyness is the common final pathway of two different forms of inhibition, one temperamental and one a result of repeated negative experiences in social settings (Asendorpf, 1989). Other researchers such as Andersson (1999) maintain that inhibition towards objects and towards people remains comparable.

The concept of inhibition is sometimes used to indicate a belief in biological underpinnings of such reactivity (see below), while shyness has more often connotations of a learning history. At least in early infancy, furthermore, it seems impossible to separate shyness in relation to social objects from the tendency to withdraw from objects, although the data presented in this chapter do not lend themselves to an analysis of these two constructs and their inter-relations. In addition, we did not follow the infants in the study beyond their first year of life. As a result, we focus in this chapter on:

- the stability of various aspects of reactivity during the first year of life;
- the stability of maternal perceptions of such characteristics as fear of novelty and reactivity;
- the extent to which these aspects of reactivity predict the emergent tendency to appear inhibited in mildly challenging situations;
- factors that might affect inhibition and shyness in the first year of life. During the first year of life, for example, the quality of mother–infant interaction may be a potent moderator of emerging inhibition.

Stability and continuity

Within the first year of life, developmentalists have identified at least two major biopsychosocial shifts, e.g., major changes of the physiological, social, and behavioural organization of the infant. Both shifts have important implications for the way infants deal with novelty. The first takes place at about 2½ months, reflecting changes in the amount of wakefulness and the degree of cortical control of subcortical activity as a result of increased myelination of primary cortical pathways (Cole and Cole, 1996: 176). The second shift, taking place between 7 and 9 months is characterized by onset of crawling with the necessary preconditions such as myelination of motor neurons to lower trunk, legs, and hands, increased wariness towards novelty, fear of heights, and observable social referencing in conditions of uncertainty (Cole and Cole, 1996: 216). Therefore, simple (homotypic) continuity in levels of inhibition through the first year of life is highly unlikely.

However, in their famous New York Longitudinal Study, Thomas and Chess (1977) identified approach–withdrawal as one basic dimension of temperament and many researchers have found that parental reports of approach–withdrawal are stable over the period from 3 months to 3 years of age (Hagekull and Bohlin, 1981; McDevitt and Carey, 1981; Peters-Martin and Wachs, 1984); although it is not clear how much of that stability is actually attributable to stable biases in the maternal informants. Kagan and his colleagues (Garcia Coll, Kagan, and Reznick, 1984; Kagan, Reznick, Snidman, Gibbons and Johnson, 1998) have relied on observational techniques rather than maternal report measures to explore individual differences in approach–withdrawal tendencies from age 2, however, and they too have emphasized the stability of behavioural inhibition, as defined by a tendency to show reluctance, withdrawal, and fearfulness especially when encountering novel situations, objects, or people. Unfortunately, however, their stability coefficients are based on selected extreme groups and this leaves open the possibility that there may be no stability across the preschool years in an unselected sample (Kagan, Reznick and Snidman, 1988).

The physiological basis and behavioural correlates of inhibition and shyness

Whatever the empirical evidence of stability from early infancy, conceptual analyses of behavioural inhibition and its physiological substrates imply that some degree of stability should be evident. According to Kagan the tendency to retreat to a familiar person rather than to explore unfamiliar stimuli reflects a largely innate temperamental characteristic which is linked to a specific neurophysiological reactivity. 'We suggest, albeit speculatively, that most of the children we called inhibited belong to a qualitatively distinct category of infants who were born with a lower threshold for limbic-hypothalamic arousal to unexpected changes in the environment or novel events that cannot be assimilated easily' (Kagan, Reznick and Snidman, 1988a: 171). Recent advances in neuroscience make such an hypothesis plausible, although 'honest disagreement surrounds the conceptualization of infant reactivity as a continuum of arousal or as two distinct categories' (Kagan, 1997: 140), and the data reveal some unexpected measure-specific trends, with motor activity scores tending to be continuous whereas distress/crying scores are not. Obviously, reactivity depends on a large number of neural links and pathways, and this increases both the potential for genetically transmitted differences and the possibility for complex environmental influences.

The links between physiological reactivity and behavioural inhibition have been pursued in three fairly independent lines of inquiry, namely hemispheric activation patterns, cardiovascular activation, and the activity of the hypothalamic-adreno-cortical axis. We review each of those areas briefly in the following paragraphs.

In their research on the neural correlates of inhibited behaviour, first of all, Fox and his co-workers (Fox, 1991; Fox, Davidson and Davidson, 1984; see Schmidt and Tasker, this volume, Chapter 3) have focused on *differences in hemispheric asymmetries*, reasoning that negative emotionality is associated with more activity in the right frontal lobe whereas positive emotional states are associated with left frontal lobe activity. Dawson and her colleagues (Dawson, Panagiotides, Grofer and Hill, 1991; Dawson, Panagiotides, Grofer-Klinger and Hill, 1992) noted that this asymmetry and the general activity levels of the two hemispheres are independent dimensions, with general activity correlated with the amount of distress observed when infants are separated from their mothers. Their observations of infants in the Strange Situation revealed a significant correlation between frontal lobe activity and the rating of disorganized behaviour (Main and Solomon, 1990), whereas asymmetry was especially effective in predicting the expression of negative emotion in situations which elicit such emotions.

Second, patterns of *cardiovascular activity* were among the earliest correlates of behavioural inhibition reported by Kagan and his co-workers (Kagan *et al.*, 1984). Infants later described as inhibited showed higher and more stable heart rates than infants who were later classified as uninhibited. However, outside the Kagan laboratory and with samples not selected to represent the least and most inhibited children, no direct relationship between cardiovascular activity and behavioural inhibition has been found (Asendorpf and Meier, 1993; Calkins and Fox, 1992; Stevenson-Hinde and Marshall, 1999).

Porges (1983, 1991) has suggested using the activity of the vagus, which mediates fast parasympathetic responses to challenges, as an index of different levels of reactivity to stimulation. The activity of the vagus is commonly assessed using an electrocardiogram to extract the respiratory sinus arrhythmia component from the overall variability recorded. Porges and his colleagues (Porges, Doussard-Roosevelt and Maiti, 1994) have shown that vagal activity is associated with a number of psychological functions related to reactivity and emotional expression, thus bearing implications for the development of behavioural inhibition. For example, infants whose vagal tone changed little during social and attention-getting tasks at 7 to 9 months of age had more behavioural or emotional problems at 3 years of age (Porges, Doussard-Roosevelt, Portales and Greenspan, 1996). Similarly, 'normal' infants and those who had difficulty regulating their states between 8 and 11 months of age had different baseline levels of vagal tone (DeGangi, DiPietro, Greenspan and Porges, 1991). Interestingly, baseline vagal tone and the suppression of vagal tone during the attention- demanding tasks were significantly correlated in the normal infants but not among the infants with regulatory disorders. However, baseline vagal tone did not differ significantly between consistently inhibited and uninhibited toddlers in another study (Rubin, Hastings, Stewart, Henderson, and Chen, 1986).

Third, Gunnar and her colleagues have studied the *activity of the hypothalamic-adreno-cortical axis* (HPA; Gunnar, 1989), reasoning that, because cortisol levels rise after stressful experiences and infants have different thresholds of reactivity, stressful events should produce different levels of cortisol among inhibited and non-inhibited children.

Empirical findings on temperamental factors and HPA activation are mixed (Gunnar, Mangelsdorf, Larson and Hertsgaard, 1989; Schölmerich, 1994). This may in part be explained by complicated relationships with other variables (such as attachment), and the rapid developmental change (Larson, Gunnar, and Hertsgaard, 1991). The circadian variation in cortisol levels that is typical among adults emerges during the first 3 or 4 months and gradually stabilizes over the first year of life (Spangler, 1991). The early ability to mount a massive reaction to challenge appears to presage a more modulated and fine-grained reactivity of that same system later in the first two years of life (Gunnar, Brodersen, Krueger, and Rigatuso, 1996; Stansbury and Gunnar, 1994) and it seems likely that the intensity of stress reactions to painful stimuli such as inoculations can be modulated by the presence of caretakers. As Gunnar *et al.* (1996: 886) note, 'with the development of specific attachments, human parents should be able, through their presence, to inhibit cortisol elevations to many stressors, perhaps even to mildly painful stimuli like inoculations'. The cortisol reaction is of special interest in the present context because it is sensitive to novelty. Stimuli that have been presented repeatedly should no longer elicit a cortisol response and thus we may expect a systematic relationship between HPA activation and fear of novelty.

While research on the physiological underpinnings of behavioural inhibition appears pivotal for the temperamental interpretation of this behavioural style, the summary indicates that there is still very little direct evidence on the physiological roots of behavioural inhibition early in development. However, there seem to be sufficient meaningful links to concepts involving closely related aspects to warrant further study and to maintain the basic theoretical conceptions.

Relationships between inhibition and other emotional characteristics

It remains unclear whether inhibition should be viewed as a distinct reaction tendency (Kagan, Reznick and Snidman, 1989) or whether tendencies to withdraw from novel stimuli are best viewed as part of a broader array of temperamental characteristics. Little is currently known about the relation between approach–withdrawal and other aspects of infant emotionality, although negative and positive emotionality appear to be relatively independent of one another (Belsky, Hsieh, and Crnic, 1996; Haynie and

Lamb, 1995). Tendencies to approach or withdraw from novel stimuli, situations, or people can be viewed as indices of negative emotionality, so significant correlations with behavioural inhibition appear likely.

On a behavioural level, van den Boom (1989) has identified irritability as a dimension of temperament that is associated with subsequent fear of novelty. According to van den Boom, irritability influences the infant's arousal system and activates the fear component of that system more often than the exploratory component. An infant who is highly irritable in early infancy is thus less likely to explore or attend to novel stimuli than a non-irritable infant is.

Infant irritability should, of course, also shape the patterns of infant–parent interactions. For example, irritable infants will spend more time in states of negative emotion and thus will not enjoy positive social stimulation as frequently as other infants. Infant irritability as reported by mothers may be of special interest, since it includes links to two pathways into shyness and inhibition. First, infants with neuropsychological risks such as a low threshold for stimulation will receive higher scores based on their proneness to colic or digestive problems. Second, it may reflect maternal attributions, and thus be a social-interactive risk factor. We know that physiological reactivity can be mediated by especially sensitive caregiving (Schneider and Suomi, 1992), and it seems likely that infants with a vulnerable physiology will suffer most from insensitive caretaking. To our knowledge, no researchers have directly assessed the moderating effects of parent–infant interaction on the development of behavioural inhibition, and the associations between mother–infant interaction and aspects of infant temperament are not clear. Some researchers claim that mother–infant interaction (and subsequent security of attachment, for example) reflect dyadic characteristics whereas temperament is a characteristic of the individual, but the two seem to be conceptually unrelated (see Vaughn *et al.*, 1992).

Summary of research questions

Kagan's (1997) suggestion that individual differences in behavioural inhibition can be traced to differences in the level of limbic-hypothalamic arousal has fostered research aimed at identifying children with different patterns of frontal lobe activation, heart rate reactivity, and adrenocortical sensitivity. Other researchers (van den Boom, 1989) have shown that individual differences in related behavioural tendencies – including irritability and negative emotionality – can be discerned in infancy as well (Belsky *et al.*, 1996; Haynie and Lamb, 1995). What remains unclear is the extent to which individual differences in these varied dimensions are empirically interrelated, and whether they can be viewed as the precursors of individual differences in behavioural inhibition. The aim of our study was thus to explore associations among indices of psychophysiological reactivity, infant irritability, negative emotionality, fear of novelty, behavioural inhibition, and mother–infant interaction. Specifically, we examined the longitudinal stability of the biopsychological temperamental and behavioural markers themselves over the first year of life. We then examined relations among scores in the different domains before exploring the extent to which individual differences in behavioural inhibition could be predicted from earlier measures of the presumed precursors.

Method

We recruited 73 families with 3-month-old infants into a longitudinal study using mass mailings and newspaper advertisements. All participants were first-born Caucasian infants from upper-middle class two-parent families. Fifty-eight (28 girls and 30 boys) of the original 73 subjects completed the 13-month visit to the laboratory and are included in the present analyses. Drop-out was not systematically related to any of the 4-, 5-, or 7-month assessments.

At 4 months of age, mothers were contacted by telephone, and they were asked about symptoms of irritability they had observed in their infants. Subsequently, infants and their mothers were seen in the laboratory when the infants were 5, 7, 10, and 13 months of age. During each laboratory visit, mothers completed the Infant Characteristics Questionnaire (ICQ; Bates, Freeland and Lounsbury, 1979) and answered additional questions concerning the fear of novelty. At 7, 10, and 13 months of age, the infants were filmed while encountering a series of emotion-eliciting stimuli. When the infants were 13 months of age, mothers completed the 90-item Attachment Q-set (AQS; Waters and Deane, 1985). Finally, during the 13-month laboratory visit, Garcia Coll, Kagan and Reznick's (1984) inhibition battery was administered.

Maternal report measures

The *symptoms of irritability* about which we inquired included: (1) frequent constipation, (2) colic, (3) respiratory or skin allergies, (4) light or uneasy sleep patterns , (5) emotional irritability (i.e., fussy, cranky) , (6) easy distress or disturbance by changes in the environment, and (7) inconsolability. We recorded the number of symptoms that mothers reported.

Maternal ratings of infant temperament

Mothers completed Bates *et al.*'s (1979) ICQ, and an additional set of questions related to infant temperament when their children were 5, 7, 10, and 13 months of age. Scores on the sub-factors described by Bates *et al.* were first computed, but except for the Fussy-difficult and Unadaptability sub-factors, these had low coefficients of internal consistency (alphas = .03

to .56). After examining and comparing our findings with those reported by Bates *et al.* (1979), we decided to omit items number 7 ('reaction to bath'), 8 ('reaction to solid food'), 15 ('activity'), and 19 ('cuddle/hold'), which contributed little to the original factor solution (Bates *et al.*, 1979: 796), and then reassessed internal consistency. Composites with internal consistency coefficients (Cronbach's alpha) below .60 were excluded from further analyses. The following composites were reliable: Fussy/difficult at 5, 7, 10, and 13 months of age (alphas = .84 to .86); Unpredictable at 7, 10, and 13 months of age (alphas = .66 to .72), and Persistent at 10 and 13 months of age (alphas = .63 to .77). Several items from the Unadaptability subscale (which was not used independently) were included in the Fear-of-novelty scale described below.

Fear of novelty

Composite variables were constructed to measure the mothers' perceptions of their children's fear of novelty at 5, 7, 10, and 13 months of age. The composites at each age included three items from the ICQ ('How does your baby respond to new playthings?', 'How does your baby typically respond to a new person?', and 'How does your baby typically respond to being in a new place?') and two additional questions ('Does your baby adjust within 5 minutes to new surroundings?' and 'What is your baby's general response to new situations – the initial reaction to new stimuli, new food, people, places, toys, or procedures?') to which the mothers responded using the same seven-point scale. When visited in their homes, mothers were also asked open-ended questions about their infants' reactions to novel stimuli; their responses to this question were coded (0 = never, 1 = sometimes, 2 = often fearful of new situations), and were included in the fear-of-novelty scale. None of the items included in the fear-of-novelty scale was included in any of the other measures of temperament. The coefficients of internal consistency (Cronbach's alphas) for the fear-of-novelty scales at each age were high (.79 to .85).

Observational measures

Infants' emotional reactivity

The infants were presented with an array of positive and negative stimuli in the laboratory when they were 7, 10, and 13 months of age. Emotional expressiveness was coded using Izard and Dougherty's (1980) AFFEX System from videotapes of these sessions, and at each age two composite variables, indexing the duration of positive emotional expressions and the duration of negative emotional expressions, were computed (see Haynie and Lamb, 1995, for further details). The composite measures were internally reliable (.65 < alphas < .74) and the correlations between them were low

(-.05 to -.20), indicating that positive and negative emotional expressiveness were largely independent dimensions.

Mother–infant interaction

The exact procedures followed were described by Schölmerich, Fracasso, Lamb and Broberg (1995) and so they are only briefly summarized here. Mothers and infants were observed in their homes using an updated version of Belsky's (Belsky, Rovine and Taylor, 1984) observational procedure, in which a number of maternal and infant behaviours were coded on a 20 second observe/10 second record interval basis. The observed behaviours were later combined to yield a summary index of interactional harmony (Isabella and Belsky, 1991).

Psychophysiological measurements

Assessment of heart rate and vagal tone

Before presentation of the emotion-eliciting stimuli at each age, electrodes were placed on the infants' chests, and 5 minutes of heart rate data were collected using transkinetic telemetry while the infants sat on their mothers' laps in an awake, quiet, nondistressed state. During the entire laboratory protocol, heart rate data were recorded continuously and, after the emotion-eliciting episodes, another five minutes of baseline were recorded before the electrodes were removed. In this report, only the baseline data are used in comparative analyses. The ECG signal was stored on tape and later analysed using a Vagal Tone Monitor to derive measures of mean heart rate and vagal tone. The measure of vagal tone was computed using Porges's algorithm for filtering the respiratory sinus arrhythmia (RSA) out of the ECG signal based on complex filtering and detrending functions. This index has been used by other researchers and constitutes a better indicator of vagal nerve activity than other ways of estimating RSA. The exact procedures followed are described in greater detail by Fracasso, Porges, Lamb and Rosenberg (1994).

Cortisol measurement

Salivary cortisol was collected by inserting a swab laced with Kool-aid crystals into the infant's mouth when she or he arrived at the laboratory for the 5-month visit. The saliva obtained was then squeezed into a needleless syringe, frozen, and stored for subsequent analysis. The procedure was explained and demonstrated for the mothers, and they were asked to obtain saliva on four other occasions during the study. One probe was taken when the child first woke up in the morning, and a second one at the same time of day as the infant was scheduled to visit our laboratory. More details can be found in Schölmerich (1994).

Behavioural inhibition

As suggested by Kagan and his co-workers (Garcia Coll *et al.*, 1984), the 13-month laboratory visit began with a 20-minute-long observation of the children's behaviour when presented with a variety of novel stimuli. An initial free-play episode (1) was followed by a stranger episode (2), a robot episode (3), another free-play episode (4), and a clown episode (5). A number of measures indexing proximity to the mother and the latency to approach novel objects were scored from videotaped records. A principal component analysis showed that most behaviours in the two 'non-threatening' free-play observations (episodes 1 and 4) were unrelated to behaviour in episodes 2, 3, and 5. A composite measure of inhibition was then constructed using the measures of proximity to the mother in episodes 1, 2, 3, and 5, the latency to play with the stranger or touch the robot in episodes 2, 3, and 5, and the latency to approach the stranger/robot in episodes 2, 3, and 5. The internal consistency of this measure (Cronbach's alpha) was .84.

Results

Stability within domains

As expected and repeatedly reported by other researchers (e.g., Rothbart, 1981), the correlations among maternal ratings of infant temperament were relatively stable over the first year of life. When we examined correlations across ICQ scores and maternal ratings of the fear of novelty at 5, 7, 10, and 13 months of age, we found that the lowest correlation on the fussiness subscale was $r = .61$ between 5 months and 13 months and the highest $r = .83$ between 7 and 10 months of age. Similarly, fear-of-novelty correlations ranged between .46 and .63, and the correlations between fear of novelty and fussiness were in the same range.

A similar picture emerged when we looked at laboratory-based measures of affective behaviour. Positive and negative emotionality during the emotion-eliciting procedures were moderately correlated and the correlations tended to increase over time, although expressions of positive and negative emotionality were relatively independent of each other.

The biopsychological markers of reactivity showed essentially the same pattern of gradually increasing stability. For example, cardiac activity appeared relatively stable during the second half of the first year of life, with correlations among adjacent assessments (3 months apart) between $r = .50$ and $r = .55$ for vagal tone, and between $r = .32$ and $r = .57$ for heart period (Fracasso *et al.*, 1994). While means of heart period increased over time as expected, no such mean change was found for vagal tone. This may contribute to the slightly earlier relative stability of vagal tone and supports the validity of vagal tone as an index of autonomic reactivity. Combined baseline (home and pretest-laboratory) cortisol measures from adjacent time points were more highly correlated later rather than earlier in the year (r = .15 from 5 to 7 months of age, r = .51 from 7 to 10 months, and r = .58 from 10 to 13 months) (Schölmerich, 1994), thus showing a picture quite comparable to the cardiac measures.

Mother–infant interaction was assessed only at 7 and 10 months of age, but measures of the extent of harmonious interactions on the two occasions were significantly intercorrelated (r = .56) (Schölmerich *et al.*, 1995).

In summary, an expected picture of increasing stability over the first year of life emerged, compatible with the view that those characteristics undergo a process of shaping during this period and that there is ample variability to allow environmental input to have influence on the emergent personality. Certainly this is neither a random nor a deterministic process. However, we feel assured that our measurements were or became sufficiently reliable to warrant considering their interrelationships.

Relations across domains and measures

For those maternal report measures which appeared to be sufficiently stable over time (fussiness, unpredictability, and fear of novelty) we computed composite scores based on all available times of measurement with the exception of the assessment concurrent with the measurement of the target behaviour at 13 months (5, 7, and 10 months of age for most variables). Persistence was not sufficiently stable over time and was therefore not included in the analysis. The number of symptoms of irritability reported by mothers at 4 months of age was the only singular variable, since this information was collected only once. Measures of positive and negative emotionality were combined separately. Heart period and vagal tone measures were significantly intercorrelated, but we did not combine them for theoretical reasons (Stevenson-Hinde and Marshall, 1999). Thus there were three measures of autonomic system reactivity (vagal tone activity, heart period measurement, and cortisol reactivity). Finally, the score describing harmony in mother–infant interactions was combined from the observations at 7 and 10 months.

As Table 4.1 shows, some significant interrelationships across domains emerged. Fussiness was significantly related to unpredictability and fear of novelty, to number of symptoms of irritability, to positive emotional expressiveness, and to interactional harmony. Fear of novelty was correlated with number of symptoms of irritability, and interactional harmony. Negative emotional expressiveness was related to positive emotional expressiveness, and heart period was correlated with vagal tone.

Both cardiac measures were independent of the cortisol index, and all three indices of autonomic functioning were unrelated to any other combined measures in the study. In sum, maternal report measures (fussiness, unpredictability, fear of novelty, and number of symptoms of irritability) showed relatively more relationships among themselves than with variables

Table 4.1 Correlations among composites of precursors of inhibition in the first year of life

	Fussiness	Unpredict- ability	Fear of novelty	Symptoms of irritability	Negative emotionality	Positive emotionality	Heart period	Vagal tone	Cortisol	Interactional harmony
Fussiness		.611 **	.530 **	.513 **	.093	-.415 **	.030	.228	-.119	-.317 *
Unpredictability	.611 **		.200	-.118	-.250	-.005	.164	-.191	-.236	-.236
Fear of novelty	.530 **	.152		.461 **	.257	-.177	-.148	-.139	-.085	-.381 *
Symptoms of irritability	.513 **	.200	.461 **		.228	-.183	.042	-.053	-.119	-.258
Negative emotionality	.093	-.118	.257	.228		-.309 *	.077	.120	-.119	-.258
Positive emotionality	-.415 **	-.250	-.177	-.183	-.309 *		-.042	-.143	.197	-.090
Heart period	.030	-.005	-.148	.042	.077	-.042		.623 **	-.052	.160
Vagal tone	.228	.164	-.139	-.053	.120	-.143	.623 **		-.049	.050
Cortisol	-.119	-.191	-.085	-.119	.197	-.052	-.049	.046	.046	.043
Interactional harmony	-.317 *	-.236	-.381 *	-.258	-.090	.160	.050	.043	.089	.089

** Correlation is significant at the 0.01 level (2-tailed).
* Correlation is significant at the 0.05 level (2-tailed).

outside this cluster. Fussiness and fear of novelty from maternal reports showed relations to interactional harmony, which was an observed index, and fussiness was correlated with observed positive emotional expressiveness. It appears that maternal ratings of infant fussiness link across domains more than any other scale from the temperament questionnaire.

Predicting inhibition during the first year

Finally, to test the relative contribution of the predictor variables from the different sources for behavioural inhibition, we employed a regression analysis with the laboratory-based index of behavioural inhibition as the dependent and the following composite variables as predictors: *vagal tone* (5 to 10 months, physiological measurement), *heart period* (5 to 10 months, physiological measurement), and levels of *cortisol* (5 to 10 months, physiological measurement), *harmony of mother–infant interactions* at home (7 and 10 months, observation), *negative emotional expressiveness, positive emotional expressiveness, fear of novelty, fussiness, unpredictability*, and *number of reported symptoms* (4 months, maternal report). Two variables emerged as significant predictors of behavioural inhibition, negative emotional expressiveness and number of symptoms of irritability. The regression model including both predictor variables yielded $r = .446$ and thus negative emotional expressiveness and number of symptoms of irritability explained approximately 20 per cent of the variance in behavioural inhibition. Table 4.2 summarizes the results of this analysis including zero order and partial correlations of the predictors with inhibition.

The correlations between inhibition and the two significant predictors, negative emotionality and symptoms of irritability, reveal that there is no direct zero order association between symptoms of irritability and inhibition. Only if entered after negative emotionality do symptoms of irritability increase the precision of the prediction. In other words, among infants who match expectations about a relationship between negative emotionality and inhibition, higher scores on symptoms of irritability are more common.

Table 4.2 Regression analysis predicting behavioural inhibition

	Unstandardized coefficients		Standardized coefficients	t	Sig.	Correlations		
	B	Std. error	Beta			Zero-order	Partial	Part
(Constant)	.436	.462		.944	.351			
Negative emotionality	.242	.087	.399	2.782	.008	.329	.398	.389
Symptoms of irritability	-.711	.331	-.309	-2.150	.037	-.218	-.318	-.301

Inspection of scatter plots reveals that those who obtain high residual values when predicting inhibition on the basis of negative emotionality have lower scores on symptoms of irritability.

All other variables did not contribute over and above the two indices described above. Specifically, the physiological measures did not contribute to the prediction of behavioural inhibition, and the score indexing the harmony of mother–infant interaction was unrelated to the target variable

Summary

Our efforts yielded a picture of emerging stability and coherence during the first year of life within psychophysiological indices, behavioural assessments, and maternal perceptions of infant temperament. However, contrary to popular expectations, individual differences in physiological indices of reactivity as well as temperamental characteristics as reported by mothers were relatively ineffective in predicting behavioural inhibition at the end of the first year. Only laboratory-based negative emotional expressions and the number of symptoms of irritability reported by mothers contributed significantly to the prediction of behavioural inhibition. This supports the view that during early development, behavioural inhibition and shyness gradually emerge from a broader background of negative emotionality. Interestingly, however, the maternal report at 4 months of age on symptoms of early irritability, such as sleep regulatory problems, digestive problems, emotional instability, colic, and inability to adapt to new surroundings proved to be another significant predictor over and above negative emotionality.

In summary, our findings suggest that behavioural inhibition reflects one aspect of the child's orientation to the social and non-social world with important implications for the future development of shyness, but individual differences are only gradually consolidating during the first year of life. There is ample opportunity for complex interactions, and a reductionist position linking shyness or inhibition to differences in specific aspects of physiological reactivity or difficulties in mother–infant interactions is not supported by our data. Individual differences in negative emotionality early in life require further study to improve our understanding of the precursors of behavioural inhibition and, later in life, of shyness.

References

Andersson, K. (1999) 'Reactions to novelties: developmental aspects', Unpublished doctoral dissertation, Uppsala University.

Asendorpf, J.B. (1989) 'Shyness as a final common pathway for two different kinds of inhibition', *Journal of Personality and Social Psychology*, 57: 481–92.

Asendorpf, J.B. (1990) 'The development of inhibition during childhood: evidence for a two-factor model', *Developmental Psychology*, 26: 721–30.

Asendorpf, J.B. and Meier, G.H. (1993) 'Personality effects on children's speech in everyday life: sociability-mediated exposure and shyness-mediated reactivity to social situations', *Journal of Personality and Social Psychology*, 31: 125–35.

Asendorpf, J.B. and van Aken, M.A.G. (1991) 'Correlates of the temporal consistency of personality patterns in childhood', *Journal of Personality*, 59: 689–703.

Bates, J.E., Freeland, C.A.B. and Lounsbury, M.L. (1979) 'Measurement of infant difficultness', *Child Development*, 50: 794–803.

Belsky, J., Hsieh, K.-H. and Crnic, K. (1996) 'Infant positive and negative emotionality: one dimension or two?', *Developmental Psychology*, 32: 289–98.

Belsky, J., Rovine, M. and Taylor, D.G. (1984) 'The Pennsylvania infant and family development project, III: the origins of individual differences in infant–mother attachment: maternal and infant contributions', *Child Development*, 55: 718–28.

Calkins, S.D. and Fox, N.A. (1992) 'The relations among infant temperament, security of attachment, and behavioral inhibition at twenty-four months', *Child Development*, 63: 1456–72.

Cole, M. and Cole, S.R. (1996) *The Development of Children*. (3rd edn.), New York: W.H. Freeman and Company.

Dawson, G., Panagiotides, H., Grofer, L. and Hill, D. (1991, March) 'Individual differences in generalized frontal activity are related to intensity of infant emotional expression', Paper presented at the Society for Research in Child Development, Seattle, WA.

Dawson, G., Panagiotides, H., Grofer-Klinger, L. and Hill, D. (1992) 'The role of frontal lobe functioning in infant self-regulatory behavior', *Brain and Cognition*, 20: 152–75.

DeGangi, G.A., DiPietro, J.A., Greenspan, S.I. and Porges, S.W. (1991) 'Psychophysiological characteristics of the regulatory disordered infant', *Infant Behavior and Development*, 14: 37–50.

Fox, N.A. (1991) 'If it's not left, it's right: electroencephalograph asymmetry and the development of emotion', *American Psychologist*, 46: 863–72.

Fox, N.A. and Davidson, R.J. (1984) 'Hemispheric substrates of affect: a developmental model', in N.A. Fox and R.J. Davidson (eds) *The Psychobiology of Affective Development* (pp. 353–82), Hillsdale, NJ.: Erlbaum.

Fracasso, M.P., Porges, S.W., Lamb, M.E. and Rosenberg, A.A. (1994) 'Cardiac activity in infancy: reliability and stability of individual differences', *Infant Behavior and Development*, 17: 277–84.

Garcia Coll, C.T., Kagan, J. and Reznick, J.S. (1984) 'Behavioral inhibition in young children', *Child Development*, 55: 1005–19.

Gunnar, M.R. (1989) 'Studies of the human infant's adrenocortical response to potentially stressful events', in M. Lewis and J. Worobey (eds) *Infant Stress and Coping (New Directions for Child Development*, Vol. 45, pp. 3–18), San Francisco: Jossey-Bass.

Gunnar, M.R., Brodersen, L., Krueger, K. and Rigatuso, J. (1996) 'Dampening of adrenocortical responses during infancy: normative changes and individual differences', *Child Development*, 67: 877–89.

Gunnar, M.R., Mangelsdorf, S., Larson, M. and Hertsgaard, L. (1989) 'Attachment, temperament, and adrenocortical activity in infancy: a study of psychoendocrine regulation', *Developmental Psychology*, 25: 355–63.

Hagekull, B. and Bohlin, G. (1981) 'Individual stability in dimensions of infant behavior', *Infant Behavior and Development*, 4: 97–108.

Haynie, D.L. and Lamb, M.E. (1995) 'Positive and negative emotional expressiveness in 7-, 10-, and 13-month-old infants', *Infant Behavior and Development*, 18: 257–9.

Isabella, R.A. and Belsky, J. (1991) 'Interactional synchrony and the origins of infant–mother attachment: a replication study', *Child Development*, 62: 373–84.

Izard, C.E. and Dougherty, L. (1980) *A system for identifying affect expression by holistic judgement (AFFEX)*, Newark, DE: University of Delaware.

Jones, W.H., Briggs, S.R. and Smith, T.G. (1986) 'Shyness: conceptualizations and measurement', *Journal for Personality and Social Psychology*, 51: 629–39.

Kagan, J. (1997) 'Temperament and the reactions to unfamiliarity', *Child Development*, 68: 139–43.

Kagan, J., Reznick, J.S., Clarke, C., Snidman, N. and Garcia Coll, C. (1984) 'Behavioral inhibition to the unfamiliar', *Child Development*, 55: 2212–25.

Kagan, J., Reznick, J.S. and Snidman, N. (1988) 'Biological bases of childhood shyness', *Science*, 240: 167–71.

Kagan, J., Reznick, J.S., and Snidman, N. (1989) 'Issues in the study of temperament', in G.A. Kohnstamm, J.E. Bates and M.K. Rothbart (eds) *Temperament in Childhood* (pp. 113–44), New York: Wiley.

Kagan, J., Reznick, J.S., Snidman, N., Gibbons, J. and Johnson, M.O. (1988) 'Childhood derivatives of inhibition and lack of inhibition towards the unfamiliar', *Child Development*, 59: 1580–9.

Kagan, J., Snidman, N. and Arcus, D. (1998) 'Childhood derivatives of high and low reactivity in infancy', *Child Development*, 69: 1483–93.

Larson, M., Gunnar, M.R. and Hertsgaard, L. (1991) 'The effects of morning naps, car trips, and maternal separation on adrenocortical activity in human infants', *Child Development*, 62: 362–72.

Main, M. and Solomon, G. (1990) 'Procedures for identifying infants as disorganized/disoriented during the Ainsworth Strange Situation', in M.T. Greenberg, D. Cicchetti and E. M. Cummings (eds) *Attachment in the Preschool Years: Theory, Research, and Intervention* (pp. 121–60), Chicago: University of Chicago Press.

McDevitt, S.C. and Carey, W.B. (1981) 'Stability of ratings vs. perceptions of temperament in one- and two-year-old children: development and standardization', *Journal of Child Psychology and Psychiatry*, 21: 37–46.

Peters-Martin, P. and Wachs, T. (1984) 'A longitudinal study of temperament and its correlates in the first 12 months', *Infant Behavior and Development*, 7: 285–98.

Porges, S.W. (1983) 'Heart rate patterns in neonates: a potential diagnostic window to the brain', in T. Field and A. Sostek (eds) *Infants Born at Risk* (pp. 3–22), New York: Grune and Stratton.

Porges, S.W. (1991) 'Vagal tone: an automatic mediator of affect', in J. Garber and K. A. Dodge (eds) *The Development of Emotion Regulation and Dysregulation* (pp. 111–28), Cambridge: Cambridge University Press.

Porges, S.W., Doussard-Roosevelt, J.A. and Maiti, A.K. (1994) 'Vagal tone and the physiological regulation of emotion', in N. A. Fox (ed.) *The Development of Emotion Regulation. Biological and Behavioral Considerations* (Monographs of the Society for Research in Child Development, Vol. 59, Nos. 2–3, Serial No. 240, pp. 167–87).

Porges, S.W., Doussard-Roosevelt, J.A., Portales, A.L. and Greenspan, S.I. (1996) 'Infant regulation of the vagal "brake" predicts child behavior problems: a psychobiological model of social behavior', *Developmental Psychobiology*, 29: 697–712

Rothbart, M.K. (1981) 'Measurement of temperament in infancy', *Child Development*, 52: 569–78.

Rubin, K.H., Hastings, P.D., Stewart, S.L., Henderson, H.A. and Chen, X. (1986) 'The consistency and concomitants of inhibition: some of the children, all of the time', *Child Development*, 68: 467–83.

Schneider, M.L. and Suomi, S.J. (1992) 'Neurobehavioral assessment in rhesus monkey neonates (Macaca mulatta): developmental changes, behavioral stability, and early experience', *Infant Behavior and Development*, 15: 155–77.

Schölmerich, A. (1994, July) 'Infants' adrenocortical reactivity, observations of behavior, and mother–infant interaction in the first year of life', Paper presented at the IXth Biennial Meeting of the International Society for Infant Studies, Paris, France.

Schölmerich, A., Fracasso, M.P., Lamb, M.E. and Broberg, A.G. (1995) 'Interactional harmony at 7 and 10 months of age predicts security of attachment as measured by Q-sort ratings', *Social Development*, 4: 62–74.

Spangler, G. (1991) 'The emergence of adrenocortical circadian function in newborns and infants and its relationship to sleep, feeding, and maternal adrenocortical activity', *Early Human Development*, 25: 197–208.

Stansbury, K. and Gunnar, M.R. (1994) 'Adrenocortical activity and emotion regulation', in N.A. Fox (ed.) *The Development of Emotion Regulation. Biological and Behavioral Considerations.* (Monographs of the Society for Research in Child Development, Vol. 59, Nos. 2–3, Serial No. 240, pp. 108–34).

Stevenson-Hinde, J. and Marshall, P.J. (1999) 'Behavioral inhibition, heart period, and respiratory sinus arrhythmia: an attachment perspective', *Child Development*, 70: 805–16.

Thomas, A. and Chess, S. (1977) *Temperament and Development*, New York: Brunner/Mazel.

van den Boom, D.C. (1989) 'Neonatal irritability and the development of attachment', in G.A. Kohnstamm, J.E. Bates and M.K. Rothbart (eds) *Temperament in Childhood* (pp. 299–318), New York: Wiley.

Vaughn, B.E., Stevenson-Hinde, J., Waters, E., Kotsaftis, A., Lefever, G.B., Shouldice, A., Trudel, M. and Belsky, J. (1992) 'Attachment security and temperament in infancy and early childhood: some conceptual clarifications', *Developmental Psychology*, 28: 463–73.

Waters, E. and Deane, K.E. (1985) 'Defining and assessing individual differences in attachment relationships: Q-methodology and the organization of behavior in infancy and early childhood', in I. Bretherton and E. Waters (eds) *Growing Points of Attachment Theory and Research* (Monographs of the Society for Research in Child Development, Vol. 50, Nos. 1–2, Serial No. 209, pp. 41–65).

5 Childhood and adolescent shyness in long-term perspective

Does it matter?

Margaret Kerr

In most western cultures, parents are concerned about children who seem to be shy. They worry about the child's social adjustment, and the implications that the child's shyness might have for the future. Developmentalists, as well, consider interactions with peers necessary to normal social development, and they usually consider shy or socially withdrawn behaviour an obstacle to normal development (Dodge, 1986; Rubin and Rose-Krasnor, 1992; Rubin and Stewart, 1996; Rubin, Stewart and Coplan, 1995; Selman, 1985). In this chapter, I look at whether these notions are supported when a long-term perspective is taken. Using data from a birth-to-midlife study, I examine the links between childhood shyness and middle adulthood adjustment.

The role of shyness in social development

The idea that peer interactions are important has a long history in developmental theory. Decades ago, theorists such as Jean Piaget, George Herbert Mead, and Harry Stack Sullivan suggested, in one way or another, that peer interactions are a necessary mechanism through which young children can learn to take another's point of view, to understand other people's feelings, to negotiate, and to anticipate the consequences of their actions (Mead, 1934; Piaget, 1926; Sullivan, 1953). Experimentally, peer interactions have been found to improve children's abilities to understand another's point of view (Damon, 1977; Doise, Mugny and Perret-Clermont, 1975), which seems to be important because the lack of understanding of different aspects of interpersonal relationships has been linked to maladaptive social behaviour (e.g., Dodge, 1986; Rubin and Rose-Krasnor, 1992; Selman, 1985). These studies and others (see Hartup, 1992; Rubin and Coplan, 1992 for reviews) have led to the suggestion that social development will be disrupted if, for whatever reason, children do not interact with peers as much as others their age do (Rubin and Stewart, 1996). Shyness is one reason why they would not.

Peer relations are also considered to be vitally important in adolescence, and shyness could interfere with developing a close peer network then, as

well. Adolescent peer relationships continue the process
sensitive to others' perspectives and feelings (Berndt, 1
and they tend to last longer than younger children's fri
Cairns, 1994). Thus adolescent friendships should he
form lasting friendships and intimate relationships i
extent that these hypothesized mechanisms are import
interferes with this developmental process, shyness shou
unsatisfactory adult friendships and intimate relationshi

What we know about the links between childhood shyness and adult functioning

There is some longitudinal evidence that childhood shyness can delay important life transitions such as marrying, having children, and entering into stable careers (Caspi, Elder and Bem, 1988; Kerr, Lambert and Bem, 1996). Caspi and colleagues (Caspi *et al.*, 1988) used data from the Berkeley Guidance Study to examine the life courses of shy American children who were born in the late 1920s. They identified shy children from mothers' reports of behaviour at ages 8–10 and then compared them with non-shy children on adult measures. They found that shy boys married, had children, and entered into stable careers later than non-shy boys. Shy girls were not slow to marry or have children, but they tended to drop out of the workforce when they married and not return to work later as the non-shy girls did.

Later, my colleagues and I looked at the same issues using data from the present sample – people who were born near Stockholm in the mid-1950s (Kerr *et al.*, 1996). In this sample, too, shy boys were slower to marry and start families, but shy girls were not. Unlike in the previous study, for boys, childhood shyness was not connected to the age of entry into a stable career. For girls, however, the situation was different. None of the shy girls earned a university degree, whereas 44 per cent of the non-shy girls did, and this was independent of family socioeconomic status and of intelligence.

In both studies, then, shyness was associated with delayed marriage and parenthood for males but not for females. Both studies attributed these findings to traditional sex role expectations in which boys were expected to take the initiative in establishing romantic relationships. Shy boys might have progressed more slowly from less to more serious relationships because of hesitating to initiate relationships with girls, or because of having awkward early experiences.

In the domain of education and career, the links between shyness and later life seem to be tied to cultural attitudes about shyness and their influence on the customs that surround education and career entry. I have developed these ideas more thoroughly elsewhere (Kerr, in press), but, in brief, the fact that shyness hindered both boys' and girls' careers in the American sample maps onto one of the most salient features of American culture: the valuing of bold, assertive behaviour, particularly in the workplace. Shy men took longer to establish themselves and shy women preferred to avoid the workplace altogether. Swedish culture, on the other hand, favours more reserved behaviour and is more tolerant of shyness (e.g., Daun, Mattlar, and Alanen, 1989). Because its career-related customs are consistent with these values, there was no delayed entry into stable careers for shy Swedish boys. But Swedish women in this particular sample faced a special situation. When they came of age in the early 1970s women were expected, for the first time in history, to enter the labour force and be self-supporting, regardless of whether they married or not (Sandlund, 1971). Our findings seem to indicate that this was more difficult for shy women than for non-shy women.

What we don't know about the links between childhood shyness and adult functioning

Despite these findings, there are a couple of reasons to continue to question how problematic childhood shyness actually is in the long run. First, little is known about the psychological, social, and economic effects of shyness over the life course, even in the domains in which delayed transitions have been documented. Can we assume that shyness has caused females no problems in their romantic or sexual relationships just because they married at the same time as their peers? On the other hand, are shy males who married late unhappy or unsatisfied with their close relationships? One could easily argue that delayed marriage could be more of an advantage than a disadvantage. Many questions remain about the actual life situations of adults who were shy as children: whether they are happy and emotionally well-adjusted; whether they are satisfied with their close relationships, including their partner relationships; whether they are sexually well-adjusted; and whether they have more economic stress than their peers.

A second reason to continue to question whether childhood shyness is problematic in the long run, is that little is known about the life-course sequelae of early- versus later-developing shyness. Although early-developing, fear-based shyness and later-developing, self-conscious shyness have been distinguished theoretically and empirically (Bruch, 1989; Bruch, Giordano and Pearl, 1986; Buss, 1986; Cheek, Carpentieri, Smith, Rierdan and Koff, 1985; Schmidt and Robinson, 1992), the studies of long-term correlates have, so far, used childhood shyness measures from only one narrow age range. However, there are reasons to believe that early- and later-developing shyness might be differently related to long-term outcomes.

Early- versus later-developing shyness

Buss's (1986) theoretical distinction between early- and later-developing shyness has received considerable support and converges with other lines of research. The idea is that shyness that emerges early in childhood is temperamentally fear-based – a reaction that is similar to the concept 'behavioural inhibition to the unfamiliar' (e.g., Kagan, Reznick and Snidman, 1987, 1988; see Kagan, this volume, Chapter 2), if the unfamiliarity is social in nature. According to Buss, this form of shyness predominates for the first 4 or 5 years of life, before children have a well-developed ability to take another person's perspective, realize that other people have a perspective of them, and begin to worry about how they are being perceived by others. Probably the best recommendation for the concept of fear-based shyness is its similarity to behavioural inhibition. There is a large subject literature that has grown up around that construct in which inhibition has been linked to physiological features that suggest higher sympathetic nervous system tone. For example, compared with uninhibited children, inhibited children show more pupillary dilations and muscular tension in response to cognitive tasks and mild stress; higher heart rates; and higher levels of cortisol and norepinephrine (Kagan, Arcus, Snidman, and Rimm, 1995; Kagan and Reznick, 1986; Kagan *et al.*, 1988; Kagan *et al.*, 1987). All these indicate low thresholds for fear-like reactions.

According to Buss (1986), the shyness that emerges after children have started to think of themselves as social objects is rooted in self-consciousness rather than fear. This argument has been developed more fully by others. For instance, it has been suggested that the pubertal changes that occur in early adolescence might spur the development of self-conscious shyness (Cheek *et al.*, 1985), and that adolescent shyness is rooted in intense self-consciousness that is experienced during middle childhood and early adolescence (Bruch, 1989). Cross-sectional studies seem to bear this out because from middle childhood onward, shyness is related to low self-esteem, low social self-confidence, and low social skills (Cheek and Melchior, 1990; Crozier, 1981, 1995; Jones and Russell, 1982; Lawrence and Bennett, 1992; Miller, 1995). It is seldom, however, that researchers are able to examine early and later shyness in the same individuals.

What should we expect from early- versus later-developing shyness?

One could argue that early-emerging, temperamentally-based shyness should be particularly troublesome in the long run because it is present from the beginning, which gives it the chance to affect development throughout childhood. One could also reason that its biological basis should make it particularly resistant to change. Indeed, in small samples of children who were selected because they were extremely inhibited or uninhibited, just over half remained inhibited from 21 months to 7 years, and they had higher incidences of anxiety disorders and phobias than the others (Hirshfeld *et al.*, 1992) and were more likely to have multiple disorders themselves or in their families (Biederman *et al.*, 1993; Rosenbaum *et al.*, 1991). It is possible, then, that early-developing shyness is the foundation for later problems.

I argue differently, however. I propose that there are two key features of early, fear-based shyness that should be important in minimizing its long-term psychological, social, and economic impacts. One is the fact that the symptoms are avoidable, and avoiding them can be reinforcing because it is associated with pleasant experiences. People who experience the negative emotions of fear or anxiety when in new social situations will learn, over time, to avoid those situations and will also learn that avoiding them is associated with the pleasant experience of relief from fear and anxiety. If children associate the pleasant experience of relief from fear and anxiety with avoiding people, then (to the extent that being alone is accepted by those around them, so that other negative experiences do not arise as a result of avoiding social interaction) they should come to enjoy being alone. This should increase their sense of personal control. Even if they have few social encounters, they should not be unhappy or unsatisfied with life. In addition, fear-based shyness should disappear more readily than self-conscious shyness, or at least it should become less important in the self-definition of shyness. Rather, it should be transformed into simply an aspect of a person's habits or preferences. Hence, fear-based shyness should be less strongly related to later-developing self-conscious shyness than adolescent self-conscious shyness is to adult shyness.

Another key feature of early, fear-based shyness that should be important for determining its long-term implications is the fact that fear-based inhibition to the unfamiliar seems to subside when people and situations become familiar (Asendorpf, 1990). This means that fearfully shy people should be able to experience many interactions with familiar others that are unconnected to fearful or anxious feelings. Hence they should not necessarily be expected to have bad feelings about the interactions that they do have, particularly in close relationships, and their shyness should not necessarily affect the quality of those relationships. Consequently, fearful shyness should not be strongly or broadly linked to poor adult adjustment.

In contrast, self-conscious shyness is all about having unavoidable bad feelings about one's interactions with others and the way others think about one's self. That is the essence of the phenomenon. People with these tendencies should, almost by definition, be dissatisfied with the quality of their interactions with others. Because their avoidance of social situations centres around their own perceived inadequacies, avoiding them should not be particularly rewarding or associated with pleasant emotions. Rather the opposite. Although they will probably seek to avoid social interactions, doing so should just make self-consciously shy people more aware of their own failings. Because they see themselves as socially inadequate and because they are unable to escape these feelings by choosing solitary activities, they should feel less in control of their emotions and their behaviour. Furthermore, because a lack of perceived control can lie at the root of depression, they should be more likely to have depressive tendencies. As they navigate through adolescence and adulthood, they should have more and more unsatisfactory social interactions, including intimate relationships, and, over time, this inescapable dissatisfaction with the interpersonal aspects of their lives should make them less satisfied with life, in general.

In this study, I examine these propositions by looking at the midlife correlates of early- versus later-developing childhood shyness. I use midlife measures that are relevant either because they are connected to the domains of life in which delayed transitions have been documented or because they are connected to findings from concurrent and short-term longitudinal studies of shyness. These include:

- close relationships with friends and partners and sexual relationships;
- mental health, self-concept, and subjective well-being;
- occupational and economic circumstances.

I use shyness measures from three different age periods: early childhood, later childhood, and adolescence. In order to tap newly emerging shyness at each age period, a multiple regression approach is taken, in which shyness from previous ages is controlled. In addition, because gender differences have been found in many studies of shyness and inhibition at different stages in the life course (e.g., Crozier, 1995; Kerr *et al.*, 1994; Stevenson-Hinde and Glover, 1996) and from childhood to adulthood (Caspi *et al.*, 1988; Kerr *et al.*, 1996), gender is always included as a covariate and gender interactions are tested.

Method

Subjects

Participants were from a suburb of Stockholm. They have been part of a longitudinal study since they were born in the mid-1950s. Investigations of socioeconomic status, parents' age, mother's marital status, sibling order, gestational age and weight, and registered criminality have shown that the sample is representative of children in Swedish urban districts (Stattin and Klackenberg-Larsson, 1990). The children were seen every year until age 16 and then again at about ages 25 and 37. Up to the age of 16, all subjects were tested within 4 weeks of their birthdays. At the average age of 37, 185 subjects (91 per cent of those who were still alive) were interviewed. To determine whether the late-adolescent data were biased because of dropouts, those who participated in the data collection at age 16 were compared with those who did not on relevant childhood measures (Terman-Merrill intelligence and social background at age 5, and broad measures of internalizing and externalizing problems aggregated over ages 4 and 5). The people who participated at age 16 did not differ significantly on any of these measures from those who did not participate.

Measures

Shyness

Composite shyness measures were formed to represent three age periods in childhood. *Early childhood shyness* covered the ages of 18 months to 5 years (ratings were made at 18 months and then yearly from 3 to 5 years). In this measure, mothers' ratings of reactions to strangers were combined with psychologists' ratings of the child's behaviour during the laboratory visits. The mothers had been asked, 'How does your child respond to strangers?' The response options ranged from 'Open, friendly approach' (1) to 'Definite fear' (5). The psychologists rated behaviours that were similar to those that have been used to identify behaviourally inhibited children under similar conditions (Kagan, Reznick and Snidman, 1987, 1988). They included: ease of adjustment to the testing situation; clinging to the mother for emotional support; timidity and silence; and intensity and frequency of social responses to the experimenter. The mothers' ratings were highly consistent with the psychologists' behavioural ratings ($\alpha = .91$ for the full scale). The measures were averaged within rater and then combined. Because the mothers' ratings focused on fear of strangers and the psychologists' ratings were of behaviours that reflect behavioural inhibition, this measure can reasonably be considered a measure of fear-based shyness.

For the measure of *middle childhood shyness* (ages 6 to 11), mothers' ratings of shyness at each age were combined with psychologists' ratings at age 6 and teachers' ratings at age 10. Mothers answered the questions:'Is your child shy with strange peers?', and 'Is your child shy with strange adults?' Responses ranged from 'never' (1) to 'always' (5). The psychologists made the same behavioural ratings described above. When the children were 10 years old, their teachers rated them on a 5-point scale from 'shy-withdrawn' to 'pushing forward.' All items were standardized before the mean was calculated ($\alpha = .85$).

Adolescent shyness

Mothers' ratings of shyness with peers and shyness with adults, as described above, were taken yearly from ages 12 to 16. These were averaged to form the adolescent shyness measure ($\alpha = .91$ for the 10-item scale).

Adult shyness

At age 37, participants completed a well-known shyness scale (Cheek and Buss, 1981). The scale includes items such as: 'I feel tense when I'm with people I don't know', 'I am afraid of saying something stupid when I'm talking to others,' and 'I get nervous when I talk to authority figures' ($\alpha = .86$).

Convergent and discriminant validity of shyness measures

The pattern of relations that appears among the shyness measures, and between them and other variables, suggests that early shyness is qualitatively different from later shyness and that later shyness is connected to self-consciousness. Although middle-childhood and adolescent shyness were substantially correlated with each other (r (188) = .67, p < .001), they were less strongly related to early shyness (r (199) = .40, p < .001 and r (187) = .09, n.s., for middle-childhood and adolescent shyness, respectively). They were, however, both significantly correlated with self-reported shyness in middle adulthood, 20 to 30 years later, r (178) = .16, p < .05 and r (167) = .32, p < .001 for middle-childhood and adolescent shyness, respectively.

In addition, from middle childhood on, shyness seems to be linked to self-conscious worries but not to other types of worries. At the age of 15, the subjects rated each of 60 potential worries on 5-point scales from 'almost never worries me' (1) to 'worries me very often' (5). For the present purposes, two worries scales were formed. One was composed of 16 items that dealt with self-conscious concerns such as: appearance, not knowing enough about sex, not getting on well with other teenagers, and being made fun of by the opposite sex (a = .89). The other was composed of 24 non-self-conscious worries such as: not being good in school, not being able to stay out late, and having an operation (α = .91). These two worries scales were highly correlated with each other, r (163) = .75, p < .001.

Early shyness was uncorrelated with both measures, r (163) = -.09, n.s. and r (163) = -.10, n.s. for self-conscious and non-self-conscious worries, respectively. However, both middle-childhood and adolescent shyness were significantly correlated with self-conscious worries (r (163) = .15, p = .05 and r (163) = .22, p = .005, respectively), but not with non-self-conscious worries (r (163) = .06, n.s. and r (163) = .11, n.s., respectively). This pattern of correlations suggests that early shyness is qualitatively different from later shyness and that later shyness is connected to self-consciousness. It should be noted, further, that age-37 shyness was also significantly correlated with self-conscious worries but not with non-self-conscious worries, r (148) = .21, p = .01 and r (148) = .09, n.s., respectively. Hence, the difference between early and later shyness cannot be attributed solely to the fact that the worries measures were taken closer in time to the later shyness measures than to the early shyness measures. There are more than 20 years separating adult shyness from the worries measures, but only about 10 years separating early shyness from the worries measures.

Relationships

Friendships and social support

As a measure of the *number of friends* participants had, the mean of two free-response items was used. The items were 'How many neighbours are you so friendly with that you visit each other?' and 'How many close friends do you have, meaning people you feel comfortable and can speak freely with?'

In addition, participants rated their degree of satisfaction with their social networks: the people with whom they socialized; with whom they talked about things that bothered them; and whom they could count on if they needed help. The mean of these ratings was used as a measure of satisfaction (α = .78).

A measure of *emotional ties* to others was taken from the Mental Health Inventory (Veit and Ware, 1983). The three questions dealt with feelings during the past month of: loneliness (reversed); being loved and wanted; and having full and complete love relationships, loving and being loved. The mean of these three items was used as the measure of emotional ties (α = .72).

Partner relationships

A composite measure of *warmth and compatibility* with the mid-life partner was formed from interview questions and questionnaires (e.g., 'To give an overall impression of your relationship, how would you describe the home atmosphere?' (1 = very disharmonious, almost divorce atmosphere, 6 = unusually cordial relations, attitudes in harmony, open and warm home atmosphere); 'How often do you spontaneously cuddle or caress each other?' (1 = seldom, 5 = daily), and 'How warm are your feelings for your partner?' (1 = no warm feelings at all, 5 = very warm feelings). Items dealing with sexual relationships were excluded from this eight-item scale (α = .80).

Subjects also rated how often they talked to their partner about: things that happened at their workplaces, current events, politics, and personal matters. The response scale was a five-point scale ranging from 'very often' to 'never or nearly never'. The mean of these ratings was used as the measure of *communication*.

Sexual adjustment

As indicators of sexual adjustment, items were selected from reports given at ages 25 and 37. At both ages, subjects reported how often they engaged in sexual intercourse and how often they experienced orgasms during intercourse, and they rated their sexual adjustment with their current partner on a six-point scale from 'no sexual life together' to 'very well adjusted'. For each of these three items, the 25- and 37-year measures were averaged.

Psychological well-being

Mental health

Three measures of mental health were used. They were taken from subscales of the Mental Health Inventory (Veit and Ware, 1983). All questions directed subjects to report on their experiences of the past month. *Anxiety* was measured by ratings of, for example, being nervous or jumpy when faced with unexpected situations, being nervous in general, feeling tense, and having shaky hands (α = .88 for the nine-item scale). *Lack of control* assessed subjects' perceived lack of control over their own behaviour, their emotions, and whether things turned out well, in general. They were asked eight questions such as: 'During the past month, have you been in firm control of your behaviour, thoughts, emotions, feelings?' and 'How often, during the past month, did you feel that nothing turned out for you the way you wanted it to?' (α = .84). *Depressed mood* was assessed by questions such as: 'Did you feel depressed during the past month?' and 'How much of the time during .the past month have you felt downhearted and blue?' Four items were used (α = .91).

Self-concept

Two measures of self-concept were used. *Self-esteem* was measured with the Rosenberg Self-Esteem scale (Rosenberg, 1979). In this sample, the scale's reliability was .88. In addition, two items were averaged to represent subjects' feelings about their *physical appearance*. One was a free-response question about their appearance: 'What do you think about your appearance?' Their responses were scored from only negative comments (1) to satisfied (4). The other question was a free-response question about body image: 'How do you feel about your body?' Responses were scored from very ashamed (1) to very proud (6). These variables were standardized and averaged.

Subjective well-being

Two indicators of well-being were used. Life satisfaction was measured by a 16-item version of Neugarten *et al.*'s Life Satisfaction Index A (Neugarten, Havighurst, and Tobin, 1961). The items assessed general, global life satisfaction: 'These are the best years of my life' and 'As I look back on my life, I am fairly well satisfied' (α = .81). Positive affect was measured with the general positive affect scale of the Mental Health Inventory (Veit and Ware, 1983). The questions assessed the amount of time during the past month that subjects felt emotions such as happiness, satisfaction, and lightheartedness about their lives and daily activities (α = .92).

Occupational and economic circumstances

Occupational circumstances

Subjects were asked about the *size of their work group* – the number of people they work with each day. The *supervisory status* measure was a combination of two standardized measures: the level of supervision in subjects' work (from 'not at all' to 'head to a company') and the number of people that they were responsible for supervising.

Economic circumstances

Subjects reported their own and their spouses' monthly incomes. *Family income* was the average of the two. Hence, it represented the average earning power of adults in the household, whether subjects were partnered or single. *Financial situation* was a subjective rating of the family's financial situation: 'Financially, how are you doing?' Their answers were scored from very badly (1) to wealthy (5).

Results

Table 5.1 shows the results of simultaneous regression equations in which Shyness, Gender, and the Shyness x Gender interaction were used to predict the adult measures. For each adult measure, the model for early childhood shyness was tested first. Then, when the middle-childhood and adolescent models were tested, the earlier shyness measures and any significant interactions were included as covariates in order to assess the effects of newly-developing shyness at each age period. Table 5.2 shows the results for boys and girls separately. I will refer to these whenever the Gender x Shyness interactions in Table 5.1 are significant. Because of the relatively small sample size and the 20–30 years that elapsed between measurements, findings that are significant at the .10 level are reported.

Relationships

Friendships and social support

Table 5.1 reveals that, as predicted, early-developing shyness is unrelated to the perceived quality of midlife relationships – satisfaction with the people in one's social support network and emotional ties to others. Early-developing shyness is also unrelated to the number of friends that 37-year-olds report having. Shyness that develops in middle childhood is unrelated to these measures, as well. These findings apply to both girls and boys, as indicated by the absence of significant Gender x Shyness interactions. However, as predicted, shyness that develops in adolescence is linked to all of these measures of adult relationships. Higher levels of adolescent-developing shyness correspond to having fewer friends and emotional ties to others in midlife. Higher levels of shyness also correspond to being less satisfied with the number of people in one's social support network, but, as Table 5.2 reveals, this is more true for women than for men.

Partner relationships

As predicted, early-developing fear-based shyness is unrelated to these measures of the quality of partner relationships, whereas later-developing shyness is linked to poorer adult partner relationships. Shyness that develops in middle childhood, corresponds to less communication with the midlife partner for boys, but not girls, and shyness that develops in adolescence is linked to poorer compatibility with the midlife partner for both boys and girls.

Sexual relationships

The results for sexual relationships are also substantially consistent with predictions. Early-developing shyness is linked to less frequent sexual encounters in adulthood, but not to lower quality sexual relationships as indicated by reports of the frequency of orgasm and sexual adjustment. In contrast, adolescent-developing shyness is linked to less frequent and less satisfying sexual relationships for both men and women. Higher levels of adolescent-developing shyness corresponded to less frequent intercourse and poorer self-rated sexual adjustment with adult partners for both men and women, and to less frequent orgasms for women.

Psychological well-being

Mental health

As indicated by the Gender x Shyness interactions, the relations between early-developing shyness and all three measures of adult mental health depend upon gender. Table 5.2 reveals that the results for males are consistent with predictions. Higher levels of early-developing shyness correspond to lower anxiety in midlife, a greater sense of control, and less depression. These results do not appear for women, however. In contrast, the results for later-developing shyness are not dependent upon gender, and they show few links to these measures of adult mental health. There is, however, a link between adolescent-developing shyness and depressed mood in adulthood. No such relations appear for shyness that develops in middle childhood.

Table 5.1 Simultaneous regression equations predicting age-37 functioning from shyness that emerges at different ages

	Early childhood (18 months–5 years)			Middle childhood[1] (6–11 years)			Adolescence[2] (12–16 years)		
	Shyness	Gender	Gender x Shyness	Shyness	Gender	Gender x Shyness	Shyness	Gender	Gender x Shyness
Relationships									
Friends and social support									
Number of friends	.02	.10		-.04	.09		-.26*	.05	
Satisfaction with support	-.01	-.16*		-.11	-.16*		-.40**	-.20**	.20+
Emotional ties	.03	-.02		.00	-.02		-.27*	-.06	
Relationship with a partner									
Warmth and compatibility	.05	.07		-.07	.07		-.39**	.01	
Communication	-.05	-.19*		.02	-.19*	-.27*	-.08	-.21*	
Sexual relations									
Frequency of intercourse[3]	-.25***	-.02		-.03	-.03		-.24*	-.06	
Frequency of orgasm[3]	-.03	.62***		-.02	.63***		-.51***	.57***	.25**
Adjustment[3]	-.10	-.03		-.11	-.03		-.48***	-.11	
Psychological well-being									
Mental health									
Anxiety	.08	-.13	-.23*	.00	-.13+		.03	-.12	
Lack of control	.15	-.26***	-.29**	.02	-.26***		.03	-.26***	
Depressed mood	.03	-.21**	-.21+	-.06	-.22**		.20+	-.19*	

Table 5.1 continues

Table 5.1 (continued)

	Early childhood (18 months–5 years)			Middle childhood[1] (6–11 years)			Adolescence[2] (12–16 years)		
	Shyness	Gender	Gender x Shyness	Shyness	Gender	Gender x Shyness	Shyness	Gender	Gender x Shyness
Self-concept									
Self-esteem	-.31**	.25***	.31**	-.04		.25***	-.22*		.22**
Physical appearance	.00	.38***		-.05		.38***	-.21*		.35***
Subjective well-being									
Life satisfaction	-.06	-.10		.02		.08	-.34***		.13
Positive effect	-.12	.04	.26*	-.05		.04	-.26*		.00
Occupational and economic circumstances									
Occupational circumstances									
Size of work group	.06	-.01		-.07	-.02		-.24*	-.05	
Supervisory status	-.03	.24**		-.07	.23**		.03	.24**	
Economic circumstances									
Family income	.03	-.03		.01	-.03		.07	-.01	
Economic situation	.11	-.03		.17*	-.02		-.06	-.03	

1 Early childhood shyness and any significant interactions entered as covariates
2 Early and middle childhood shyness and any significant interactions entered as covariates
3 Mean of age-25 and age-37 measures
+ p < .10; * p < .05; ** p < .01; *** p < .001

Table 5.2 Simultaneous regression equations predicting age-37 functioning from shyness that emerges at different ages for boys and girls separately

	Boys			Girls		
	Early childhood	Middle childhood[1]	Adolescence[2]	Early childhood	Middle childhood	Adolescence
Relationships						
Friends and social support						
Number of friends	.04	.04	-.24	-.01	-.18	-.26
Satisfaction with support	-.07	-.02	-.09	.07	-.25+	-.43**
Emotional ties	.10	.02	-.21	-.05	-.01	-.26
Partner relationships						
Warmth and compatibility	-.06	-.11	-.25	.22+	-.06	-.50*
Communication	.00	-.39**	-.11	-.12	.21	-.17
Sexual relationships						
Frequency of intercourse[3]	-.21*	-.01	-.17	-.32**	-.05	-.33*
Frequency of orgasm[3]	.06	.01	-.05	-.13	-.07	-.61***
Adjustment[3]	-.03	-.11	-.44**	-.22+	-.10	-.51**
Psychological well-being						
Mental health						
Anxiety	-.24*	-.01	.02	.08	-.03	.02
Lack of control	-.26**	.05	.05	.15	.02	-.01
Depressed mood	-.27**	-.01	.10	.04	-.09	.26
Self-concept						
Self-esteem	.12	-.05	-.15	-.31**	-.06	-.28+
Physical appearance	-.05	-.04	-.17	.04	-.10	-.22

Table 5.2 (continued)

	Boys			Girls		
	Early childhood	Middle childhood[1]	Adolescence[2]	Early childhood	Middle childhood	Adolescence
Subjective well-being						
Life satisfaction	.04	-.02	-.31*	-.07	.01	-.35*
Positive effect	.23*	-.08	-.16	-.12	-.02	-.35*
Occupational and economic circumstances						
Occupational circumstances						
Size of work group	.01	-.12	-.15	.10	-.03	-.32+
Supervisory status	.08	-.13	-.04	-.22+	.01	-.01
Economic circumstances						
Family income	.05	.04	.09	-.00	-.08	-.01
Economic situation	.09	.25*	-.13	.15	.05	.03

Significant gender differences shown in bold.
1 Early shyness controlled in these models
2 Early and middle-childhood shyness controlled in these models
3 Mean of age-25 and age-37 measures
+ $p < .10$; * $p < .05$; ** $p < .01$; *** $p < .001$

Self-concept

Early-developing shyness is linked to adult self-esteem, but, again, this depends on gender. For women, higher levels of early-developing shyness correspond to lower self-esteem more than 30 years later. For men, the tendency is the opposite, which would be consistent with predictions, but the relation is nonsignificant. Consistent with predictions, however, adolescent-developing shyness is linked to more negative thoughts about one's self later in life, and this is true for both males and females. Higher adolescent-developing shyness corresponds to poorer self-esteem and more negative thoughts about one's body and general appearance.

Subjective well-being

The results concerning subjective well-being are largely consistent with predictions. Early-developing shyness is unrelated to life satisfaction. Adolescent-developing shyness is, however, related to lower life satisfaction in midlife. The same is true for positive affect, with the additional finding that higher early-developing shyness corresponds to more positive emotions in midlife for males. Higher levels of adolescent-developing shyness are linked to fewer experiences of positive emotions in midlife for both men and women.

Occupational and economic circumstances

Occupational circumstances

As Table 5.1 reveals, both early- and later-developing shyness are unrelated to having a supervisory position in middle adulthood. Being male is related to being a supervisor, but shyness does not add anything to the prediction of supervisory status. Early-developing shyness is unrelated to the size of one's work group. However, higher levels of adolescent-developing shyness are linked to working in smaller groups in middle adulthood.

Economic circumstances

These results offer no evidence that childhood shyness affects one's actual or perceived economic situation in midlife. Neither early- nor later-developing shyness was related to one's earning power, if single, or to the average earning power of one's self and one's spouse, if partnered. For subjective ratings of the economic situation of the family, middle-childhood-developing shyness was linked to a tendency to perceive one's economic situation slightly more positively.

Shyness at different ages versus shyness that develops at different ages

In this study, I have focused, conceptually, on early- versus later-developing shyness by consistently controlling for shyness at earlier points in time. How important is this, particularly given that the correlation between early shyness and adolescent shyness is close to zero? The answer to this question is clear from a glance at the correlations in Table 5.3, which are partial correlations between shyness at the two later age periods and the adult measures with only sex partialled out. They indicate what the beta slopes in

Table 5.3 Correlations between childhood shyness at different ages and 37-year functioning.

	Early childhood	Middle childhood	Adolescence
Relationships			
Friends and social support			
Number of friends	.04	-.03	-.16*
Satisfaction with support	.00	-.08	-.16*
Emotional ties	.03	.01	-.12
Relationship with a partner			
Warmth and compatibility	.05	-.04	-.24**
Communication	-.04	-.17	-.13
Sexual relations			
Frequency of intercourse[1]	-.25***	-.13	-.15*
Frequency of orgasm[1]	-.08	-.10	-.30***
Adjustment[1]	-.10	-.13	-.30***
Psychological well-being			
Mental health			
Anxiety	-.08	-.02	.03
Lack of control	-.05	.03	.08
Depressed mood	-.10	-.07	.10
Self-concept			
Self-esteem	-.09	-.10	-.19*
Physical appearance	-.03	-.08	-.21**
Subjective well-being			
Life satisfaction	.05	-.01	-.12
Positive effect	.07	-.02	-.16*
Occupational and economic circumstances			
Occupational circumstances			
Size of work group	.06	-.03	-.15+
Supervisory status	-.05	-.10	-.08
Economic circumstances			
Family income	.04	.03	.05
Economic situation	.12	.19**	.09

1 Mean of age-25 and age-37 reports

+ $p < .10$; * $p < .05$; ** $p < .01$; *** $p < .001$

Table 5.1 would have looked like if earlier shyness measures were not entered as covariates.

These correlations, particularly those for adolescent shyness, are consistently less strong than in Table 5.1 when earlier shyness is partialled out. It appears, then, that what is important for adult adjustment is the shyness that emerges in adolescence.

Discussion

This chapter has examined the long-term correlates of early- and later-developing shyness. I suggested that there are two dimensions on which early-developing, fear-based shyness and later-developing, self-conscious shyness differ that should determine their relations to adult adjustment:

• the extent to which the symptoms are avoidable and avoiding them is a pleasant experience;
• the extent to which one's interactions with familiar others are affected.

Based on these differences, I suggested that early, fear-based shyness should be linked to adulthood feelings of personal control, happiness, satisfaction with life, and fairly good relationships with others, even though interactions with others might be infrequent. In contrast, later-developing, self-conscious shyness should be linked, in adulthood, to a lack of perceived control, feelings of depression, and both few and poor-quality relationships with others.

The results support these patterns, to some degree. The only connection between early-developing shyness and adult relationships was one to less frequent intercourse. There were no relations between early shyness and any of the variables that tapped quality of relationships, either with friends, with the partner, or in the realm of sexuality. In contrast, adolescent-developing shyness was a negative predictor of nearly all measures of the frequency and the quality of interactions with friends and partners, and in the realm of sexuality. Concerning psychological well-being, early-developing shyness was clearly less problematic than later-developing shyness for males, but the same was not true for females. The results for males supported the hypotheses in that early-developing shyness was related to less anxiety, more feelings of control, fewer depressive symptoms, and more positive effect in adulthood. However, for all of these measures there were significant sex differences, and the results for females, although not strong, went in the opposite direction. In addition, for females early-developing shyness was linked to lower self-esteem in adulthood. For both sexes, however, adolescent-developing shyness was, as predicted, linked to more depressed mood, lower self-esteem, poorer attitudes about one's appearance, lower life satisfaction, and less positive affect. There is little evidence that any form of shyness is related to later occupational or economic circumstances.

These correlations, particularly those for adolescent shyness, are consistently less strong than in Table 5.1 when earlier shyness is partialled out. It appears, then, that what is important for adult adjustment is the shyness that emerges in adolescence.

These results show that shyness can have very different implications for men and women. One possible explanation for this is that the mechanism through which early-developing shyness could result in positive adjustment – through choosing solitary activities and finding that rewarding – might not work for females because they are expected to be more social than males. Perhaps it is more acceptable for boys than for girls to choose not to interact with others. If this is so, then this sheds a different light on the issue of sex differences than past research has. For instance, in an earlier study of the stability of shyness over childhood and adolescence in the present sample (Kerr *et al.*, 1994), my colleagues and I found that girls who were shy as toddlers remained more shy than average until age 16. Boys did not. We suggested, as others had before (Buss and Plomin, 1984), that shyness was more acceptable for girls than for boys, and that perhaps boys were more pressured to change. An alternative explanation, however, is that boys came to terms with their early, fear-based shyness through the mechanism hypothesized here, whereas girls, being given the message that they should not be choosing solitary activities, became self-conscious about their natural inclinations and developed a self-conscious form of shyness later on. This is also interesting in light of the earlier results showing delayed transitions to marriage for males but not for females. From those results, one could have concluded that shyness is more of an obstacle for boys than for girls. These results suggest that delayed transitions do not tell the whole story. Measures that tap adjustment more directly show very clearly that shyness was not more associated with poor adult adjustment for boys than for girls – and this was true neither of early- nor of later-developing shyness.

This study has examined later-developing shyness at two different age periods – middle childhood, when the first realization of oneself as a social object is supposed to occur, and adolescence, when issues such as puberty and sexual and romantic relationships are entering the picture. These results show clearly that adolescence is the age at which later-developing shyness becomes important for long-term adjustment. Shyness that develops in middle childhood was relatively unimportant in terms of life-course adjustment.

A particular strength of this study was the use of multiple informants as raters of shyness and the use of different informants (the subjects, themselves) as providers of the outcome measures. The study provides useful information about the relations between childhood and adolescent shyness and later adjustment. One problem with concluding that the results support the predictions that were presented, however, is that the fear-based shyness measures were taken further in time from the outcome measures than the later shyness measures were. One predictable finding in longitudinal studies is that the further apart in time the measures are taken, the weaker the associations tend to be. We should, then, expect fewer and weaker associations for early-developing shyness, which, unfortunately, is largely what I predicted. However, there are a couple of reasons to believe that the time factor is not an alternative explanation of the results. One is that measures that were taken closer in time in this study were not always more strongly related than measures that were taken further apart in time. Early shyness was uncorrelated with adolescent shyness (7–16 years apart), but adolescent shyness was substantially correlated with age-37 shyness (20–25 years apart). So proximity in time is not the only explanation. The second factor is that some of the links to early-developing shyness actually were as strong or stronger than the links to later-developing shyness for the same variable – frequency of intercourse, for example, and self-esteem for women. It appears, then, that time does not tell the whole story. Early- and later-developing shyness have different implications for adult adjustment.

It is difficult to say how much of these results are dependent upon culture. Cultural differences in the acceptance of shyness can be quite extreme and can have radically different implications for the social experiences of shy people. For example, in research with North American children, socially wary children are at risk for being rejected by their peers, becoming lonely and depressed, and feeling badly about their social skills (Boivin, Hymel and Bukowski, 1995; Rubin, Chen and Hymel, 1993). But a number of studies have shown that exactly the opposite is true in China (e.g., Chen, Hastings, Rubin, Chen, Cen and Stewart, 1998; Chen, Rubin and Li, 1999). These studies suggest that Chinese children's socially wary behaviour is valued and encouraged by parents, teachers, and peers and linked to perceptions of oneself as socially competent. Sweden is somewhere in between China and North America in its attitudes about shyness. Shyness is certainly more accepted in Sweden than in North America, because it is more consistent with the cultural values of reserve, dignity, and, above all, not thinking of one's self as better than others. Indeed, shyness provides a nice example of a phenomenon that cannot be seen apart from other factors that influence the whole person (Magnusson and Stattin, 1998). There might be a biological component, particularly for early-developing shyness, but what that means for the development of the whole person is determined by other factors – cultural, social, psychological, and biological. In long-term perspective, does shyness matter? Apparently, the answer is yes, but the questions why, when, and how still remain.

Acknowledgements

This research was supported, in part, by a grant from the Axel and Margaret Johnson Foundation. I wish to thank Håkan Stattin for facilitating work with the Swedish data.

References

Asendorpf, J.B. (1990) 'Development of inhibition during childhood: evidence for situational specificity and a two-factor model', *Developmental Psychology*, 26: 721–30.

Biederman, J., Rosenbaum, J.F., Bolduc-Murphy, E.A., Faraone, S.V., Chaloff, J., Hirshfeld, D.R., and Kagan, J. (1993) 'A 3-year follow-up of children with and without behavioral inhibition', *Journal of the American Academy of Child and Adolescent Psychiatry*, 32: 814–21.

Berndt, T.J. (1992) 'Friendship and friends' influence in adolescence', *Current Directions in Psychological Science*, 1: 156–9.

Boivin, M., Hymel, S., and Bukowski, W.M. (1995) 'The roles of social withdrawal, peer rejection, and victimization by peers in predicting loneliness and depressed mood in children', *Development and Psychopathology*, 7: 765–85.

Bruch, M.A. (1989) 'Familial and developmental antecedents of social phobia: issues and findings', *Clinical Psychology Review*, 9: 37–47.

Bruch, M.A., Giordano, S., and Pearl, L. (1986) 'Differences between fearful and self-conscious shy subtypes in background and current adjustment', *Journal of Research in Personality*, 20: 172–86.

Buss, A.H. (1986) 'A theory of shyness', in W.H. Jones, J.M. Cheek, and S.R. Briggs (eds) *Shyness: Perspectives on Research and Treatment* (pp. 39–46), New York: Plenum.

Buss, A.H., and Plomin, R. (1984) *Temperament: Early Developing Personality Traits*, Hillsdale, NJ: Erlbaum.

Cairns, R.B. and Cairns, B.D. (1994) *Lifelines and Risks: Pathways of Youth in Our Time*, Cambridge: Cambridge University Press.

Caspi, A., Elder, G.H., Jr., and Bem, D.J. (1988) 'Moving away from the world: life-course patterns of shy children', *Developmental Psychology*, 24: 824–31.

Cheek, J.M. and Buss, A.H. (1981) 'Shyness and sociability', *Journal of Personality and Social Psychology*, 41: 330–9.

Cheek, J.M., Carpentieri, A.M., Smith, T.G., Rierdan, J., and Koff, E. (1985) 'Adolescent shyness', in W.H. Jones, J.M. Cheek, and S.R. Briggs (eds) *Shyness: Perspectives on Research and Treatment* (pp. 105–15), New York: Plenum Press.

Cheek, J.M. and Melchior, L.A. (1990) 'Shyness, self-esteem, and self-consciousness', in H. Leitenberg (ed.) *Handbook of Social and Evaluation Anxiety* (pp. 47–82), New York: Plenum Press.

Chen, X., Hastings, P.D., Rubin, K.H., Chen, H., Cen, G., and Stewart, S.L. (1998) 'Child-rearing attitudes and behavioral inhibition in Chinese and Canadian toddlers: a cross-cultural study', *Developmental Psychology*, 34: 677–86.

Chen, X., Rubin, K.H., and Li, D. (1999) 'Adolescent outcomes of social functioning in Chinese children', *International Journal of Behavioral Development*, 23: 199–223.

Crozier, W.R. (1981) 'Shyness and self-esteem', *British Journal of Social Psychology*, 20: 220–2.

Crozier, W.R. (1995) 'Shyness and self-esteem in middle childhood', *British Journal of Educational Psychology*, 65: 85–95.

Damon, W. (1977) *The Social World of the Child*, San Francisco: Jossey-Bass.

Daun, Å., Mattlar, C.-E., and Alanen, E. (1989) 'Personality traits characteristic for Finns and Swedes', *Ethnologia Scandinavica*, 19: 30–50.

Dodge, K.A. (1986) 'A social information processing model of social competence in children', in M. Perlmutter (ed.) *Minnesota Symposia on Child Psychology*, Vol. 18.

Cognitive Perspectives on Children's Social and Behavioral Development (pp. 77–125), Hillsdale, NJ: Erlbaum.

Doise, W., Mugny, G., and Perret-Clermont, A. (1975) 'Social interaction and the development of cognitive operations', *European Journal of Social Psychology*, 5: 367–83.

Hartup, W.W. (1992) 'Peer relations in early and middle childhood', in V.B. Van Hasselt and M. Hersen (eds) *Handbook of Social Development: A Lifespan Perspective*, New York: Plenum Press

Hirshfeld, D.R., Rosenbaum, J.F., Biederman, J., Bolcuc, E.A., Faraone, S.V., Snidman, N., Reznick, J.S., and Kagan, J. (1992) 'Stable behavioral inhibition and its association with anxiety disorder', *Journal of the American Academy of Child and Adolescent Psychiatry*, 31: 103–11.

Jones, W.H., and Russell, D. (1982) 'The social reticence scale: an objective instrument to measure shyness', *Journal of Personality Assessment*, 46: 629–31.

Kagan, J., Arcus, D., Snidman, N., and Rimm, S. (1995) 'Asymmetry of forehead temperature and cardiac activity', *Neuropsychology*, 9: 47–51.

Kagan, J., and Reznick, J.S. (1986) 'Shyness and temperament', in W.H. Jones, J.M. Cheek, and S.R. Briggs (eds) *Shyness: Perspectives on Research and Treatment* (pp. 81–90), New York: Plenum Press.

Kagan, J., Reznick, J.S., and Snidman, N. (1987) 'The physiology and psychology of behavioral inhibition in children', *Child Development*, 58: 1459–73.

Kagan, J., Reznick, J.S., and Snidman, N. (1988) 'Biological bases of childhood shyness', *Science*, 240: 167–71.

Kerr, M. (in press) 'Culture as a context for temperament: suggestions from the life courses of shy Swedes and Americans', in T. Wachs and D. Kohnstamn (eds) *Temperament in Context*, Mahwah, NJ: Erlbaum.

Kerr, M., Lambert, W.W., and Bem, D.J. (1996) 'Life course sequelae of childhood shyness in Sweden: comparison with the United States', *Developmental Psychology*, 32: 1100–5.

Kerr, M., Lambert, W.W., Stattin H. and Klackenberg-Larson, I. (1994) 'Stability of inhibition in a Swedish logitudinal sample', *Child Development*, 65: 138–46.

Lawrence, B., and Bennett, S. (1992) 'Shyness and education: the relationship between shyness, social class and personality variables in adolescents', *British Journal of Educational Psychology*, 62: 257–63.

Magnusson, D., and Stattin, H. (1998) 'Person-context interaction theories', in W. Damon and R.M. Lerner (eds) *Handbook of Child Psychology*. Volume 1: Theoretical Models of Human Development (pp. 685–759), New York: Wiley.

Mead, G. (1934) *Mind, Self, and Society*, Chicago: University of Chicago Press.

Miller, R.S. (1995) 'On the nature of embarrassability: Shyness, social evaluation, and social skill', *Journal of Personality*, 63, 315–37.

Neugarten, B.L., Havighurst, R J., and Tobin, S.S. (1961) 'The measurement of life satisfaction', *Journal of Gerontology*, 16: 141.

Piaget, J. (1926) *The Language and Thought of the Child*, London: Routledge and Kegan Paul.

Rosenbaum, J.F., Biederman, J., Hirshfeld, D.R., Bolduc, E.A., Faraone, S.V., Kagan, J., Snidman, N., and Reznick, J.S. (1991) 'Further evidence of an association between behavioral inhibition and anxiety disorders: results from a family study of children from a non-clinical sample', *Journal of Psychiatric Research*, 25: 49–65.

Rosenberg, M. (1979) *Conceiving the Self*, New York: Basic Books.

Rubin, K.H., Chen, X., and Hymel, S. (1993) 'Socio-emotional characteristics of aggressive and withdrawn children', *Merrill-Palmer Quarterly*, 49: 518–34.

Rubin, K.H. and Coplan, R. (1992) 'Peer relationships in childhood', in M. Bornstein and M. Lamb (eds) *Developmental Psychology: An Advanced Textbook* (pp. 319–578), Hillsdale, NJ: Erlbaum.

Rubin, K.H. and Rose-Krasnor, L. (1992) 'Interpersonal problem-solving and social competence in children', in V.B. Van Hasselt and M. Hersen (eds) *Handbook of Social Development: A Lifespan Perspective* (pp. 283–324), New York: Plenum Press.

Rubin, K.H., Stewart, S.L., and Coplan, R.J. (1995) 'Social withdrawal in childhood: conceptual and empirical perspectives', in T.H. Ollendick and R J. Prinz (eds) *Advances in Clinical Child Psychology*, Vol. 17 (pp. 157–196), New York: Plenum Press.

Rubin, K.H., and Stewart, S L. (1996) 'Social withdrawal', in E J. Mash and R.A. Barkley (eds) *Child Psychopathology* (pp. 277–307), New York: Guilford Press.

Sandlund, M.B. (1971) 'The status of women in Sweden: report to the United Nations 1968', in E. Dahlström (ed.) *The Changing Roles of Men and Women* (pp. 209–302), Boston: Beacon Press.

Schmidt, L.A. and Robinson, T.N., Jr. (1992) 'Low self-esteem in differentiating fearful and self-conscious forms of shyness', *Psychological Reports*, 70: 255–57.

Selman, R.L. (1985) 'The use of interpersonal negotiation strategies and communicative competencies: a clinical-developmental exploration in a pair of troubled early adolescents', in R.A. Hinde, A. Perret-Clermont, and J. Stevenson-Hinde (eds) *Social Relationships and Cognitive Development* (pp. 208–32), Oxford: Clarendon Press.

Stattin, H., and Klackenberg-Larsson, I. (1990) 'The relationship between maternal attributes in the early life of the child and the child's future criminal behavior', *Development and Psychopathology*, 2: 99–111.

Stevenson-Hinde, J., and Glover, A. (1996) 'Shy girls and boys: a new look', *Journal of Child Psychology and Psychiatry*, 37: 181–7.

Sullivan, H.S. (1953) *The Interpersonal Theory of Psychiatry*, New York: Norton.

Veit, C.T., and Ware J.E. Jr. (1983) The structure of psychological distress and well-being in general populations, *Journal of Consulting and Clinical Psychology*, 51: 730–42.

6   Shyness in the context of close relationships

Joan Stevenson-Hinde

In infancy and early childhood 'shyness' may be viewed as one aspect of the widely studied concept of 'behavioural inhibition' – defined as a child's initial withdrawal to unfamiliar or challenging events (e.g., Kagan, 1989; 1994 and this volume, Chapter 2) – an aspect in which the events are restricted to social stimuli. With increasing age, the term 'shyness' has been applied not only to observed behaviour, but also to inner feelings. For example, Jones, Briggs and Smith (1986: 630) define shyness as 'a tendency to respond with heightened anxiety, self-consciousness, and reticence in a variety of social contexts; a person high in the trait of shyness will experience greater arousal than a person low in shyness independent of the level of interpersonal threat in the situation'. Now with young children, shyness may be assessed by means of questionnaires to parents or teachers, and results from these informants do indeed correlate significantly with each other and with direct observations (e.g., Stevenson-Hinde and Glover, 1996). However, in addition to the obvious point that questionnaires carry the risk of cross-temporal assessments being biased by relying on the same observers, we have found that mothers of securely attached children tend to over-estimate their children's shyness as compared with our observations, while mothers of insecurely attached children do the opposite (Stevenson-Hinde and Shouldice, 1990; see also Sameroff, Seifer and Elias, 1982; Stevenson-Hinde and Shouldice, 1995a; Vaughn, Taraldson, Crichton and Egeland, 1981). Since attachment is our other main interest, it was essential to avoid this sort of respondent-error in our assessments of shyness. Thus, in our own work, we tend to use questionnaires only as a 'back-up' (e.g., for screening purposes, see Stevenson-Hinde and Glover, 1996). Following Kagan's lead, we rely primarily on direct observations of behaviour. Thus direct observations will be the focus of the present chapter, with assessments of behavioural inhibition from the Madingley studies involving responses to social stimuli only, and behavioural inhibition from the other studies cited involving Kagan's more general definition.

Behavioural inhibition (BI) is seen as a temperamental construct, reflecting relatively stable individual differences in behavioural style (e.g.,

Goldsmith *et al.*, 1987). Longitudinal studies have demonstrated BI to be at least moderately stable throughout childhood (e.g., Kagan, Reznick, Snidman, Gibbons and Johnson, 1988; Kerr, Lambert, Stattin and Klackenberg-Larsson, 1994; Stevenson-Hinde and Shouldice, 1995b, 1996; Fordham and Stevenson-Hinde, 1999), twin studies have indicated a significant heritable component (e.g., DiLalla, Kagan and Reznick, 1994; see also Schmidt, Polak and Spooner, in press), and associations have been made with infant precursors of BI and genetic polymorphisms (Auerbach *et al*, 1999). Kagan and others have gone on to identify physiological correlates of BI (e.g., EEG data, cortisol levels, and cardiac functioning; reviewed in Marshall and Stevenson-Hinde, in press; Schmidt and Tasker, this volume, Chapter 3), with models focusing on variation in the excitability of neural circuits in the limbic system and the amygdala playing a central role (e.g., Davidson and Rickman, 1999; LeDoux, 1995).

Yet in spite of all the above reasons for viewing BI as an aspect of a child's temperament, BI does of course vary – across time (see above references), across measures (e.g., Reznick, Gibbons, Johnson and McDonough, 1989), and across contexts (Stevenson-Hinde, 1989, 1998) – leaving room for environmental influences. As I have suggested earlier, one may view any given temperamental characteristic as lying along a continuum, in which the susceptibility to environmental influences lies within limits from 0 per cent to 100 per cent. Furthermore, the position of any given characteristic on such a continuum may change with age. Thus, BI 'may be relatively *independent* of relationships from 0–6 months, then *modified* by attachment relationships and social reinforcement, and finally *relatively fixed*' (Stevenson-Hinde, 1988: 75).

Indeed, 'biological considerations do not imply that behaviour is *determined* by genetic factors which are or were selected in evolution, but rather by a continuous interplay between those factors and experiential ones' (Hinde and Stevenson-Hinde, 1991: 54; see also Vaughn and Bost, 1999). This statement reflects the central thesis of this chapter, namely of a continuous interplay between BI and experience. Since experience within close family relationships is particularly salient in the early years (e.g., Cassidy and Shaver, 1999), the present chapter will consider BI in relation to mother/child interactions, the quality of attachment to mother, and feelings of self-worth.

An ethological perspective

However, before moving on, I should acknowledge the ethological context of our work at Madingley, and set both BI and attachment behaviour in that perspective. To start with, fear of the unfamiliar is a ubiquitous characteristic, not only within our own species, but also over a broad range of species, ranging from pumpkinseed sunfish to other primates (e.g., Gosling and John, 1999; Stevenson-Hinde, Stillwell-Barnes and Zunz, 1980; Wilson, Coleman, Clark and Biederman, 1993). This is, of course, the approach taken by John Bowlby (e.g., 1982), who considered attachment behaviour, conspicuous in stressful situations, to be a ubiquitous characteristic of many species, including humans.

Second, such a common characteristic within and across species suggests that fearful behaviour may have been selected for during the course of evolution. The argument is that individuals who exhibited fear of the unfamiliar would have been more apt to survive and leave offspring who in turn reproduce – i.e., to have increased their inclusive fitness – compared with those who did not. In harmony with this view, Stevenson, Batten and Cherner (1992) have shown that fears concerning harm possibly relevant during the course of evolution (e.g., fear of the unknown, fear of animals, fear of danger) have significant heritability estimates, while modern-day fears not involving risk of life (e.g., fear of criticism, fear of medical procedures) do not. Thus, the propensity to show BI may have been guided by natural selection, with the function being protection from harm (Stevenson-Hinde and Shouldice, 1996). Again, this reflects Bowlby's suggestion that attachment behaviour and its complement, caregiving behaviour, have almost certainly been selected for during the course of evolution (Bowlby, 1982).

Third, as Bowlby argued:

> It is against this picture of man's environment of evolutionary adaptedness that the environmentally stable behavioural equipment of man is considered. Much of this equipment, it is held, is so structured that it enables individuals of each sex and each age-group to take their places in the organised social group characteristic of the species ... not a single feature of a species' morphology, physiology, or behaviour can be understood or even discussed intelligently except in relation to that species' environment of evolutionary adaptedness.
>
> (Bowlby, 1982: 64)

We shall apply this argument first to the occurrence of 'irrational fears of childhood' and then to the individual consistency found in both BI and attachment behaviour.

In considering the fears of childhood, such as fear of strangeness, separation, noise, sudden approach, or darkness, Bowlby disagreed with the analysts of his day such as Klein or Freud who labelled them as unrealistic, irrational or abnormal. Instead Bowlby argued that our tendency to fear what had been dangers in the environments in which we evolved is 'to be regarded as a natural disposition of man ... that stays with him in some degree from infancy to old age ... . Thus it is not the presence of this tendency in childhood or later life that is pathological; pathology is indicated either when the tendency is apparently absent or when fear is aroused with unusual readiness and intensity' (Bowlby, 1973: 84). Similarly, attachment behaviour in times of stress should not be viewed as a sign of weakness, at any age. Long before research began on the role of attachment in adulthood, Bowlby wrote 'such tendencies ... are present not only during childhood but throughout the whole span of life. Approached in this way, fear of being separated unwillingly from an attachment figure at any phase of the life-cycle ceases to be a puzzle, and instead, becomes classifiable as an instinctive response to one of the naturally occurring clues to an increased risk of danger' (Bowlby, 1973: 86). In one of his final contributions, Bowlby continued in this vein:

> Once we postulate the presence within the organism of an attachment behavioural system regarded as the product of evolution and having protection as its biological function, many of the puzzles that have perplexed students of human relationships are found to be soluble. ... Instead, an urge to keep proximity or accessibility to someone seen as stronger or wiser, and who if responsive is deeply loved, comes to be recognised as an integral part of human nature and as having a vital role to play in life. Not only does its effective operation bring with it a strong feeling of security and contentment, but its temporary or long-term frustration causes acute or chronic anxiety and discontent. When seen in this light, the urge to keep proximity is to be respected, valued, and nurtured as making for potential strength, instead of being looked down upon, as so often hitherto, as a sign of inherent weakness.
>
> (Bowlby, 1991: 293)

Turning to the consistency in individual differences in both BI and patterns of attachment, is there a relevant evolutionary argument here as well? Wilson, Clark, Coleman and Dearstyne (1994) have suggested how frequency-dependent selection may have produced 'phenotypically inflexible genotypes', as well as 'phenotypically plastic genotypes'. Referring to 'shyness' and 'boldness', characteristics found in a wide range of species and not unlike 'high BI' and 'low BI', Wilson *et al.* argue that in a constant environment, the inflexible shy and bold individuals should replace the plastic form. 'If the opportunities for risk-prone and risk-averse individuals are temporally variable, however, natural selection will promote a mixture of innate and facultative forms, whose relative proportions will depend on the magnitude of temporal variation' (p. 445). This suggestion is compatible with Kagan's approach to BI – that children who are extreme, with either high or low BI, should be treated as if qualitatively different from each other and from children in the mid-range (Kagan, Snidman and Arcus, 1998).

A similar argument may be applied to consistent individual differences in quality of attachment, reflected in the three basic patterns: Avoidant, Secure, and Ambivalent. 'It is evident that the particular pattern taken by any one child's attachment behaviour turns partly on the initial biases that infant and mother each bring to their partnership and partly on the way that each affects the other during the course of it' (Bowlby, 1982: 340). After presenting data, Bowlby continues, 'By the time the first birthday is reached both mother and infant have commonly made so many adjustments in response to one another that the resulting pattern of interaction has already become highly characteristic' (Bowlby, 1982: 348). In addition to the immediate characteristics of the infant, the behaviour of the caregiver is determined by 'the particular sequence of environments, from infancy onwards, within which development takes place' (Bowlby, 1982: 378). In more recent terminology, 'patterns of attachment represent nascent facultative reproductive strategies that evolved to promote reproductive fitness in particular ecological niches' (Belsky, 1999: 150). But a pattern required for the 'biological desiderata' of increasing inclusive fitness need not be the same as a pattern fitting 'cultural desiderata' (e.g., in Bielefeld where an Avoidant pattern was the norm compared with Regensburg where a Secure pattern predominated; Grossmann, Fremmer-Bombik, Rudolph and Grossmann, 1988). And it was the Secure pattern which Bowlby, as a practising psychiatrist, saw as absolutely basic for 'psychological well-being'. These three desiderata – biological, cultural, and psychological – while influencing each other, may differ, especially in modern industrialized societies (Hinde and Stevenson-Hinde, 1991).

A fourth ethological issue is the postulation that fearful behaviour – like attachment behaviour or exploratory behaviour – is organized as a distinct motivational system within individuals (e.g., Stevenson-Hinde, 1991; Stevenson-Hinde and Shouldice, 1993). Such a behaviour system may have a unique threshold of arousal within each individual (Stevenson-Hinde and Shouldice, 1996: 242, Fig. 11.1). A 'fear behaviour system', like other behaviour systems, is 'distinguished on the basis of common causation ... [and is] usually found to subserve a particular biological function' (Baerends, 1976: 721–3). A behaviour systems approach stresses organization within and between systems: 'In the study of behaviour as well as neuroscience the investigator must typically deal with interlocking *networks* of organisational processes, rather than being satisfied with simple linear conceptualisations' (Fentress, 1991: 78). Within a behaviour systems approach, activation of a 'fear behaviour system' would lead to activation of the 'attachment behaviour system'. Attachment behaviour would lead to proximity to the caregiver, which would in turn deactivate the fear system, enabling activation of an exploratory or social system (e.g., Bowlby, 1982; with data from Greenberg and Marvin, 1982). Thus, 'Activation of a fear behaviour system may lead to activation of an attachment behaviour system in all infants or young children, many times over. Furthermore, such activation will occur in the context of close relationships, with influences being mutual during the course of development' (Stevenson-Hinde, 1991: 325–6).

Just as attachment behaviour towards a caregiver may be distinguished from BI, so also may separation anxiety, which tends to appear independently of BI in the course of development (Bowlby, 1982).

> The simplest form in which the distinction can be stated is that, on the one hand, we try at times to *withdraw or escape* from a situation or object that we find alarming, and, on the other, we try to *go towards or remain*

with some person or in some place that makes us feel secure. The first type of behaviour is commonly accompanied by a sense of fright or alarm, and is not far from what Freud had in mind when he spoke of 'realistic fear'. ... The second type of behaviour is, of course, what is termed here attachment behaviour. So long as the required proximity to the attachment-figure can be maintained, no unpleasant feeling is experienced. When, however, proximity cannot be maintained ... the consequent searching and striving are accompanied by a sense of disquiet, more or less acute; and the same is true when loss is threatened. In this disquiet at separation and at threat of separation Freud in his later work came to see 'the key to an understanding of anxiety'.

(Bowlby, 1982: 330)

We shall return to this point with the model put forward at the end of the chapter.

Assessing the quality of behaviour

Assessments of BI and attachment behaviour involve differing contexts. Whereas BI assessments involve behaviour in *unfamiliar* and challenging situations such as meeting a stranger, attachment assessments involve behaviour to a *well-known* caregiver, usually mother. The attachment focus is on how a child uses mother as a 'secure base' when distressed, typically observed during separation/reunion episodes within the Ainsworth strange situation. Thus, a behaviourally inhibited child – who would withdraw when a stranger entered and, after being left alone, would not be comforted by the stranger – might nevertheless be relatively easily soothed by mother after separation from her, and hence judged securely attached. Indeed, this would be expected if brought up by a mother who was sensitively responsive (see the meta-analysis by DeWolff and van IJzendoorn, 1997).

In our own studies, BI as well as attachment is assessed in terms of quality as opposed to quantity (see Figure 6.1). That is, instead of measuring the frequency of responses or latency to first occurrence of a particular response, we apply ratings scales to both verbal and non-verbal behaviour, thereby indexing a child's behavioural style along the lines of temperament theorists such as Thomas and Chess (reviewed in Goldsmith *et al.*, 1987). Such ratings may be made in the home or laboratory (see Fordham and Stevenson-Hinde, 1999). We repeatedly view a video-taped sequence – first, to get an overview, then for rating verbal behaviour, then for non-verbal behaviour, and finally for a global rating. Such coding can be applied over a wide age range, and we have used it at 2.5 years (Stevenson-Hinde and Shouldice, 1990), 4.5 and 7 years (Marshall and Stevenson-Hinde, 1998), and 10 years (Fordham and Stevenson-Hinde, 1999). What does change with age is the nature of the challenge – with older children not simply being invited to approach the

LOW	MEDIUM	HIGH
1 2 3	| 4 5 6 |	7 8 9

norm for age

Verbal behaviour

ready verbal responsiveness	minimal responsiveness
clear voice, spontaneous	soft, 'tight' voice
initiations and/or full extensions	no initiations

Non-verbal behaviour

relaxed posture	tense posture, nervous gestures, fidgeting
ease of orientation to S	physical/visual avoidance
open facial expression	tense face, tight lips, wary look
relaxed smile	ambivalent smile

Figure 6.1 BI ratings applied to our samples aged 2.5 to 10 years – based on behaviour towards a stranger

stranger 'to see what is in my hand', but rather being asked conversational questions, ending with a request to stand up and 'sing your favourite song'.

Similarly, in assessing attachment it is the quality rather than the quantity of behaviour that counts. Reunion episodes are viewed over and over, in order to classify how the child organizes his or her behaviour to mother following the stress of separation. A Secure child greets mother's return with full gaze and positive affect. Interactions are calm, while also intimate and indicative of a special relationship. The two main insecure patterns may be contrasted with this, and indeed with each other. Whereas the Avoidant child shows minimal responses and maintains neutrality, the Ambivalent child emphasizes dependence on mother, with angry/whiny resistance and/or immature behaviour (from the Cassidy and Marvin coding system for 2.5- to 4.5-year-olds, 1992).

Physiological functioning and BI from an attachment perspective

Before exploring direct relations between BI and attachment, it should be pointed out that attachment status may be used as an adjunct to clarify predicted relations between BI and physiological functioning. As noted above, Kagan and his co-workers have hypothesized that differences in reaction to novelty between inhibited and uninhibited children arise from variation in the excitability of neural circuits in the limbic system, which in turn affect cardiac pacemaker activity and provide a rationale that inhibited children should show consistently higher heart rate than uninhibited children. This rationale has been supported by some studies, but not all (see Stevenson-Hinde and Marshall, 1999).

We suggest that those studies which do support the predicted relation between BI and autonomic functioning may have a high proportion of children who are securely attached to their mothers. Within our own sample of children selected for Low, Medium, or High BI (as indicated in Figure 6.1), we found that it was only the Secure children who showed the predicted relations – with the high BI group having significantly lower heart period (or higher heart rate) than the low BI group. A characteristic of Secure children is that, through interactions with a sensitively responsive caregiver, they are able to express their emotions in a relaxed and open manner, without the need to develop any particular strategy. With such 'emotional coherence' (Grossmann and Grossmann, 1991: 108), Secure children should exhibit a more direct relation between autonomic functioning and behaviour to strangers than should insecure children. Indeed, our insecure children did not show any significant relations between BI and HP (Stevenson-Hinde and Marshall, 1999).

Mother/child interactions related to BI and attachment

Some relations between high BI and parent/child interactions have been reported, although it would be useful to have more data here. For example, BI has been associated with parental over-protection, over-control, and less allowance of psychological autonomy or failure to encourage independent opinions (see Figure 6.2). Furthermore, such interactions are similar to those associated with the development of an Ambivalent pattern of attachment: interfering, inconsistent, and unpredictable (reviewed in Cassidy and Berlin, 1994). With an unpredictable caregiver, 'infants live with the constant fear of being left vulnerable and alone ... the anxiety associated with this fear of separation lasts beyond infancy as well.' (Weinfield, Sroufe, Egeland and Carlson, 1999: 78). Thus, given the similarities in mothering style, the two child 'outcomes' – BI and Ambivalent attachment – are likely to co-occur. We should add that the direction of effect here is likely to be two-way:

BI ◀──▶ mothering style ◀──▶ Ambivalent attachment.

BI and attachment

We have seen how mothering style may provide a developmental reason for the co-occurrence of BI and a particular pattern of attachment – Ambivalent. An additional reason for expecting this pattern to be associated with BI concerns how Ambivalently attached children express their emotions.

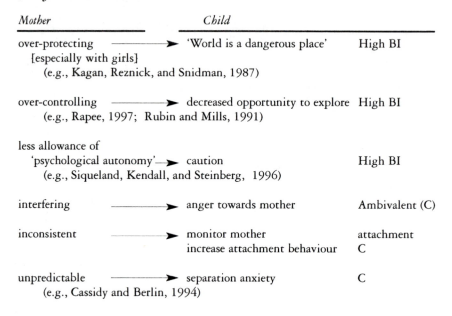

Mother	*Child*	
over-protecting ———————▶ [especially with girls] (e.g., Kagan, Reznick, and Snidman, 1987)	'World is a dangerous place'	High BI
over-controlling ———————▶ (e.g., Rapee, 1997; Rubin and Mills, 1991)	decreased opportunity to explore	High BI
less allowance of 'psychological autonomy'——▶ (e.g., Siqueland, Kendall, and Steinberg, 1996)	caution	High BI
interfering ———————▶	anger towards mother	Ambivalent (C)
inconsistent ———————▶	monitor mother increase attachment behaviour	attachment C
unpredictable ———————▶ (e.g., Cassidy and Berlin, 1994)	separation anxiety	C

Figure 6.2 Aspect of mothering style associated with child's behaviour High behavioural inhibition (BI) and an ambivalent pattern of attachment (C)

Suppose we have three children with similar underlying predispositions to BI. In practice, the Secure (B) child who expresses emotions openly may receive a higher BI rating than the Avoidant (A) child who tries very hard to appear neutral, thereby hiding his emotions. However, the Ambivalent (C) child, with the strategy of over-emphasising emotions and dependence, might 'overplay' emotions and be observed to be the most fearful. Thus, we have two distinct reasons for predicting a relation between BI and Ambivalent attachment.

This prediction is supported by results involving both infants and young children (see Figure 6.3). When significant relations occur, they involve an association between high BI and the Ambivalent (C) pattern. In our normal sample of 2.5-year-olds, the Very Secure (B3) children were observed to be the least fearful, and the Ambivalent children the most fearful. Furthermore, our own studies suggest that relations between BI and attachment are more apt to appear with samples which ensure a good proportion of high BI children. That is, whereas in our 'normal' sample the relations found at 2.5 years disappeared at 4.5 years, significant relations at 4.5 years did occur within a sample selected to contain a good proportion of children with high BI, and the relations held at 7 years (see Figure 6.4). Note that, as expected, the ratings of this selected sample tend to be above 4, which was the 'norm for age', and that BI decreased over the samples, from 4.5 to 7 years (Marshall and Stevenson-Hinde, 1998). At both ages, BI in Ambivalent

Infancy   Level of BI
   (Calkins and Fox, 1992)
      BI at 24 months with SS pattern at 14 months   A < C**
   (Kochanska, 1998)
      BI at 13–15 months with contemporaneous SS pattern   A < C*

Early childhood
   (Stevenson-Hinde and Shouldice, 1990)
      BI at 30 months with contemporaneous SS pattern   B3 < C***
   but not later in the same sample
   (Stevenson-Hinde and Shouldice, 1993)
      BI at 4.5 years with contemporaneous SS pattern   n.s.

   With a sample SELECTED for high/low BI
   (Stevenson-Hinde and Marshall, 1999)
      BI at 4.5 years with contemporaneous SS pattern   A < C*
      BI at 7 years with SS pattern at 4.5 years   A < C*

* $p < .05$;   *** $p < .001$, two-tailed
n.s. – no significant differences

Figure 6.3 The level of behavioural inhibition (BI) associated with particular patterns of attachment observed in the strange situation (SS): Avoidant (A), Ambivalent (C) or Very Secure (B3).

children was significantly greater than BI in Avoidant children. Consistent with predictions, Avoidant children showed the lowest BI.

In addition to the three main patterns of attachment identified in Ainsworth's original study (Ainsworth, Blehar, Waters, and Wall, 1978), Figure 6.4 includes two more recently identified insecure patterns: Controlling, characterized by the child rather than mother structuring the reunion episode; and Insecure-other reflecting insecurity but with no particular pattern or a mixture of patterns. The Insecure-other pattern, as well as the Disorganized pattern (not represented here since only one child in the sample showed it), has been particularly associated with disorder (see chapters in Cassidy and Shaver, 1999), and here the highest BI ratings occurred in children classed as Insecure-other, with Ambivalent children coming next. The association between high BI, an Ambivalent pattern, an Insecure-other pattern, and the development of anxiety disorder warrants further study.

Conclusions

Thus, BI is seen as a temperamental characteristic influenced by and possibly influencing mothering style, particularly over-protection and control. Similarly, insensitive mothering, involving interference and unpredictability, is related to an insecure Ambivalent pattern of attachment in the child, which in turn is related to BI.

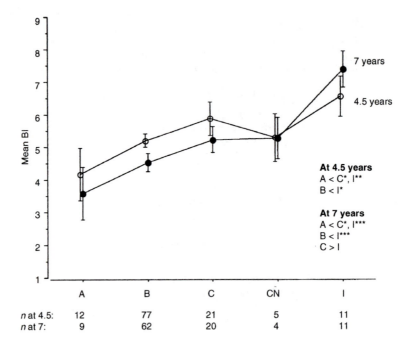

At 4.5 years
A < C*, I**
B < I*

At 7 years
A < C*, I***
B < I***
C > I

n at 4.5:   12   77   21   5   11
n at 7:   9   62   20   4   11

* = p < .05; ** = p < .01; *** = p < .001, two-tailed

Figure 6.4 Mean ratings of behavioural inhibition (BI) taken at 4.5 years and
          again at 7 years, over five patterns of attachment assessed at 4.5 years.
          Avoidant (A), Secure (B), Ambivalent (C), Controlling (CN) and
          Insecure-other (I)

After reviewing the studies from the Harvard group, which followed up
children with high BI and their families, Turner, Beidel, and Wolff (1996)
suggested that high BI which was stable over time could be related to the
development of disorder, as follows:

Stable, High BI ——▶ Vulnerability ——▶ Anxiety disorder

They pointed out that stable, high BI is not a *necessary* condition for
disorder, since an uninhibited child may develop anxiety; and furthermore
that high BI is not a *sufficient* condition, since additional input is required.
From the studies they reviewed, high parental anxiety was seen to be a
vulnerability factor. Now this could be passed on to the child genetically, by
modelling parental behaviour, and/or by parental failure to provide a
predictable, secure base. As we have seen, the latter would engender
separation anxiety, which I have argued above is conceptually distinct from
BI but co-occurs with BI. Furthermore, anxiety concerning attachment

figures could be particularly devastating to a behaviourally inhibited child. Therefore, one may conclude that an insecure Ambivalent attachment (and possibly Insecure-other attachment) along with stable, high BI may be a powerful combination for the development of anxiety disorder.

Author note

I am grateful to the Sub-Department of Animal Behaviour at Madingley for providing an ethological context and a secure base over the years and to those with whom I have worked there (as indicated in the above references), particularly Robert Hinde, who has also read the manuscript more than once.

References

Ainsworth, M.D.A., Blehar, M.C., Waters, E. and Wall, S. (1978) *Patterns of Attachment*, Hillsdale, NJ: Erlbaum.

Auerbach, J., Geller, V., Lezer, S., Shinwell, E., Belmaker, R.H., Levine, J. and Ebstein, R.P. (1999) 'Dopamine D4 receptor (D4DR) and serotonin transporter promoter (5-HTTLPR) polymorphisms in the determination of temperament in 2-month-old infants', *Molecular Psychiatry*, 4: 369–73.

Baerends, G.P. (1976) 'The functional organization of behaviour', *Animal Behaviour*, 24: 726–38.

Belsky, J. (1999) 'Modern evolutionary theory and patterns of attachment', in J. Cassidy and P.R. Shaver (eds) *Handbook of Attachment: Theory, Research, and Clinical Applications* (pp. 141–61), New York: Guilford Press.

Bowlby, J. (1973) *Attachment and Loss, Vol 2: Separation, Anxiety and Anger*, London: Hogarth Press.

Bowlby, J. (1982) *Attachment and Loss, Vol 1: Attachment*, 2nd edn, London: Hogarth Press.

Bowlby, J. (1991) 'Postscript', in C.M. Parkes, J. Stevenson-Hinde and P. Marris (eds) *Attachment across the Life Cycle* (pp. 293–7), London: Routledge.

Calkins, S.D. and Fox, N.A. (1992) 'The relations among infant temperament, security of attachment, and behavioral inhibition at twenty-four months', *Child Development*, 63: 1456–72.

Cassidy, J. and Berlin, L. J. (1994) 'The insecure/ambivalent pattern of attachment: theory and research', *Child Development*, 65: 971–91.

Cassidy, J. and Marvin, R.S. (1992) *Attachment Organization in Preschool Children: Procedures and Coding Manual*, Seattle: MacArthur Working Group on Attachment.

Cassidy, J. and Shaver, P.R. (eds) (1999) *Handbook of Attachment: Theory, Research, and Clinical Applications*, New York: Guilford Press.

Davidson, R.J. and Rickman, M. (1999) 'Behavioral inhibition and the emotional circuitry of the brain', in L.A. Schmidt and J. Schulkin (eds) *Extreme Fear, Shyness, and Social Phobia* (pp. 67–87), Oxford: Oxford University Press.

DeWolff, M.S. and van IJzendoorn, M.H. (1997) 'Sensitivity and attachment: a meta-analysis on parental antecedents of infant attachment', *Child Development*, 68: 571–91.

DiLalla, L.F., Kagan, J. and Reznick, J.S. (1994) 'Genetic etiology of behavioral inhibition among 2-year-old children', *Infant Behavior and Development*, 17: 405–12.

Fentress, J.C. (1991) 'Analytical ethology and synthetic neuroscience', in P. Bateson (ed.) *Development and Integration of Behaviour* (pp. 7–120), Cambridge: Cambridge University Press.

Fordham, K. and Stevenson-Hinde, J. (1999) 'Shyness, friendship quality, and adjustment during middle childhood', *Journal of Child Psychology and Psychiatry*, 40: 757–68.

Goldsmith, H.H., Buss, A.H., Plomin, R., Rothbart, M.K., Thomas, A., Chess, S., Hinde, R.A. and McCall, R.B. (1987) 'Roundtable: what is temperament?', *Child Development*, 58: 505–29.

Gosling, S.D. and John, O.P. (1999) 'Personality dimensions in nonhuman animals: a cross-species review', *Current Directions in Psychological Science*, 8: 69–75.

Greenberg, M.T. and Marvin, R.S. (1982) 'Reactions of preschool children to an adult stranger: a behavioral systems approach', *Child Development*, 53: 481–90.

Grossmann, K., Fremmer-Bombik, E., Rudolph, J. and Grossmann, K.E. (1988) 'Maternal attachment representation as related to patterns of infant–mother attachment and maternal care during the first year', in R.A. Hinde and J. Stevenson-Hinde (eds) *Relationships within Families: Mutual Influences* (pp. 241–62), Oxford: Clarendon Press.

Grossmann, K.E. and Grossmann, K. (1991) 'Attachment quality as an organizer of emotional and behavioral responses in a longitudinal perspective', in C.M. Parkes, J. Stevenson-Hinde and P. Marris (eds) *Attachment across the Life Cycle* (pp. 93–114), London: Routledge.

Hinde, R.A. and Stevenson-Hinde, J. (1991) 'Perspectives on attachment', in C.M. Parkes, J. Stevenson-Hinde and P. Marris (eds) *Attachment across the Life Cycle* (pp. 52–65), London: Routledge.

Jones, W.H., Briggs, S.R. and Smith, T.G. (1986) 'Shyness: conceptualization and measurement', *Journal of Personality and Social Psychology*, 51: 629–39.

Kagan, J. (1989) 'The concept of behavioral inhibition to the unfamiliar', in J.S. Reznick (ed.) *Perspectives on Behavioral Inhibition* (pp. 1–23), Chicago: University of Chicago Press.

Kagan, J. (1994) *Galen's Prophecy*, New York: Basic Books.

Kagan, J., Reznick, J.S. and Snidman, N. (1987) 'The physiology and psychology of behavioral inhibition in children', *Child Development*, 58: 1459–73.

Kagan, J., Reznick, J.S., Snidman, N., Gibbons, J. and Johnson, M.O. (1988) 'Childhood derivatives of inhibition and lack of inhibition to the unfamiliar', *Child Development*, 59: 1580–9.

Kagan, J., Snidman, N. and Arcus, D. (1998) 'The value of extreme groups', in R.B. Cairns, L.R. Bergman and J. Kagan (eds) *Methods and Models for Studying the Individual: Essays in Honor of Marian Radke-Yarrow* (pp. 65–80), Thousand Oaks, CA: Sage.

Kerr, M., Lambert, W.W., Stattin, H. and Klackenberg-Larsson, I. (1994) 'Stability of inhibition in a Swedish longitudinal sample', *Child Development*, 65: 138–46.

Kochanska, G. (1998) 'Mother–child relationship, child fearfulness, and emerging attachment: a short-term longitudinal study', *Developmental Psychology*, 34: 480–90.

LeDoux, J. E. (1995) 'Emotion: clues from the brain', *Annual Reviews of Psychology*, 46: 209–35.

Marshall, P.J. and Stevenson-Hinde, J. (1998) 'Behavioral inhibition, heart period, and respiratory sinus arrhythmia in young children', *Developmental Psychobiology*, 33: 283–92.

Marshall, P.J. and Stevenson-Hinde, J. (in press), 'Behavioral inhibition: physiological correlates', in W.R. Crozier and L.E. Alden (eds) *International Handbook of Social Anxiety*, Chichester, Sussex: John Wiley.

Rapee, R.M. (1997) 'The potential role of child-rearing practices in the development of anxiety and depression', *Clinical Psychology Review*, 17: 47–67.

Reznick, J.S., Gibbons, J.L., Johnson, M.O. and McDonough, P.M. (1989) 'Behavioral inhibition in a normative sample', in J.S. Reznick (ed.) *Perspectives on Behavioral Inhibition* (pp. 25–49), Chicago: University of Chicago Press.

Rubin, K.H. and Mills, R.S.L. (1991) 'Conceptualizing developmental pathways to internalizing disorders in childhood', *Canadian Journal of Behavioural Science*, 23: 300–17.

Sameroff, A.J., Seifer, R. and Elias, P.K. (1982) 'Sociocultural variability in infant temperament ratings', *Child Development*, 53: 164–73.

Schmidt, L.A., Polak, C.P. and Spooner, A.L. (in press) 'Biological and environmental contributions to childhood shyness: a diathesis-stress model', in W.R. Crozier and L.E. Alden (eds) *International Handbook of Social Anxiety*, Chichester, Sussex: John Wiley.

Siqueland, L., Kendall, P.C. and Steinberg, L. (1996) 'Anxiety in children: perceived family environments and observed family interaction', *Journal of Clinical Child Psychology*, 25: 225–37.

Spangler, G. and Grossmann, K.E. (1993) 'Biobehavioral organization in securely and insecurely attached infants', *Child Development*, 64: 1439–50.

Stevenson, J., Batten, N., and Cherner, M. (1992) 'Fears and fearfulness in children and adolescents: a genetic analysis of twin data', *Journal of Child Psychology and Psychiatry*, 33: 977–85.

Stevenson-Hinde, J. (1988) 'Individuals in relationships', in R.A. Hinde and J. Stevenson-Hinde (eds) *Relationships within Families: Mutual Influences* (pp. 68–80), Oxford: Clarendon Press.

Stevenson-Hinde, J. (1989) 'Behavioral inhibition: issues of context', in J.S. Reznick (ed.) *Perspectives on Behavioral Inhibition* (pp. 125–38), Chicago: University of Chicago Press.

Stevenson-Hinde, J. (1991) 'Temperament and attachment: an eclectic approach', in P. Bateson (ed.) *Development and Integration of Behaviour* (pp. 315–29), Cambridge: Cambridge University Press.

Stevenson-Hinde, J. (1998) 'The individual in context', in R.B. Cairns, L.R. Bergman and J. Kagan (eds) *Methods and Models for Studying the Individual: Essays in Honor of Marian Radke-Yarrow* (pp. 123–32), Thousand Oaks, CA: Sage.

Stevenson-Hinde, J. and Glover, A. (1996) 'Shy girls and boys: a new look', *Journal of Child Psychology and Psychiatry*, 37: 181–7.

Stevenson-Hinde, J. and Marshall, P.J. (1999) 'Behavioral inhibition, heart period, and respiratory sinus arrhythmia: an attachment perspective', *Child Development*, 70: 805–16.

Stevenson-Hinde, J. and Shouldice, A. (1990) 'Fear and attachment in 2.5-year-olds', *British Journal of Developmental Psychology*, 8: 319–33.

Stevenson-Hinde, J. and Shouldice, A. (1993) 'Wariness to strangers: a behavior systems perspective revisited', in K.H. Rubin and J. Asendorpf (eds) *Social Withdrawal, Inhibition, and Shyness in Childhood* (pp. 101–16), Hillsdale, N.J.: Erlbaum.

Stevenson-Hinde, J. and Shouldice, A. (1995a) '4.5 to 7 years: fearful behaviour, fears and worries', *Journal of Child Psychology and Psychiatry*, 36: 1027–38.

Stevenson-Hinde, J. and Shouldice, A. (1995b) 'Maternal interactions and self-reports related to attachment classifications at 4.5 years', *Child Development*, 66: 583–96.

Stevenson-Hinde, J. and Shouldice, A. (1996) 'Fearfulness: developmental consistency', in A. J. Sameroff and M. M. Haith (eds) *The Five to Seven Year Shift: The Age of Reason and Responsibility* (pp. 237–52), Chicago: University of Chicago Press.

Stevenson-Hinde, J., Stillwell-Barnes, R. and Zunz, M. (1980) 'Subjective assessment of rhesus monkeys over four successive years', *Primates*, 21: 66–82.

Turner, S.M., Beidel, D.C. and Wolff, P.L. (1996) 'Is behavioral inhibition related to the anxiety disorders?', *Clinical Psychology Review*, 16: 157–72.

Vaughn, B.E. and Bost, K.K. (1999) 'Attachment and temperament: redundant, independent, or interacting influences on interpersonal adaptation and personality development?', in J. Cassidy and P.R. Shaver (eds) *Handbook of Attachment: Theory, Research, and Clinical Applications* (pp. 198–225), New York: Guilford Press.

Vaughn, B.E., Taraldson, B.J., Crichton, L. and Egeland, B. (1981) 'The assessment of infant temperament: a critique of the Carey Infant Temperament Questionnaire', *Infant Behavior and Development*, 4: 1–17.

Weinfield, N.S., Sroufe, L.A., Egeland, B. and Carlson, E.A. (1999) 'The nature of individual differences in infant-caregiver attachment', in J. Cassidy and P.R. Shaver (eds) *Handbook of Attachment: Theory, Research, and Clinical Applications* (pp. 68–88), New York: Guilford Press.

Wilson, D.S., Clark, A.B., Coleman, K. and Dearstyne, T. (1994) 'Shyness and boldness in humans and other animals', *Trends in Ecology and Evolution*, 9: 442–6.

Wilson, D.S., Coleman, K., Clark, A.B. and Biederman, L. (1993) 'Shy–bold continuum in Pumpkinseed Sunfish (Lepomis gibbosus): an ecological study of a psychological trait', *Journal of Comparative Psychology*, 107: 250–60.

7 Shyness and adaptation to the social world of university

Jens B. Asendorpf

The transition to university is a life transition (Elder, 1985) that is particularly suited for the study of shyness in adulthood. The new social world of university offers freshmen many opportunities for socializing with peers, making friends, dating, falling in love, and finding a partner. Therefore the university is for most students not only an academic environment but also an attractive social setting. Consequently, the contact with and the importance of parents and siblings are expected to decrease after a short phase when they may be used as a source of support for coping with this life transition. Thus, in general, the life transition is expected to enlarge students' social network, particularly with regard to peers, and to change their relationships with family members.

Shyness and the transition to university

For shy first-year students, the social world of university is a setting that frequently makes them acutely shy for two reasons. First, the university is initially an *unfamiliar* social setting where they meet strangers and have to act in large, unfamiliar groups; both kinds of situations are known to be key elicitors of shyness (Russell, Cutrona and Jones, 1986; Zimbardo, 1977). Second, the university is continuously a *social-evaluative* setting where students are evaluated for intellectual, social, and sexual attractiveness by their peers, and for intellectual competence by their teachers; social-evaluative situations are also known to be potent elicitors of shyness (Schlenker and Leary, 1982).

Asendorpf (1989) experimentally varied both the unfamiliarity and the social-evaluative content of dyadic interactions between students in a waiting-room paradigm and found that both the unfamiliarity of the interaction partner and the prospect of social evaluation made the students shy. According to Asendorpf's common pathway model, acute state shyness is the final common pathway for two different kinds of inhibitory processes: inhibition to the unfamiliar, and inhibition due to fear of being ignored or rejected by others. This view is consistent with Gray's (1982, 1987) model of behavioural inhibition where inhibition is aroused by novel stimuli and by conditioned cues for frustrative nonreward and punishment. Within Gray's model, state shyness is inhibition in social situations.

When this perspective on state shyness is applied to interindividual differences in trait shyness, that is, the enduring tendency to react with state shyness more than others, one might expect two different types of chronically shy people. *Temperamentally shy* people have a low threshold or a steeper response gradient for behavioural inhibition for physiological reasons and therefore become more easily or more intensely shy in both unfamiliar and social-evaluative situations. *Experientially* shy people have often experienced social neglect or rejection in the past and therefore have higher expectations of becoming ignored or rejected by others, including strangers and unfamiliar groups (see Asendorpf and Meier, 1993, and Asendorpf and van Aken, 1994, for evidence for these two types of shyness in childhood). In both cases, a stable disposition of reacting in a shy manner to both unfamiliar and evaluative situations results. Thus, theoretical considerations and empirical findings strongly suggest that the first months at university are a period that maximizes differences between shy and non-shy students.

A few short-term longitudinal studies followed students over the first year at university and studied their social-emotional adaptation to the new environment. In a path-breaking study, Cutrona (1982) repeatedly assessed loneliness in UCLA freshmen. Most students tended to report loneliness in the first term but had recovered at the end of the freshman year. However, about one-fifth of the participants in her study remained lonely all year long. They tended to attribute their loneliness to personal rather than external causes at the initial assessment. Unfortunately Cutrona (1982) did not assess shyness, but it is not a far-fetched assumption that her chronically lonely students were shy, given a strong correlation between trait shyness and trait loneliness (the enduring trait to feel lonely; e.g., Jones, Freeman and Goswick, 1981).

Shaver, Furman and Buhrmester (1986) assessed characteristics of Denver freshmen's loneliness, social network, and perceived support in each quarter of the first academic year. They observed a drop in perceived relationship quality with friends and romantic partners in the first term and a subsequent recovery to the initial level (assessed one month before university started). State loneliness (reports of feeling lonely during the past few days) showed correspondingly an increase in the first term and a decrease to the initial level later on. In contrast, the quality of relationships with family members did not decrease; instead, a slight increase was observed from summer to first term, with no change thereafter. State loneliness showed a much stronger cross-sectional correlation with reported problems in relationship initiation in the first term than before or after. The interindividual differences in state loneliness were much less stable between summer and spring than the interindividual differences in trait loneliness (reports of having experienced loneliness during the past few years), which remained highly stable throughout the study. Again, shyness was not assessed in this study, but state and trait shyness might have shown a similar pattern: stable trait shyness and an increase in state shyness during the first term due to problems with the initiation of new peer relationships.

A similar result was obtained by Hays and Oxley (1986) who studied Utah freshmen's social networks and adaptation to university during their first term. The best network predictor of self-perceived college adaptation was the percentage of students in the network. Together, these three studies suggest that the establishment of relationships with fellow students is the main social task during the transition to university. Failure to achieve this task is accompanied by state loneliness, and the risk for failure may be enhanced in shy students.

Shyness effects in the Berlin Relationship Study

In the remainder of this chapter I report findings from the *Berlin Relationship Study*, a longitudinal study of students' personality and social relationships as they changed over the course of the first 18 months at Humboldt University, Berlin. Asendorpf and Wilpers (1998) reported results for a first cohort of 132 students. Because men were under-represented in this sample due to self-selection for the study, a year later a second cohort of 39 men who underwent identical assessments was added, yielding a better sex-balanced longitudinal sample of 92 females and 79 males, aged 18–24 years. A study of sample selectivity in terms of the Big Five factors of personality showed that the sample was biased towards higher conscientiousness scores. Because conscientiousness was not significantly related to shyness, this sampling bias is not problematic for the present analyses. More details about the sampling procedure and selection effects are reported by Asendorpf and Wilpers (2000).

Distinguishing shy from non-shy participants

Most studies of trait shyness rely on correlational or regression analyses because these methods respect the full range of shyness. The results are nearly always interpreted in terms of high versus average shyness because it is in high shyness that most people are interested. However, correlational and regression approaches cannot, in fact, distinguish between these two different interpretations. Therefore I present the findings for shyness here in terms of an *asymmetric extreme group approach*. This compares the 25 per cent most shy participants with the 50 per cent participants below the shyness median. Significant differences between these two groups can unequivocally be attributed to effects of high shyness.

Shyness was assessed during the first week at university and 6, 12, and 18 months later by means of a short five-item scale. The five items were mixed with the 60 items of the NEO-FFI (Costa and McCrae, 1989) and were answered on a 5-point scale with an agreement format 1 (*not at all*) to 5 (*completely*). The items and their psychometric characteristics at the first assessment are presented in Table 7.1. The items formed a highly homogeneous scale with the exception of the final item that showed a lower (but still acceptable) correlation with the rest of the scale. Dropping this item increased the internal consistency of the scale but decreased most shyness effects that are reported below. Therefore the item was not dropped (Asendorpf and Wilpers, 1998, had also retained this item for the same reasons).

An analysis of the shyness means showed that the average shyness score in the sample decreased significantly from the first assessment ($M = 2.84$) to the second assessment ($M = 2.62$, and then continued to decrease only slightly to a final $M = 2.57$ (these figures differ slightly from those reported by Asendorpf and Wilpers (1998) due to the larger size of the sample for the present study). Also, the 6-month stabilities increased from .81 to .86. The initially decreasing shyness and the increasing stability of the interindividual differences in shyness suggest that the shyness ratings at the first assessment included a state component due to the highly unfamiliar university setting. This state effect was not as marked as for loneliness in the study by Shaver *et al.* (1986), probably because the instruction asked for self-ratings with regard to the past few months rather than to the past few days in the Shaver *et al.* (1986) study.

In order to pull out the enduring trait component from the shyness ratings, these ratings were averaged for each participant across the four assessments. The two groups of shy and non-shy participants were then formed on the basis of these aggregated shyness scores (upper 25 per cent and lower 50 per cent of the distribution). This procedure resulted in 43 shy and 85 non-shy participants; 24 per cent of the males and 26 per cent of the females were classified as shy. Subsequently, significant differences between the shy and the non-shy group in various dependent variables were interpreted as effects of high shyness on these variables.

Table 7.1 The shyness scale

Item	M	SD	r_{it}[a]
I feel shy in the presence of others	2.83	.99	.73
I feel inhibited when I am with other people	2.74	.88	.76
I easily approach others (-)	2.89	1.01	.75
It is easy for me to get in touch with strangers (-)	3.08	1.05	.73
I feel uneasy at parties and in large groups	2.67	1.21	.37

$N = 171$. The data refer to the first assessment.
Items marked (-) were inverted
Cronbach's $\alpha = .84$.
a Corrected item-total correlation.

This approach seems appropriate in this case because path analyses by Asendorpf and Wilpers (1998) showed that shyness exerted effects on various relationship measures but was not affected by them during the course of the study. Thus, shyness can be viewed as an antecedent rather than as a consequence of the observed differences with some confidence.

Shyness effects on social relationships

The participants' social relationships were assessed every three months from a social network perspective. In the first assessment, they were asked to list all persons who were currently important to them. To minimize errors of omission, we presented 14 categories of relationship to them as retrieval cues (e.g., friends from their former high school). All listed persons were identified by their initials, relationship category, sex, age, and relationship duration. Also, the quality of the participant's relationship with each person during the last three months was rated on eight scales (see Asendorpf and Wilpers, 1998, for details). For example, each person was rated for perceived available support, operationalized by the item 'If I have problems, I would turn to this person to talk about my problems' which was rated on a 5-point scale ranging from 1 = never to 5 = always.

In the subsequent six assessments, the participants received a printout of their previous relationship questionnaire, excluding the ratings of relationship quality. They were asked to delete those persons whom they did not consider important any more, to check the data for the remaining persons for correctness, and to add new persons who were currently important to them. Subsequently, they rated the revised list of persons on the eight scales of relationship quality since the last assessment.

From these data, various measures of relationship quality were derived, e.g., size of the total network, number of peers (peers were defined as non-siblings aged 18–27 years), number of old peers (pre-university relationship initiation), number of new peers (relationship initiation at or after the first day at university), perceived available support from the mother. I do not present here a systematic overview of all significant shyness effects for these variables but instead present the main results, as much theory-driven as possible.

From the above literature review, two main hypotheses about the effects of shyness on the students' relationships can be derived. First, shyness is expected to interfere with the main social task of freshmen, namely establishing new peer relationships. Thus, shy students are expected to show a slower increase of new peer relationships. Second, shy students are expected to stick more than non-shy students to their family members and old friends because (a) these are familiar people that they can deal with more easily and (b) the shy students are less distracted from these familiar relationships by new peer relationships. Thus, shy students are expected to decrease their contact with family members and old friends less than non-shy students.

These hypotheses were fully confirmed for peer relationships, but not for family relationships. Figure 7.1 plots the groupwise changes in the number of old, pre-university peer relationships and in the number of new peer relationships that were formed after becoming a university student. For old peer relationships, a significant shyness x linear trend interaction confirmed that the initial difference between non-shy and shy students (non-shy students had more pre-university peer relationships) decreased and, in fact, disappeared. As expected, non-shy students dissolved old peer relationships

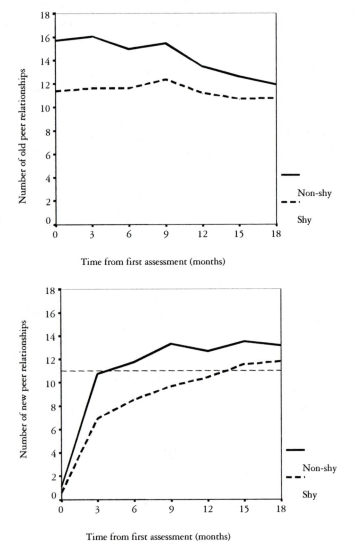

Figure 7.1 Change in the number of old and new peer relationships after entering university, by shyness

at a fairly constant rate after the third month at university whereas shy students showed no evidence for relationship termination. Also, as expected, non-shy students initiated new peer relationships much faster than shy students. Already after three months, the non-shy students had eleven new peers included into their social network whereas shy students needed four times as long to achieve this. However, the shyness x linear trend interaction was not significant. Instead, a significant shyness x quadratic trend indicated a non-linear change of the difference between shy and non-shy students. As Figure 7.1 shows, shy students' peer network increased all the time during the 18 months of observation whereas the non-shy students did not add more new peers to their network after 9 months than they lost. Because of their steadier network growth and because of the fact that they did not dissolve old peer relationships, the shy students had only slightly fewer peers in their network at the end of the study than the non-shy students (3.1 peers fewer, a nonsignificant difference with an effect size of 0.26 standard deviations).

The bottom line of these results is that shyness leads to a slower adaptation to the new social world of university, but in the long run to a similar peer network (if we had observed longer, the peer networks of shy and non-shy students might have been found to be equally large). This finding squares nicely with the description of shyness in infancy and early childhood by Thomas and Chess (1977) who called shy children 'slow-to-warm-up children'. Shy students are indeed slow-to-warm-up when they face new peers.

The number of relationships is only one aspect of the quality of the peer network. What about the quality of the relationships? Perhaps there is a trade-off between number and quality such that shy students have transitionally fewer peer relationships but of a higher quality in terms of closeness, support and love? This assumption was not supported by our data. The students rated the closeness of their relationship with all people in their network, how much they would turn to them for help if they had a problem (perceived available support; see Asendorpf and Wilpers, 2000, for details), whether they were in love with that person, whether they had a steady sexual partner, and how often they had sex with that partner during the last month (scores on that scale referred to 1 = *once a month*, 2 = *several times per month*, 3 = *once a week*, to 4 = *several times a week*).

The results for these variables of relationship quality are presented in Table 7.2. Because no significant shyness x time effects were observed, it is sufficient to report the average differences across the seven assessments. Shy students perceived their peer relationships as less close and supportive than non-shy students. Although this might be attributed to a negative bias in reporting, the virtually identical means for interpersonal conflict are inconsistent with this interpretation. Instead, it seems that the reported differences are valid. Thus, the shy students had not only transitionally fewer peer relationships but also continuously poorer relationships in terms of closeness and support.

Table 7.2 Differences between shy and non-shy students in terms of peer relationship quality

Relationship quality	Non-shy		Shy		Effect size
	M	SD	M	SD	d
Perceived relationship closeness[a]	3.24	0.33	3.12	0.33	0.35*
Perceived available support[a]	2.52	0.43	2.27	0.36	0.56*
Perceived interpersonal conflict[a]	1.64	0.35	1.69	0.37	n.s.
In love (yes/no)	0.61	0.34	0.35	0.35	0.72*
Steady sexual partner (yes/no)	0.46	0.45	0.20	0.35	0.60*
Frequency of sex with partner	2.82	0.92	3.27	1.01	0.41(*)

Note: Data refer to 85 non-shy and 43 shy students. The results are averaged over all seven assessments
a Average across all peer relationships on a 5-point scale.
n.s. not significant
(*) $p = .10$ * $p < .05$

This finding applies in particular to love relationships. Shy students reported they were currently in love in only 35 per cent of the cases whereas twice as many non-shy students were in love (overall, 49 per cent of the students were in love at any point in time during the 18 months of observation; this finding attests to the importance of this life stage for finding a love partner). Similarly, 20 per cent of the shy students but 46 per cent of the non-shy students reported a steady sexual partner. Together, these results for falling in love and partnership support the general conclusion that shy students had difficulties in initiating peer relationships of all kinds, including close, supportive, and loving ones.

One finding warns against an over-simplistic picture of shy students having poorer relationships. They tended to have more sex with their partner, if they had one (see Table 7.2). The effect was only marginally significant but it should be noted that the sample size for this comparison was less than half as large as for the other tests because most students had no partner; the size of the effect is respectable. Trivial interpretations such as more spatially distant relationships among the non-shy can be excluded because there was not even a marginal difference between the shy and the non-shy students in terms of the location of their partner (living in the same house vs. living in the same town vs. living in different towns).

This finding is interesting both psychologically and biologically. Psychologically it suggests that shy students either have more intense partnerships or feel obliged to assure the partner of themselves through frequent sex because they fear that the partner may leave. The intensity and the assurance hypothesis cannot be tested with our data because the closeness and support ratings were close to the maximum of the scale for nearly all participants (a ceiling effect), and because we did not assess fear of separation among the shy, or how they tried to cope with it.

Biologically the finding is interesting because it suggests a mechanism through which shyness might have survived natural selection. Although the shy appear to have problems in securing a mate, if they mate, they seem to invest more heavily in terms of sex, increasing the likelihood for reproduction, at least in former times when contraceptives were not available. Through this trade-off between mating and investment in the mate, they might have achieved the same fitness potential as the non-shy. This is surely an interesting hypothesis worth pursuing further.

So far, the results are fully consistent with the view that shy students have transitional problems with the initiation of peer relationships, including love and sex relationships, and, therefore, stick more closely to old friendships. The additional hypothesis that they also stick more closely to family members was not supported, however. On average, students' reported contact with parents and siblings decreased over the first 18 months at university, and this was true for both shy and non-shy students. Shy students started off with nonsignificantly higher contact with family members but tended to reduce this contact nonsignificantly more than non-shy students; at the end of the observation period, they had as much contact with their family as non-shy students. This applied to mother, father, and siblings as well.

Contact with family is related not to shyness but instead to conscientiousness (see Asendorpf and Wilpers, 1998; more recently this finding has been supported by a large-sample cross-sectional study of 18–30-year-old Germans; Neyer, 1999). Thus, it seems that shyness particularly affects peer relationships, not family relationships. The family relationship hypothesis was in part built on a principle of compensation: if shy students have problems with initiating peer relationships, they might therefore stick more closely to familiar relationships such as parent and sibling relationships and old friendships. It seems that this compensatory principle acts only within the domain of peer relationships. Family relationships were not affected. This result attests to the more general finding that family relationships have a life of their own, independent of peer relationships (see, e.g., Asendorpf and Wilpers, 2000, for the independence of attachment styles to parents versus peers). The ultimate reason for this independence may be the very different functions of family and peer relationships in terms of genetic relatedness and significance for reproducing one's genes (see Trivers, 1972).

Shyness effects on loneliness

Loneliness was assessed seven times concurrently with the relationship assessments by a 10-item version of the UCLA loneliness scale with high reliabilities (a >.89). Overall, the loneliness ratings showed the same pattern of change as the shyness scores. They dropped significantly from an average of 1.92 on a 5-point scale at the first assessment to 1.80 at the second assessment, and then decreased only slightly to a final 1.74. Thus, loneliness was low on average even at the first assessment. Also similarly to the shyness measurement, the 6-month stabilities of the interindividual differences in loneliness increased from an initial .77 to a final .87. At any point in time, loneliness was moderately strongly correlated with shyness (r = .54 to r = .60, with no trend in time). Therefore, marked differences between the shy and the non-shy group were expected.

As Figure 7.2 shows, non-shy participants had very low loneliness scores whereas shy students had somewhat higher (but by no means very high) scores. The difference was significant with a large effect size of d = 1.6. In addition, the shyness x quadratic trend was significant. Figure 7.2 indicates that loneliness in shy students was particularly high at the first assessment, dropped considerably, but increased slightly after the second assessment whereas non-shy students' loneliness decreased more or less over the whole observation period. Thus, most shy and non-shy students were initially somewhat more lonely than they were later on but shy students did not fully recover from loneliness. In terms of Cutrona's (1982) study, there were some chronically lonely students in the shy group, but very few, if any, in the non-shy group.

In order to investigate this interpretation more closely, chronically lonely students were identified by average loneliness scores above the mid-point of the scale (3) during the last three assessments (thus, after one year at university). Only 2 per cent of the non-shy students were chronically lonely but 21 per cent of the shy students were (a highly significant difference). Only a minority of the shy students were chronically lonely, to be sure, but shyness was a risk factor for being chronically lonely.

The time trends for loneliness suggest that shy students' loneliness was not due to problems with peer relationships in general because shy students were fairly successful in establishing peer relationships in the long run (see Figure 7.1). Instead, loneliness in the shy participants may be attributed to problems in close relationships with family members and/or peers. This assumption is also consistent with the literature on loneliness that clearly shows that feeling lonely is due to a lack of close relationships, not to a small number of relationships (see, e.g., Marangoni and Ickes, 1989).

The hypothesis that a lack of close relationships, including love relationships and parental relationships, mediated the relation between shyness and loneliness was tested by hierarchical regression. For four types of relationships (with parents, siblings, same-sex peers, and opposite-sex peers) the *maximum* perceived available support across all relationships of that type was computed. Low maximum support is expected to be more closely related to loneliness than low mean support because mean support can be relatively low for those who have a large number of relationships of a particular type including a few highly supportive ones (see also Asendorpf and Wilpers, 2000). In such cases where the maximum is much higher than the mean,

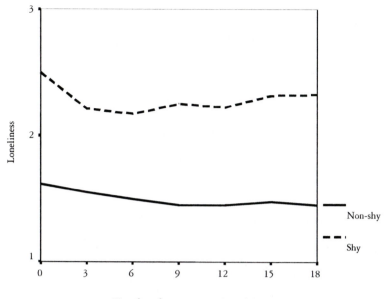

Figure 7.2 Change in loneliness after entering university, by shyness

loneliness is not expected to be high. Indeed, maximum support showed consistently more negative correlations with loneliness than mean support.

In addition to available support as an indicator of a close relationship, being currently in love (yes/no) may also be related to loneliness because in an early stage of a love relationship, being in love may reduce loneliness but the relationship may not yet provide high support because this requires trust in the partner which needs time to develop.

Five relationship predictors were entered step by step in a hierarchical regression analysis: available support from parents, siblings, same-sex peers, and opposite-sex peers, and being in love. At a final step, shyness was entered. The rationale of this procedure is to detect the incremental predictive validity of each type of relationship and to see whether shyness additionally explains variance in loneliness. The results were similar for all assessments, with no clear age trends in the overall predictive power or the contribution of individual predictors. Therefore I present here only the result for the first assessment (see Table 7.3).

All five relationship predictors were risk factors for loneliness independently of each other at least marginally. Thus, loneliness increased when students felt that they could not turn to parents, siblings, same-sex peers, or opposite-sex peers, and being in love tended to reduce loneliness independently of availability of support. Together, the relationship variables explained 22 per cent of the variance in loneliness which corresponded to a multiple correlation of .47. For other variables of relationship quality such as maximum felt closeness or maximum interpersonal conflict, the explained variance was smaller. Another 18 per cent of the variance in loneliness was predicted by shyness. Thus, shyness predicted nearly as much specific variance as all the relationship predictors.

In other words, the effect of shyness on loneliness was only partly mediated by relationship quality. What was not mediated by relationship quality can be attributed to a tendency of shy students to feel more lonely than others, given the same perceived support and love. Such feelings may arise, for example, from a history of social neglect or rejection in the past that continues to affect their current feelings despite more recent social acceptance, or from unrealistic ideals about relationships.

Effects of leaving one's home town

Because shy people fear unfamiliar environments, it may be expected that shy students were under-represented among those who had left their home town in order to study in Berlin. However, in Germany applicants for popular subjects such as psychology or medicine are assigned to universities according to (a) their high school degree, (b) a priority for their home town, and (c) a waiting list score, in this order of importance. This system works against the expected shyness effect because bright shy students from other towns who applied for popular subjects were often assigned to Berlin despite their preferences. Despite this counteracting bias, non-Berliners were significantly under-represented in the shy group (25 per cent) as compared to the non-shy

Table 7.3 Prediction of loneliness by relationship quality and shyness through hierarchical regression

		Adjusted		Change statistic	
Step	Predictor	R	R^2	R^2_{change}	p
1	Support from parents	0.24	0.059	0.059	0.004
2	Support from siblings	0.27	0.074	0.016	0.130
3	Support from same-sex peers	0.42	0.175	0.101	0.001
4	Support from opposite-sex peers	0.45	0.203	0.029	0.029
5	In love (yes/no)	0.47	0.220	0.017	0.092
6	Shyness	0.63	0.395	0.175	0.001

$N = 171$ at first assessment. If no parents or siblings were included in the network, support was defined as a missing value.

group (37 per cent). (To increase power, this analysis was undertaken for all 312 students who participated in the first assessment.)

Other predictions concern the effect of leaving one's home town on relationships and loneliness. It may be expected that non-Berliners would feel particularly lonely at least initially and also may have had particular problems in initiating new peer relationships. In addition, this effect may be assumed to be more marked for shy students. The results did not confirm these assumptions. As Figure 7.3 indicates, non-Berliners' loneliness was initially not higher than Berliners' loneliness, and even tended to drop more strongly (a nonsignificant effect). This applied to both shy and non-shy participants.

Leaving one's hometown tended to reduce loneliness slightly after three months at university, and was not a risk factor for shy students. This becomes most obvious when the same type of analysis was completed for the number of new peers (see Figure 7.4).

Both non-shy and shy non-Berliners engaged transitionally in more new peer relationships than Berliners (as indicated by a significant home town x quadratic trend), and this tendency had probably tended to reduce their loneliness. Two reasons for this finding come to mind. First, students who had moved to Berlin might have been self-selected for higher sociability. This could be tested by a comparison of the Berliners and non-Berliners in self-

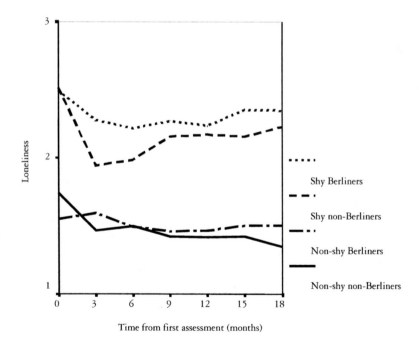

Figure 7.3 Change in loneliness after entering university, by shyness and home town

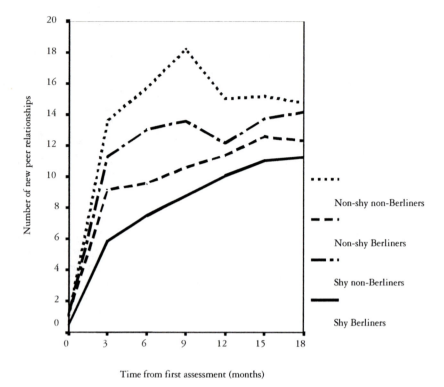

Time from first assessment (months)

Figure 7.4 Change in the number of new peer relationships after entering university, by shyness and home town

rated extraversion and sociability at the first assessment (see Asendorpf and Wilpers, 1998, for these scales). However, the two groups did not differ even marginally in these scores.

Therefore, another interpretation seems valid. The spatial distance from their old peers had motivated the non-Berliners to invest more in getting to know new peers than the Berliners for whom many old peers were still available for interaction. Thus, moving to another town with the accompanying loss of interaction opportunities presented a challenge rather than a risk factor for the movers. Interestingly, this applied to shy students as well. Leaving one's home town does not seem to be a risk factor for shy students.

Discussion

This first detailed study of shy students' transition to university confirmed many expectations that were derived from Gray's theory of behavioural inhibition. Shy students were slow to warm up with their new peers at university. They increased their peer network in the long run nearly as much as the non-shy students, but they needed more time to establish new peer relationships. Because they did not dissolve pre-university relationships, they had at the end of the study nearly as many peer relationships as the non-shy students. Thus, with regard to the number of peer relationships, shy students differed from non-shy students mainly in the pace of their network growth.

More serious problems for some shy students were indicated by the results for love relationships and loneliness. Whereas the majority of the non-shy students reported being in love at any point in time, only one-third of the shy students did so, and shy students were particularly unlikely to have a steady sexual partner. Consequently, a substantial number of shy students were chronically lonely whereas chronic loneliness was extremely rare among non-shy students. From a developmental task perspective, the findings indicate that the more difficult the age-appropriate developmental task was, the more shyness prevented students from fulfilling this task.

It seems clear that this overall result cannot be attributed only to shy students' problems in dealing with the unfamiliarity of the new social world of university. In addition, social-evaluative anxieties about not being an attractive love partner probably contributed to the specific problems of the shy. Interestingly, if they succeeded in finding a love partner, they engaged in more sex than the non-shy students. Either shy students have more intense partnerships or feel obliged to assure the partner of themselves through frequent sex because they fear that the partner may leave.

It is important to note that the study ended 18 months after the beginning of university studies. If we had observed the students for a longer time, we might have come to the conclusion that even for love relationships and loneliness, shyness only slowed down the process of falling in love, having sex, and having children but did not affect the final outcomes of this process. Perhaps the shy students engaged in as many stable partnerships and had as many children at, say, age 40 as the non-shy students.

In fact, such a result is expected from a re-analysis of the Berkeley Guidance Study by Caspi, Elder and Bem (1988). A total of 182 boys and girls who were born in 1928–9 in Berkeley, California, were followed up until age 40. At ages 8–10, 28 per cent of the boys and 30 per cent of the girls were classified as shy. At age 40, the formerly shy boys had married three years later than formerly non-shy boys and had become fathers four years later than their non-shy peers. But they were just as likely to be married, have stable marriages, and have as many children as the non-shy group at age 40. Similar effects were not found for shy girls, and this can be attributed to the traditional gender roles in that generation (see Kerr, this volume, Chapter 5). It can be expected, however, that the increasing pressures in current western societies for women to fulfil traditional male roles have largely erased this gender difference today.

From such a long-term perspective, shyness may be viewed as a personality trait that slows down social developmental processes in both men and women in contemporary western societies, leading to transitional problems such as loneliness. It is interesting and as yet largely unexplored whether this slowing down has positive effects in addition to the transitional negative effects. Despite the current view in western societies that change and high speed are intrinsically good, there are sufficient examples from biology and psychology that tell us the opposite. For example, the intellectual capacity of *homo sapiens* seems to be attributable to delayed brain maturation that increased the capacity for learning; wise decisions require more time because they are based on a more in-depth exploration of the present state and its alternatives. In the relationship arena, quickly formed romantic relationships are not necessarily the more lasting ones, and early parenthood often goes along with poor parenting quality. Perhaps the relationships of shy adults are more enduring than those of their non-shy counterparts, as the results of the present study on old peer relationships suggest (see Figure 7.1). Can a shy partner be trusted more than a non-shy partner? Research on adults' shyness has been biased towards a focus on social-emotional problems; more studies are needed of the potential of shy people (see Schmidt and Tasker, this volume, Chapter 3).

Despite the possibility of this potential and the often transitional nature of problems of shy people, there is one finding of the present study that may present the most serious problem for the shy. Shyness predicted a large portion of variance in loneliness even when support and love in the most significant relationships were statistically controlled for. Thus, shy students face a real risk for loneliness even when they have a love partner and their significant relationships are supportive. It may be that we have neglected important aspects of relationship quality in our analyses, but it is also possible that shy people tend to experience more loneliness and other negative affective states than non-shy people even if they have relationships of the same quality. This negative affective bias is obvious in analyses of all kinds of self-related cognition – self-reflective processes (Asendorpf, 1987, 1989), self-efficacy expectations (Hill, 1989), attributions of outcomes of own behaviour (Johnson, Petzel and Johnson, 1991), and memory encoding about self-related events (Mansell and Clark, 1999); however, relationship quality was not controlled in these studies. My personal view is that in order to understand chronic shyness and its effects on subjective experience and observable behaviour properly, we must consider contributions of a different relationship quality (both positive and negative) and of a deeply-rooted negative social self-esteem, and take into account that these two factors covary and interact and also have some life of their own.

This chapter has dealt with the transition to the *social world* of university. There may be additional, important contributions of shyness to the transition to the *intellectual world* of university. This topic has been largely unexplored in the literature (but see Crozier, 1997), but one can easily generate hypotheses about the difficulties that shy students experience in large-group settings such as lectures and seminars, and in social-evaluative settings such as examinations, and how these difficulties interfere with learning and achievement. If alternative learning styles such as learning in public versus private settings, and alternative testing such as oral versus written examinations are taken into account, a longitudinal study into how shy students differ from non-shy students in learning and achievement would be worth pursuing.

References

Asendorpf, J.B. (1987) 'Videotape reconstruction of emotions and cognitions related to shyness', *Journal of Personality and Social Psychology*, 53: 542–9.

Asendorpf, J.B. (1989) 'Shyness as a final common pathway for two different kinds of inhibition', *Journal of Personality and Social Psychology*, 57: 481–92.

Asendorpf, J.B. and Meier, G.H. (1993) 'Personality effects on children's speech in everyday life: sociability-mediated exposure and shyness-mediated reactivity to social situations', *Journal of Personality and Social Psychology*, 64: 1072–83.

Asendorpf, J.B. and van Aken, M.A.G. (1994) 'Traits and relationship status', *Child Development*, 65: 1786–98.

Asendorpf, J.B. and Wilpers, S. (1998) 'Personality effects on social relationships', *Journal of Personality and Social Psychology*, 74: 1531–44.

Asendorpf, J.B. and Wilpers, S. (2000) 'Attachment security and available support: closely linked relationship qualities', *Journal of Social and Personal Relationships*, 17: 115–38.

Caspi, A., Elder, G.H., Jr. and Bem, D.J. (1988) 'Moving away from the world: life-course patterns of shy children', *Developmental Psychology*, 24: 824–31.

Costa, P.T. and McCrae, R.R. (1989) *The NEO PI/FFI Manual Supplement*, Odessa, FL: Psychological Assessment Resources.

Crozier, W.R. (1997) *Individual Learners: Personality Differences in Education*, London: Routledge.

Cutrona, C.E. (1982) 'Transition to college: loneliness and the process of social adjustment', in L.A. Peplau and D. Perlman (eds) *Loneliness: A Sourcebook of Current Theory, Research, and Therapy* (pp. 291–309), New York: Wiley.

Elder, G.H., Jr. (1985) 'Perspectives on the life course', in G.H. Elder, Jr. (ed.) *Life Course Dynamics: Trajectories and Transitions*, 1968–1980 (pp. 23–49), Ithaca, NY: Cornell University Press.

Gray, J.A. (1982) *The Neuropsychology of Anxiety: An Enquiry into the Functions of the Septo-hippocampal System*, Oxford: Oxford University Press.

Gray, J.A. (1987) 'Perspectives on anxiety and impulsivity. a commentary', *Journal of Research in Personality*, 21: 493–509.

Hays, R.B. and Oxley, D. (1986) 'Social network development and functioning during a life transition', *Journal of Personality and Social Psychology*, 50: 305–13.

Hill, G.J. (1989) 'An unwillingness to act: behavioral appropriateness, situational constraint, and self-efficacy in shyness', *Journal of Personality*, 57: 871–90.

Johnson, J.M., Petzel, T.P. and Johnson, J.E. (1991) 'Attributions of shy persons in affiliation and achievement situations', *Journal of Psychology*, 125: 51–8.

Jones, W.H., Freemon, J.E. and Goswick, R.A. (1981) 'The persistence of loneliness: self and other determinants', *Journal of Personality*, 49: 27–48.

Mansell, W. and Clark, D.M. (1999) 'How do I appear to others? Social anxiety and processing of the observable self', *Behaviour Research and Therapy*, 37: 419–34.

Marangoni, C., and Ickes, W. (1989) 'Loneliness: a theoretical review with implications for measurement', *Journal of Social and Personal Relationships*, 6: 93–128.

Neyer, F.J. (1999) 'Die Persönlichkeit junger Erwachsener in verschiedenen Lebensformen (The personality of young adults in different living patterns)', *Kölner Zeitschrift für Soziologie und Sozialpsychologie*, 51: 491–508.

Russell, D., Cutrona, C.E. and Jones, W.H. (1986) 'A trait-situational analysis of shyness', in W.H. Jones, J.M. Cheek and S.R. Briggs (eds) *Shyness: Perspectives on Research and Treatment* (pp. 239–49), New York: Plenum Press.

Schlenker, B.R. and Leary, M.R. (1982) 'Social anxiety and self-presentation: a conceptualization and model', *Psychological Bulletin*, 92: 641–69.

Shaver, P., Furman, W. and Buhrmester, D. (1986) 'Transition to college: network changes, social skills, and loneliness', in S.W. Duck and D. Perlman (eds) *Understanding Personal Relationships* (pp. 193–219), London: Sage.

Thomas, A. and Chess, S. (1977) *Temperament and Development*, New York: Brunner & Mazel.

Trivers, R. (1972) 'Parental investment and sexual selection', in B. Campbell (ed.) *Sexual Selection and the Descent of Man* (pp. 136–79), Chicago, IL: Aldine-Atherton.

Zimbardo, P.G. (1977) *Shyness*, Reading, MA: Addison-Wesley.

8 'u r a lot bolder on the net'

Shyness and Internet use

*Lynne D. Roberts, Leigh M. Smith and
Clare M. Pollock*

Over the past two decades the prevalence of shyness in young adults in western societies has risen from 40 per cent to 48 per cent. This increase has been attributed to social, economic and technological presses reducing the need for face-to-face contact between individuals in everyday life, and limiting the opportunities to develop and practise social skills, and form intimate relationships (Carducci, 1999; Carducci and Zimbardo, 1995; Henderson and Zimbardo, 1998). Indeed, Carducci and Zimbardo (1995: 82) describe technology as 'ushering in a culture of shyness' where technology is changing or replacing personal communication. At the same time they describe computer-mediated communication (CMC) as 'the perfect medium for the shy' (p. 82) as a result of the greater control over the communication process, the absence of time constraints in preparing messages and the absence of direct observation by others.

Does Internet use enhance or impede social interactions for shy individuals? In this chapter we will present a series of three studies that examine how shy people are using CMC, and the effect this is having on their behaviour both on-line (when connected to the Internet) and off-line (in 'real life'). First, given the newness of the technology, we will briefly describe CMC and the social virtual environments accessible over the Internet.

Computer-mediated communication

Communication in cyberspace occurs through CMC. A message from one individual is sent to one or more people via computer networks. The geographic location of communication partners is immaterial providing all have access to the Internet via computer and modem. Dyads, small groups, and large networks can use CMC.

CMC can be synchronous or asynchronous. Synchronous CMC is real-time communication and is most frequently associated with computer chat-based environments such as Internet Relay Chat (IRC), Multi-User Dimensions (MUDs), web-based chats, talkers and chat-rooms. Asynchronous CMC is a form of delayed communication where communication partners do not need to be simultaneously on-line. Frequently used forms of asynchronous CMC are email and newsgroups.

CMC can occur in text, graphic, audio, or video formats, or a combination of these. However, due to bandwidth restrictions, CMC is predominantly text-based at present. Text-based CMC is less formal than most forms of writing, and has been characterized as 'written speech' (Marvin, 1995). Text is supplemented by the use of paralinguistic cues (e.g. exclamation marks and ellipsis) and emoticons (e.g. 'smilies') to express emotions and aid in the interpretation of messages. The incorporation of speech patterns transforms the static text into active text (Greller and Barnes, 1993).

Socio-emotional communication has been widely reported in text-based virtual environments accessible via the Internet. High rates of self-disclosure, emotional/social support, and sense of community have been reported in newsgroups (Baym, 1998; McKenna and Bargh; 1998; Salem, Bogat and Reid, 1997; Walther and Boyd, in press; Winzelberg, 1997), discussion groups (Sharf, 1997), MUDs (Reid, 1994; Ryan, 1995) and IRC (Reid, 1991). Acquaintanceships, friendships, romantic and sexual relationships frequently develop in newsgroups (Parks and Floyd, 1996) and MUDs (Parks and Roberts, 1998). In some instances the interpersonal bonding of members in computer-mediated groups surpasses that of comparable face-to-face groups, a phenomenon called 'hyperpersonal' communication (Walther, 1996).

However, while socio-emotional communication on-line may flourish, the effect of on-line involvement on off-line life is less than clear. Some psychologists (e.g. Griffiths, 1998; Young, 1998) warn of the dangers of long periods of time spent on-line and the potential for 'Internet addiction'. In the first published longitudinal survey of Internet use, Kraut, Patterson, Lundmark and Kiesler (1998) reported that increased Internet use was associated with reduced communication with family members, reduced social circles and increased depression and loneliness. While concluding that the Internet had a negative effect on social involvement and psychological well-being, they noted that for the socially isolated, Internet use may increase social participation and psychological well-being. Consistent with this, McKenna and Bargh (1998) reported that individuals with stigmatized identities benefited from the opportunity to belong to on-line groups. Self-disclosure and support on-line resulted in over half of those surveyed self-disclosing embarrassing problems to others in their off-line lives.

Shyness and the Internet

Shy individuals can access all types of mainstream virtual environments. In addition, they may use virtual environments that are specifically set up to attract shy individuals and meet shyness-related needs. Sites on the Internet that provide information and resources for shy people range from World Wide Web pages developed by shyness professionals (e.g. http://www.shyness.com/) to pages developed by shy individuals themselves. These web-sites frequently contain links to other shyness-related web-sites, newsgroups, and discussion groups and may provide details of where to obtain treatment for shyness.

Some shy individuals are using shy-specific virtual environments to meet and interact with other shy people. These environments include newsgroups and discussion groups. For example, the newsgroup alt.support.shyness is a busy newsgroup (more than 100 postings each day) where shy individuals can post messages to other shy individuals. Members may ask questions, and offer and receive advice and support. Responding to a survey on newsgroup use, one poster to alt.support.shyness noted:

> I often feel uncomfortable asking my friends/acquaintances for help with being shy because I don't want this fact to ruin my friendships, as it sometimes has done in the past. I received more diversified opinions and support when online, and this also helps me – I ask for help 'into the air' (one might say) and receive many replies, as opposed to asking one person for help and getting one reply - which is usually not enough to help. In short, I prefer asking for help online than asking my friends for help.
>
> (Walther and Boyd, in press)

Shy individuals may find that shyness is not an issue for them when on-line. There are anecdotal accounts of reduced shyness in social synchronous virtual environments such as IRC (Albright and Conran, 1995; Reid, 1991) and MUDs (Turkle, 1995). Shy individuals typically assume a protective self-presentation style to cope with their social anxiety (Arkin, Lake and Baumgardner, 1986). The self-presentational theory of social anxiety (Leary 1986; see also Leary, this volume, Chapter 9) states that where situational factors are likely to interfere with the communication process, the individual reduces his or her self-presentational concerns as any social interaction difficulties may be attributed to the interfering factor. When using CMC, the absence of non-verbal cues, the time taken to type messages and the variable response time in sending and receiving messages are all likely to be interfering factors in the communication process. As public self-consciousness has been hypothesized as a 'necessary antecedent' to social anxiety (Fenigstein, Scheier and Buss, 1975), a reduction in public self-consciousness may result in a reduction in the shyness experienced on-line.

In their off-line lives shy people have smaller social support and friendship networks and report fewer, more passive interactions than the non-shy (Jones and Carpenter, 1986). Shy individuals can become trapped in a cycle of shyness where their protective self-presentation style and negative cognitions do not provide them with the opportunities to experience successful social interactions (Cheek and Melchior, 1986). CMC may provide them with the opportunity to break the cycle, increase their social and friendship circles, and experiment with less-shy behaviours. Those who are shy but also have a high need for sociability have the most difficulties in social situations (Arkin and Grove, 1990; Cheek and Buss, 1981). It is possible that CMC would most appeal to those shy people who also have a high need for sociability that is not being met in their off-line lives.

Little is known about the effect of reduced shyness on-line on shyness off-line. Some authors have provided anecdotal reports suggesting that shyness off-line may decrease following the adoption of a less-shy persona on-line (e.g. Turkle, 1995; Wallace, 1999). Virtual environments such as MUDs provide a setting for identity play where an individual can try on new identities and behaviours as part of a psychosocial moratorium period. Turkle (1995: 185) argued that over time, 'slippages' occur where the multiple identities merge with the individual's notion of the real self. Positive reinforcement received for less-shy behaviour may result in the generalization of that behaviour to off-line settings (Wallace, 1999).

In direct contrast to the notion of increased psychological well-being and decreased shyness resulting from Internet use, some researchers warn of the dangers of Internet use for shy individuals. Young, Pistner, O'Mara and Buchanan (1999) surveyed 35 therapists who had treated clients with mental health problems related to their Internet use. One area of dysfunction identified from qualitative responses was shy individuals' dependence on on-line relationships at the expense of off-line life. This was attributed to the anonymity of virtual environments providing shy individuals with a safe and secure environment for social interaction. Carducci and Zimbardo (1995) warned of the dangers of shy individuals using CMC as a way of avoiding face-to-face social interaction, claiming that these new technologies provide only the illusion of human connectedness. Carducci (cited by DeWees, 1996) suggested that 'Shy people should log off of their computers and log on to life'. Even Turkle (1995), a proponent of the positive changes that can result from Internet use, has noted that positive changes may not always occur. She provided a case study of 'Stewart', a shy individual with health problems who despite successful social interactions on-line was unable to make improvements off-line.

No empirical research on the use of virtual environments by shy individuals, or the effect this has on shyness, was located in a search of traditional and on-line psychology journals by the authors. Given the paucity of empirical research on shy people's use of CMC, it is difficult to assess the two conflicting positions. Does Internet use enhance or impede off-line social interactions for shy individuals? Research is needed that examines the use of virtual environments by shy individuals and the effect this has on their lives. As a starting point, this chapter looks at findings on shyness that emerged from a series of three studies conducted by the authors. Only the portions of the studies that directly address shyness are reported here. For further information on other aspects of these studies see Roberts, Smith and Pollock (1996, 1997a and b). The first two studies provide a phenomenological account of shy individuals' experiences on-line, and the effects on their off-line lives. The final study provides an empirical examination of shyness on- and off-line over the first 6 months of Internet use.

Studies 1 and 2

The first two studies examined social interaction via CMC in two synchronous social text-based virtual environments, MOOs (MUDs, Object Oriented; Study 1) and IRC (Study 2). Both of these environments support dyadic, small-group and many-to-many communication. Users of these environments select the name by which they wish to be known (frequently referred to as a 'nick' or 'handle'), providing a level of anonymity to their on-line interactions. In addition, on MOOs individuals can create and describe their own characters, homes and possessions.

Methodology

Subjects

A total of 101 individuals who use text-based virtual environments took part in these two studies. Research participants ranged in age from 14 to 57 years, the majority were male (68.3 per cent) and educated to tertiary level. Experience in text-based virtual environments ranged from 1 day to 5 years.

Procedure

Grounded theory methodology (Glaser and Strauss, 1967) guided the procedures for this research. Theoretical sampling was used to select a wide range of past and present users of MOOs and IRC. Semi-structured interviews were conducted on-line or face-to-face. All interviews were logged or audio-recorded. Triangulation of data was achieved through the use of interviews, participant observation, postings to MOO mailing lists and IRC newsgroups, and MOO and IRC documentation. Transcripts, logs of interviews and postings were coded and analysed using the QSR NUD*IST (QSR, 1995) program. Grounded theories of social interaction in MOOs and IRC were developed from the analyses.

Results

Results from these studies are presented in the form of direct quotes from interviews interwoven with research findings. All quotes appear in italics. Minor changes have been made to the spelling or grammar of some quotes in accordance with research participants' wishes and to enhance readability. Explanatory notes have been inserted in roman text in parentheses within the quotes where necessary.

Emergent themes from this grounded theory research were the disinhibited use of on-line text-based environments by shy individuals and the carry-over effect on their off-line lives. Research participants were not asked during the interview if they were shy. However, some research participants volunteered the information that they were shy in their everyday lives. This information was usually forthcoming at two points in the interview: either when they were asked if there were any ways in which their behaviour or interaction with others on-line differed from that off-line, or when asked what effect their on-line involvement had on their off-line lives. It should be noted that while these research participants self-identify as shy, no clinical judgements were made by the researchers as to the degree of severity or type of shyness.

The self-described extent of shyness varied among those research participants who self-identified as shy. While some experienced shyness only when initiating conversations with strangers, others reported persistent difficulties in social interactions. Regardless of the degree of shyness experienced in their off-line lives, none of the research participants described themselves as shy on-line.

When asked how their on-line behaviour and social interactions differed from those off-line, most research participants responded that they were less inhibited or less conservative on-line. For example, one respondent noted that '*It makes me a bit more daring I think ...*', while another commented that '*I'm a lot less conservative. I guess I don't want to be conservative, and I am a little fearful at what they will think of me when I am me, in real life.*' Respondents found it easier to overcome their shyness in virtual environments: '*on the MOO I find it definitely easier to overcome my natural shyness. In real life I turned down many chances of friendship only out of shyness.*' In virtual environments they were able to practise assertive communication. A university lecturer who runs classes in MOOs commented how she had '*seen very shy, scared students really glow in a MOO environment ...*'. It should be noted that disinhibited behaviour on-line was reported by many research participants, not just those who are shy (see Roberts *et al.*, 1997a).

Shy individuals form a range of relationships in virtual environments, from friendships to romantic and sexual relationships. One MOOer noted how she used on-line sexual relationships to help overcome her shyness in intimate situations:

> *Well I find it hard to express myself sometimes ... there are times when I just can't find the words ... that is one of those times ... I want to learn to say things a bit more eloquently ... like in romance novels ...*<giggle> *it forces me to find alternative ways of saying things ... It helps me to overcome my shyness because it is a very awkward subject to talk about ... especially to rp* (real people – as opposed to virtual people on MOOs)... .

Another MOOer interviewed noted how a shy classmate had used the MOO to initiate an off-line date. The formation of intimate on-line relationships provided shy individuals with the opportunity to experience intimacy in a non-threatening environment.

Research participants attributed the ease of social communication and disinhibited behaviour on-line to a number of factors inherent in anonymous, text-based virtual environments. They could not be seen when interacting in text, and in turn did not have to look at the people with whom they were interacting. As one respondent noted: '*I think that being on here, it is just easier to be open because you aren't looking someone right in the face ... Me, I am very shy irl ... So on here I can talk without being shy ...*'. Not looking the other in the face means that difficulties in making or maintaining eye contact in off-line interpersonal situations are removed: '*Copper_Guest doesn't worry about eye contact or anything like that. ... while on the moo, that is.*' The anonymity associated with not being seen and with using a nickname provides a form of protection against 'real life' identification: '*I was a lot more shy when I first started on the net ... but at least now I can crack corny jokes on the net without feeling embarrassed ... the net protects your real identity ... as long as they don't know you in person:*'.

A second factor contributing to disinhibited behaviour was the perceived absence of judgement of oneself by other virtual inhabitants. As one research participant noted, in virtual environments '*I am not as afraid that I might offend ppl ... or as afraid of what they think of me ...*'. This results in individuals feeling free to discuss difficult personal situations in their lives that they may feel unable to discuss with their off-line family and friends. One MOOer commented: '*I've been able to deal with some personal issues on here that I could never deal with irl*' ... (provides the example of being able to talk about being raped in the past) ... '*I don't know what it was that made me talk about it, but I just felt comfortable telling these people ... it was kinda like my rl friends would judge me or something.*' As a result of the acceptance and support obtained on-line, this MOOer was able to talk later to her family about the rape.

Related to the inability to see communication partners on-line and the perceived absence of judgement is a reduction in the fear of being rejected. One research participant observed that '*obviously on the computer one is in no danger of being ridiculed or made fun of – the others can't see you so there is no real danger of rejection.*' These factors combine to reduce performance pressure for shy individuals. Because all that others can judge the individual on is what they type, public self-awareness is reduced: '*Don't have to worry about your appearance, don't have to worry about meeting the person in real life and have to interact with the person on a daily basis. The person you met on the net could be on the other side of the world, across the state, anywhere. Don't have to worry about gender variables, about culture. Don't really have to worry about how rich you are. It is just what you say, you don't have to worry about how you say, your words, you don't have to worry about your voice. Everything other than what you type.*' In this way, on-line text-based environments provide shy individuals with the perception of a safe environment in which to interact socially with others.

Disinhibited behaviour on-line had carry-over effects in the off-line lives of some of the shy individuals interviewed. In one case, the discrepancy between on-line and off-line social interaction was so marked that it had provided the impetus for change: *'well ... IRC has made it obvious where my RL deficiencies are ... so they slap me in the face whenever I do something in RL'*. For this individual who claimed that prior to IRC use he had no social life, on-line friendships were his only friendships. Acknowledging the limitations of his on-line friendships, *'IRC life is easier and shallower and a good precursor to RL friendships. But it is not a substitute'*, he had made off-line contact with some of his geographically dispersed on-line friends. However, he noted *'I still don't* (have an off-line social life). *But IRC, among its many functions, acts as a support group for those who don't have a life.'*

Others noted how successful social interaction in virtual environments had translated to increased confidence in their social interaction skills: *'I used to be quite shy and awkward in RL ... my experiences online have given me much more confidence and it definitely shows in RL. ... 'Now when people meet me, they have a hard time believing that I was ever really shy or awkward.'* One research participant noticed the decrease in self-consciousness: *'I'm less self conscious ... can talk about almost anything irl now. I was VERY shy ... well, I still can be, but not nearly as much'*. Intimate topics of conversation were perceived as less stressful than they had been: *'I think I am more outgoing and I chat about sex more freely now and I can understand people's perspectives more, since I have chatted to so many people.'*

Research participants attributed positive changes in off-line social interaction to their on-line experiences. One attributed the change to improved communication skills: *'... just that dealing with real people through this medium has given me the ability to relate and deal with them in RL as well without having to feel so unsure of myself as I used to be.'* Complementing this was interaction with on-line friends in off-line environments: *'I would say though that meeting people off-line whom I have been close to and seeing that they are not all that much different than the person I knew on-line makes a big difference.'*

Not all changes in off-line were positive. Some noted the time spent on-line displaced time previously spent sleeping, working, studying, or with people off-line. In some cases, on-line life was seen as an escape from problems off-line. As one MOOer commented: *'It is an escape from rl ... and any escape can take over your life if you let it ... Fantasy is always more pleasant than RL stuff.'*

Discussion

The results of this research suggest that shy individuals are less inhibited in their behaviour and social interaction in text-based virtual environments than in their off-line lives and, as a result, were able to develop a range of relationships on-line. Less inhibited behaviour on-line was attributed to the perception of IRC and MOOs as safe environments in which to interact. Self-presentational concerns and performance pressure were reduced for shy individuals as they could not be seen by their communication partners, did not have to engage in eye contact, and could remain anonymous. These factors resulted in a perceived absence of judgement and reduced fear of rejection by communication partners.

The perception shy individuals have of not being judged by others in virtual environments means they may be ideal environments for shy individuals to practise the behaviours which they find the most difficult. Interactions with members of the opposite sex are especially likely to elicit shyness (Crozier, 1979, 1986; Pilkonis, 1977; Russell, Cutrona and Jones, 1986). Given the frequency of opposite-sex relationships in virtual environments (Parks and Floyd, 1996; Parks and Roberts, 1998), interaction in text-based virtual environments may be particularly beneficial for shy individuals who experience difficulties in communicating with members of the opposite sex.

Through experiencing successful social interactions in virtual environments, some shy individuals were able to improve, or change their perception of their communication skills, resulting in decreased shyness in off-line social interactions. Caution needs to be exercised in generalizing from the results of the research presented here. First, the research project did not set out specifically to examine the behaviour of shy individuals in text-based virtual environments. Only the comments from those research participants who self-identified as shy have been included here. Given the prevalence of shyness in western societies, it is likely that many more of the research participants were shy, but were not identified as such in this research. It is possible that the experiences of those who self-identified as shy to the researcher differ from those who did not. Second, this research examined social interaction in only two of many virtual environments. It is possible that the findings are situationally specific, and social interaction in other types of virtual environments may have a different effect, or no effect, on shyness. Third, this research provides a picture of on- and off-line shyness at one point in time. It is not known whether changes in shyness off-line following successful interactions on-line will be maintained over time. Further research is required to determine whether it is possible to generalize from the findings of this research. As a first step towards this goal, Study 3 was designed to test empirically hypotheses developed from Studies 1 and 2.

Study 3

Study 3 was a longitudinal investigation of new Internet users, following their progress for their first 6 months on-line. The results from Study 1 and Study 2 suggested that shy individuals are less inhibited in their behaviour and social interaction in text-based virtual environments than in their off-line lives. Through experiencing successful social interactions with others in the virtual environments of IRC and MOOs, some shy individuals were able to change the perception of their own interpersonal skills, resulting in decreased shyness in off-line social interactions. Given these findings it was hypothesized that shy individuals would experience lower levels of shyness on-line, resulting in a reduction in shyness off-line after 6 months of Internet use.

Shy individuals who also have a high need for sociability have the most difficulties in social situations (Arkin and Grove, 1990; Cheek and Buss, 1981). CMC may most benefit these shy individuals whose sociability needs are not being met in their off-line lives. Shy individuals who have a low need for sociability may receive all (or more than) their desired level of social interaction in their everyday lives. It was hypothesized that the greatest reductions in shyness would be recorded for individuals who are both shy and sociable.

Method

Research participants

The research participants in this study were 70 people who had obtained their first Internet account during the month immediately prior to taking part in the research. They were recruited through advertisements placed with Australian Internet Service Providers, an information page on the Internet, and postings to newsgroups whose primary focus is assisting new Internet users. Survey respondents (54.3 per cent male, 45.7 per cent female) ranged in age from 14 to 65 years ($M = 37.26$ years, $SD = 12$ years). The majority were married (51.7 per cent), lived in Australia (65.7 per cent), and were educated to tertiary level ($M = 13.93$ years, $SD = 3.15$ years).

Procedure

The research design for Study 3 was a longitudinal study with measures administered via surveys on the World Wide Web at three points in time: during the research participants' first ('Newbie' survey), fourth ('Midbie' survey) and seventh ('Oldbie' survey) month on-line. Each survey consisted of a range of measures related to Internet use or personality, including shyness and sociability. Research participants were asked to rate their shyness and sociability in 'real' life (off-line) on the Newbie and Oldbie surveys. Off-line shyness and sociability were not measured on the Midbie survey as the focus of the research was on long-term changes in these measures. Research participants were also asked to rate their shyness and sociability in cyberspace (on-line) on the Midbie and Oldbie surveys. On-line shyness and sociability were not measured on the Newbie survey as research participants were new to Internet use and on-line social interaction was unlikely to have stabilized.

Measures

The measures of interest for this chapter are shyness and sociability. Shyness was measured using a shortened 5-item version (see Schmidt and Fox, 1995) of the Revised Cheek and Buss Shyness Scale (Cheek, 1983). Shyness on-line was measured using the same 5-item scale with each item prefaced with 'In CYBERSPACE'. Sociability was measured using the Cheek and Buss (1981) Sociability Scale, a 5-item measure of sociability based on the desire to be with others. Sociability on-line was measured using the same 5-item scale with each item prefaced with 'In CYBERSPACE'. In this study both the shyness (α = .71) and sociability scales (α = .81) had acceptable reliability for research purposes.

Results

Scores on the off-line shyness scale on the Newbie survey ranged from 0 to 19 (M = 8.10, SD = 3.99) and were normally distributed. Males and females did not significantly differ in their shyness scores, and all further analyses combine the two groups. Groups of high-shy and low-shy individuals were selected on the basis of their off-line shyness score on the Newbie survey: scores equal to or below the 25th percentile (score of 6) were classified as low-shy, and equal to or above the 75th percentile (score of 10.25) were classified as high-shy.

Repeated measures ANOVAs using the General Linear Model (GLM) were conducted to examine changes in shyness scores across the four conditions (shyness off-line, first month; shyness on-line, fourth month; shyness on-line, seventh month; shyness off-line, seventh month) for the high- and low-shy groups separately. Changes in shyness across time and settings for both high- and low-shy groups are depicted graphically in Figure 8.1.

For the low-shy group (n = 17) there was no significant difference in shyness scores across settings and time.

For the high-shy group (n = 10), there was a significant main effect for condition (Pillais trace $F(3, 7)$ = 33.19, p < .001; η^2 = .93; observed power of .99 at α = .05). Post hoc pairwise comparisons revealed significant differences in shyness across settings and time. High-shy individuals experienced lower levels of shyness on-line (Midbie M = 7.10, SD = 3.48; Oldbie M = 5.80, SD = 2.57) than off-line (Newbie M = 13.60, SD = 2.59).

Every member of the high-shy group reported decreased shyness on-line, ranging from 4 to 14 units on the shyness scale. This resulted in high- and low-shy individuals experiencing similar levels of shyness on-line. An independent samples t-test confirmed that shyness on-line did not significantly differ for the high- and low-shy groups. This finding, combined

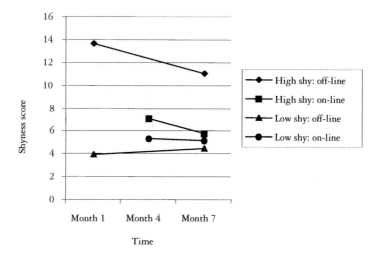

Figure 8.1 Changes in shyness scores over time for low- and high-shy
            groups in on- and off-line settings

with the absence of a significant correlation between shyness off-line in the
Newbie survey and shyness on-line in the Oldbie survey, indicates that
shyness on-line cannot be predicted from shyness scores off-line.

As a group, the high-shy individuals experienced a significant decrease in
shyness off-line over time. Post hoc pairwise comparisons confirmed that off-
line shyness after 6 months' Internet use ($M = 11.00$, $SD = 3.83$) was
significantly less than initial off-line shyness ($M = 13.60, SD = 2.59$). While
the majority of the high-shy group members experienced decreased shyness
off-line after 6 months of Internet use (range 1 to 7 units on the shyness
scale), two (18.18 per cent) reported a small increase in shyness (2 units on
the shyness scale).

When groups are selected on the basis of extreme scores on a measure,
there is an increased risk of a regression to the mean effect. The standard error
of prediction calculated for this sample indicated that the difference in
shyness scores between the Newbie and Midbie surveys could not be solely
accounted for by measurement error. The first hypothesis was supported: shy
individuals experienced significantly lower levels of shyness on-line, and a
significant reduction in shyness off-line after 6 months of Internet use.

To examine the possible interaction of shyness and sociability, respondents
were divided into four groups based on their off-line shyness and sociability
scores on the Newbie survey. Median points on the scales were used as cut
points for the groups. The four resulting groups are:

• high shyness score and high sociability score (hishyhisoc);

- high shyness score and low sociability score (hishylosoc);
- low shyness score and low sociability score (loshylosoc);
- low shyness score and high sociability score (loshyhisoc).

A repeated measures ANOVA (GLM) with shyness score as the repeated measure within subjects factor and shyness/sociability grouping as the between subjects factor was conducted. There were significant main effects for condition (Pillais trace $F(3,40)$ = 11.48, p < .001; η^2 = .46; observed power of .99 at α = .05 and shyness/sociability grouping across conditions (Pillais trace $F(9,126)$ = 3.29, p = .001; η^2 = .19; observed power of .98 at α = .05).

To test the hypothesized decrease in shyness for individuals high in shyness and sociability, a repeated measures t-test was conducted. Shyness significantly reduced from the first month on-line (Newbie survey: M = 11.11, SD = 1.05) to the seventh month on-line (Oldbie survey: M = .11, SD = 2.67, $t(8)$ = 2.45, $p<.05$). However, a similar significant decrease in shyness was also found for individuals high in shyness but low in sociability (Newbie survey: M = 14.70, SD = 2.54; Oldbie survey M = 12.00, SD = 3.86, $t(9)$ = 2.54, $p<.05$). Off-line shyness significantly decreased over the 6-month period regardless of sociability. This result suggests that shyness does not interact with sociability to affect shyness on- and off-line over time.

Discussion

Two main findings emerge from this study. First, the Internet provides virtual environments that free individuals from the shyness-related inhibitions they experience in off-line settings. Shy individuals are less shy on-line, with on-line shyness matching that of the non-shy. There is no relationship between an individual's level of shyness at the beginning of the survey and his or her level of shyness on-line after 6 months of Internet use. This is consistent with the disinhibition reported by research participants in Studies 1 and 2. Text-based CMC provides a 'level playing field' for social interaction for the shy and non-shy alike.

The second main finding is that for the high-shy group overall, off-line shyness decreased after 6 months of Internet use. While the majority of the group experienced decreased shyness, two reported a small increase in shyness. Again, this is consistent with findings from Studies 1 and 2, where only some individuals reported decreases in shyness off-line after experiencing successful interactions on-line.

The hypothesized interaction between shyness and sociability was not supported. Regardless of their need for sociability, shy individuals experienced decreases in shyness on-line and a resultant decrease in shyness off-line after 6 months of Internet use.

This study has a number of limitations that make it impossible to generalize from the results: non-random sampling technique, high drop-out rate over the course of the three surveys, and the resultant small sample size. However, the small sample size was offset by the large effect sizes obtained for most analyses, providing the necessary power to detect significant differences. This increases our confidence in the results. Future research replicating these results is needed before we can confidently generalize the findings to the larger population.

General discussion

We began this chapter by asking whether Internet use enhanced or impeded social interactions and psychological well-being for shy individuals. The studies presented here provide both qualitative and quantitative evidence for reduced shyness on-line for all shy individuals. As a result of successful social interactions on-line, some shy individuals also experienced a reduction in shyness off-line. These results suggest that participation in virtual environments has the potential to enhance psychological well-being for shy individuals, providing the opportunity to break the shyness cycle (Cheek and Melchior, 1986) to enhance personal, social and occupational well-being.

What are the mechanisms through which this reduction in shyness occurs? A likely pathway is that the reduction in public self-awareness experienced in virtual environments results in disinhibited behaviour on-line. On-line text-based environments provide shy individuals with the perception of a safe environment in which to interact socially with others without the confines of shyness, and to experiment with new less inhibited behaviours. Where these behaviours are reinforced by positive feedback, the individual may change his or her perception of his or her social skills and the behaviours may generalize to off-line settings (Wallace, 1999). Over time, many relationships formed in on-line virtual environments migrate to off-line settings (Parks and Floyd, 1996; Parks and Roberts, 1998), and this may increase the shy individual's off-line social network while also providing further opportunities to practise his or her new skills within off-line settings.

However, increased social competence on-line did not always result in a reduction in shyness off-line. There is the potential for shy individuals to become stuck in cyberspace, preferring virtual interaction to face-to-face interaction (Turkle, 1995; Young et al., 1999). Even where social behaviours do not transfer to off-line life, the experience of successful social interactions and the development of friendships on-line may be beneficial to individuals who have a poor, or non-existent social life off-line.

Some social interaction is better than none. Contrary to Carducci and Zimbardo (1995) we argue that CMC *is* a form of human connectedness. Just because CMC does not require face-to-face interaction does not mean that real communication is not taking place. Rather than encouraging shy individuals to 'log off' from the one environment where they are experiencing successful social interactions, as psychologists we should be examining ways to help them transfer their new social skills to off-line situations.

Currently therapists are treating shy individuals with Internet-related problems using cognitive-behavioural and interpersonal psychotherapy techniques (Young *et al.,* 1999). There is a relatively unexplored potential for the use of virtual environments and CMC as part of shyness treatment programmes. For computer-literate shy individuals, text-based virtual environments may provide a non-threatening environment in which to rehearse social skills as part of a treatment programme. Some shy individuals who will not seek treatment in off-line settings may be willing to engage in on-line therapy, with the potential for on-line therapy as a precursor to off-line therapy.

Which virtual environments can best be utilized for on-line shyness treatment programmes? Sempsey (1998a) argued that CMC in MUDs promotes disinhibition, equality of participation and lower degrees of group conformity, and may provide acceptable environments for on-line psychotherapy. King and Moreggi (1998) provided a hypothetical model of how an on-line support group for shyness could be set up utilizing MUDs, email and the World Wide Web.

Some existing virtual environments may in themselves be therapeutic. Sempsey (1998b) used MOOs' Group Environment Scale questionnaire to examine the social climates of groups within MUDs. In comparison to off-line groups, MUD groups were less formalized and structured, enabled more self-expression, diversity and change, independent action, and openness. Discussion groups related to mental health can provide information and support, although they are limited by their transient membership, potential misunderstandings due to the text-only medium, lack of interpersonal responsibility and possibility for poor advice (Miller and Gergen, 1998; Lebow, 1998). Lebow (1998) contends that virtual participation without a therapist is no substitute for therapy, resulting in greater risks and smaller gains.

Further research is required to identify the long-term effects Internet use has on the social skills and psychological well-being of shy individuals. Of particular concern is the identification of shy individuals for whom Internet use is restricting their off-line social interactions, and the development of strategies that will aid the transference of on-line communication skills to off-line settings.

Authors' note

Parts of this chapter were first presented at the International Conference on Shyness and Self-consciousness, 14–17 July 1997, Cardiff, United Kingdom.

References

Albright, J. and Conran, T. (1995, April) 'Online love: sex, gender and relationships in cyberspace', Paper presented at the Pacific Sociological Association, Seattle, Washington [On-line]. Available: http://www-scf.usc.edu/~albright/onlineluv.txt

Arkin, R.M. and Grove, T. (1990) 'Shyness, sociability and patterns of everyday affiliation', *Journal of Social and Personal Relationships*, 7: 273–81.

Arkin, R.M., Lake, E.A. and Baumgardner, A.H. (1986) 'Shyness and self-presentation', in W.H. Jones, J.M. Cheek and S.R. Briggs (eds) *Shyness: Perspectives on Research and Treatment* (pp. 189–204), New York: Plenum Press.

Baym, N.K. (1998) 'The emergence of on-line community', in S.G. Jones (ed.) *Cybersociety 2.0: Revisiting Computer-mediated Communication and Community. New Media Cultures*, Vol. 2 (pp. 35–68), Thousand Oaks, CA: Sage.

Carducci, B.J. (1999) *Shyness: A Bold New Approach*, New York: HarperCollins.

Carducci, B J. and Zimbardo, P.G. (1995) 'Are you shy?', *Psychology Today*, 28(6): 34–45, 64–70, 78–82.

Cheek, J.M. (1983) 'The revised Cheek and Buss Shyness Scale', Unpublished manuscript, Wellesley College.

Cheek, J.M. and Buss, A.H. (1981) 'Shyness and sociability', *Journal of Personality and Social Psychology*, 41: 330–9.

Cheek, J.M. and Melchior, L.A. (1986) 'Shyness and self-concept', in L.M. Hartman and K.R. Blankstein (eds) *Perception of Self in Emotional Disorder and Psychotherapy* (pp. 113–31), New York: Plenum Press.

Crozier, W.R. (1979) 'Shyness as a dimension of personality', *British Journal of Social and Clinical Psychology*, 18: 121–8.

Crozier, W.R. (1986) 'Individual differences in shyness', in W.H. Jones, J.M. Cheek and S.R. Briggs (eds) *Shyness: Perspectives on Research and Treatment* (pp. 133–45), New York: Plenum Press.

DeWees, P. (1996) 'Talking by computer may increase . . . shyness', *The Psychology Newspaper* for faculty and staff of the eight campuses of Indiana University [On-line]. Available: http://www.iuinfo.indiana.edu:80/Newspaper/06-07-96/shypeop.htm

Fenigstein, A., Scheier, M.F., and Buss, A.H. (1975) 'Public and private self-consciousness: assessment and theory', *Journal of Consulting and Clinical Psychology*, 43: 522–7.

Glaser, B.G. and Strauss, A. (1967) *The Discovery of Grounded Theory: Strategies for Qualitative Research*, Chicago: Aldine Publishing Co.

Greller, L.M. and Barnes, S. (1995) 'Groupware and interpersonal text: the computer as a medium of communication', *Interpersonal Computing and Technology: An Electronic Journal for the 21st Century*, 1(2). [On-line]. Available: http://www2.nau.edu/~ipct-j/1993/n2/greller.txt

Griffiths, M. (1998) 'Internet addiction: does it really exist?', in J. Gackenbach (ed.) *Psychology and the Internet: Intrapersonal, Interpersonal, and Transpersonal Implications* (pp. 60–76), San Diego, CA: Academic Press.

Henderson, L. and Zimbardo, P. (1998) 'Shyness', in H.S Friedman (ed.) *Encyclopedia of Mental Health* (pp. 497–509), San Diego, CA: Academic Press. [On-line]. Available: http://www.shyness.com/encyclopedia.html

Jones, W.H. and Carpenter, B.N. (1986) 'Shyness, social behavior, and relationships', in W.H. Jones, J.M. Cheek and S.R. Briggs (eds) *Shyness: Perspectives on Research and Treatment* (pp. 227–49), New York: Plenum Press.

King, S.A. and Moreggi, D. (1998) 'Internet therapy and self-help groups: the pros and cons', in J. Gackenbach (ed.) *Psychology and the Internet: Intrapersonal, Interpersonal, and Transpersonal Implications* (pp. 77–109), San Diego, CA: Academic Press.

Kraut, R., Patterson, M., Lundmark, V. and Kiesler, S. (1998) 'Internet paradox: a social technology that reduces social involvement and psychological well-being?', *American Psychologist*, 53: 1017–31.

Leary, M.R. (1986) 'The impact of interactional impediments on social anxiety and self-presentation', *Journal of Experimental Social Psychology*, 22: 122–35.

Lebow, J. (1998) 'Not just talk, maybe some risk: the therapeutic potentials and pitfalls of computer-mediated conversation', *Journal of Marital and Family Therapy*, 24: 203–6.

McKenna, K.Y.A. and Bargh, J.A. (1998) 'Coming out in the age of the Internet: identity "demarginalization" through virtual group participation', *Journal of Personality and Social Psychology*, 75: 681–94.

Marvin, L.E. (1995) 'Spoof, spam, lurk and lag: the aesthetics of text-based virtual realities', *Journal of Computer-Mediated Communication*, 1(2) [On-line]. Available: http://shum.huji.ac.il/jcmc/vol1/issue2/marvin.html

Miller, J.K. and Gergen, K.J. (1998) 'Life on the line: the therapeutic potentials of computer-mediated conversation', *Journal of Marital and Family Therapy*, 24: 189–202.

Parks, M.R. and Floyd, K. (1996) 'Making friends in cyberspace', *Journal of Communication*, 46: 80–97.

Parks, M.R. and Roberts, L.D. (1998). ' "Making MOOsic": the development of personal relationships on-line and a comparison to their off-line counterparts', *Journal of Social and Personal Relationships*, 15: 517–37.

Pilkonis, P.A. (1977) 'Shyness, public and private, and its relationship to other measures of social behavior', *Journal of Personality*, 45: 585–95.

QSR NUD*IST (Application Software Package) (1995) Melbourne, Australia: Qualitative Solutions and Research.

Reid, E. (1991) 'Electropolis: communication and community on Internet Relay Chat [On-line]', Available: http://www.ee.mu.oz.au/papers/emr/index.html

Reid, E. (1994) *Cultural formations in text-based virtual realities*, Master's thesis. Dept. of English, Cultural Studies programme, University of Melbourne. [On-line], Available: http://www.ee.mu.oz.au/papers/emr/index.html

Roberts, L.D., Smith, L.M. and Pollock, C. (1996, September) 'A model of social interaction via computer-mediated communication in real-time text-based virtual environments', Paper presented at the 31st Annual Conference of the Australian Psychological Society, Sydney, Australia.

Roberts, L.D., Smith, L.M. and Pollock, C. (1997a, July) 'Disinhibited behaviour in computer-mediated communication: the good, the bad and the ugly', Poster presented at the 5th European Congress of Psychology, Dublin, Ireland.

Roberts, L.D., Smith, L.M. and Pollock, C. (1997b, May) 'Internet Relay Chat: Virtual community or virtual wasteland?', Poster presented at the 6th Biennial Conference on Community Research and Action, University of South Carolina, Columbia, SC.

Russell, D., Cutrona, C.E. and Jones, W.H. (1986) 'A trait-situational analysis of shyness', in W.H. Jones, J.M. Cheek and S.R. Briggs (eds) *Shyness: Perspectives on Research and Treatment* (pp. 239–49), New York: Plenum Press.

Ryan, J. (1995) 'A uses and gratifications study of the Internet social interaction site LambdaMOO: talking with "dinos"', Masters thesis, Ball State University, Muncie, Indiana [On-line]. Available: http://pbpl.physics.ucla.edu/~smolin/lambda/laws_and_history/thesisw5.rtf

Salem, D.A., Bogat, G.A. and Reid, C. (1997) 'Mutual help goes on-line', *Journal of Community Psychology*, 25: 189–207.

Schmidt, L.A. and Fox, N.A. (1995) 'Individual differences in young adults' shyness and sociability: personality and health correlates', *Personality and Individual Differences*, 19: 455–62.

Sempsey, J. (1998a) 'The therapeutic potentials of text-based virtual reality', *Journal of MUD Research*, 3(2). [On-line]. Available: http://journal.tinymush.org/v3n2/sempsey.html

Sempsey, J. (1998b) 'A comparative analysis of the social climates found among face to face and Internet-based groups within Multi-User Dimensions', *Dissertations Abstracts International*, 59(3-B):1414.

Sharf, B.F. (1997) 'Communicating breast cancer on-line: support and empowerment on the Internet', *Women and Health*, 26: 65–84.

Turkle, S. (1995) *Life on the Screen: Identity in the Age of the Internet*, New York: Simon and Schuster.

Wallace, P. (1999) *The Psychology of the Internet*, Cambridge: Cambridge University Press.

Walther, J.B. (1996) 'Computer-mediated communication: impersonal, interpersonal and hyperpersonal interaction', *Communication Research*, 23: 3–43.

Walther, J.B. and Boyd, S. (in press) 'Attraction to computer-mediated support', in C.A. Lin and D.Atkin (eds) *Communication Technology and Society: Audience Adoption and Uses of the New Media*, New York: Hampton Press.

Winzelberg, A. (1997) 'The analysis of an electronic support group for individuals with eating disorders', *Computers in Human Behavior*, 13: 393–407.

Young, K.S. (1998) 'Internet addiction: the emergence of a new clinical disorder', *CyberPsychology and Behavior*, 1: 237–44.

Young, K.S., Pistner, M., O'Mara, J. and Buchanan, J. (1999, August) 'Cyber-disorders: the mental health concern for the new millennium', Paper presented at 107th APA Annual Convention, Boston, MA.

9 Shyness and the pursuit of social acceptance

Mark R. Leary and Katherine E. Buckley

Research on shyness over the past 25 years has centred on two basic questions: 'What are shy people afraid of?' and 'Why are they so inhibited?' Few researchers have asked these two questions quite so explicitly, but, in fact, most research has involved efforts to understand the social anxiety and behavioural inhibition that lie at the heart of shyness.

The self-presentational theory of social anxiety was an effort to offer an overriding perspective that tied shyness to people's concerns with others' perceptions and evaluations. According to the theory, people tend to become shy – that is, experience social anxiety and display behavioural inhibition – when they are motivated to make desired impressions on other people but doubt that they will successfully make those impressions (Leary and Schlenker, 1981; Schlenker and Leary, 1982). Thus, self-presentation theory's answer to the question, 'What are shy people afraid of?' is that they are afraid of making undesired impressions because doing so typically leads to unpleasant outcomes. The theory's answer to the second question, 'Why are shy people so inhibited?' is that quiet, inhibited behaviour is a reasonable response to situations in which one is afraid of making an undesired impression.

Empirical research has generally supported the self-presentational approach to social anxiety. As the theory predicts, the situational variables that evoke shyness appear to heighten self-presentational concerns by increasing the motivation to impression-manage or creating doubts in one's self-presentational efficacy. Furthermore, the personality variables that predict shyness likewise seem to be related to impression motivation and self-presentational doubt (for reviews, see Leary and Schlenker, 1981; Leary and Kowalski, 1995; Schlenker and Leary, 1982). In addition to accounting for the known causes and correlates of shyness, self-presentation theory also subsumes other popular models of shyness (such as those involving poor social skills and negative self-evaluations).[1]

Despite self-presentation theory's usefulness as a general explanation of shyness, not every instance in which people are concerned about other people's impressions of them causes anxiety and inhibition. All episodes of shyness seem to involve self-presentational concerns (it is difficult to imagine a person being socially anxious and inhibited who was not worried about other people's perceptions and evaluations), but people do not react shyly every time they think they will not make the kind of impression they desire to make. Put simply, self-presentational concerns are a necessary but not always sufficient cause of shyness. This consideration suggests that we are missing an important piece of the shyness puzzle, the piece that will answer more fully the questions, 'What are shy people afraid of?' and 'Why are they so inhibited?' This chapter is an effort to hunt for that missing piece.

The need for social acceptance

Human beings are among the most gregarious animals on earth. Although many species live in groups (herds, packs, flocks, schools, or whatever), few of them engage one another in social interaction with as much regularity, energy, and enthusiasm as we do. Human beings not only spend most of their lives in proximity with other people, but their interactions and relationships with one another are a central part of their everyday lives.

The universal human propensity to seek the company of other people and to establish a variety of relationships with them is likely to stem from the fact that human beings need one another for survival to a greater extent than many other animals. Lacking both ferocity and speed, our pre-human ancestors were able to survive and reproduce only by living in social groups (Tooby and Cosmides, 1992). As a result, natural selection favoured individuals who sought the company of other people.

Importantly, people living in the ancestral environment (the savannahs of Africa where most human evolution occurred) needed not only to live in the presence of other people but to form supportive and co-operative relationships with them. To do so, they needed to be the kinds of people with whom other individuals would desire to form friendships, have as group members, choose as mates, and develop other relationships. People who made an effort to be acceptable group members and relational partners thus received the benefits of group living, whereas those who did not pursue social acceptance were left to fend for themselves. As a result, selection pressures may have led human beings to develop an innate propensity to seek the acceptance of other individuals. In fact, a great deal of human behaviour can be conceptualized as efforts to foster and maintain a minimum degree of social acceptance and to avoid rejection and ostracism (Baumeister and Leary, 1995). This is not to say that all human behaviour is motivated by the desire to be accepted, but rather that the motive to seek acceptance and avoid rejection is a pervasive influence. Against the backdrop of the human quest for interpersonal connectedness, shyness poses a bit of an enigma in that it appears to interfere with the development of interpersonal relationships. Understanding this enigma may tell us a great deal about both shyness and the human pursuit of social acceptance.

Shyness and social acceptance

As we use the term here, shyness refers to an affective-behavioural syndrome characterized by social anxiety (subjective nervousness and tension) and interpersonal inhibition (reticence and passivity in social encounters) (see Leary, 1986). Virtually everyone experiences shyness at one time or another, but people differ greatly in the frequency with which they are shy and the intensity of their anxiety and inhibition. At one end of the continuum, some people are rarely nervous and inhibited in social encounters; at the other end, some are so troubled by shyness that they meet psychiatric criteria for the diagnosis of social phobia (Turner, Beidel and Townsley, 1990). Along this continuum, there is no point at which we can easily draw a line between dispositionally 'shy' and 'non-shy' individuals, so these labels (which we will use for convenience throughout this chapter) must be regarded as relative only.

Compared to people who are not shy, shy individuals appear to struggle in their quest for social acceptance. Whether one uses indicators of social contact (such as the number of daily interactions or frequency of dating), measures of close relationships (such as numbers of friends and sexual partners), or subjective appraisals of the quality of one's interpersonal life (such as self-reports of loneliness, perceived social acceptance, or a desire for relationships), shy people undoubtedly fare worse in social life than less shy people.

For example, shy (and socially anxious) people have fewer social interactions and spend less time per day, on average, interacting with other people. They have fewer friends, and their friendships take longer to develop (Asendorpf and Wilpers, 1998; see also Asendorpf, this volume, Chapter 7). In the romantic arena, shy people date less frequently, have fewer sexual experiences, and are less likely to be romantically involved at any point in time (Asendorpf and Wilpers, 1998; Jones and Carpenter, 1986; Leary and Dobbins, 1983; Prisbell, 1991; Zimbardo, 1977).

Of course, the sheer number of people's interactions and relationships may bear little relationship to the quality of their lives, and some people who are low in sociability or extraversion are quite content with relatively few social contacts and relationships (Cheek and Buss, 1981). However, shy people are not as satisfied with their interpersonal lives as non-shy people. Shyness correlates highly (typically around .50) with feelings of loneliness (Cheek and Busch, 1981; Jones, Freemon and Goswick, 1981; Neto, 1992), reflecting a perceived deficiency in the number or closeness of their social relationships. Importantly, shyness is related to loneliness vis-à-vis all types of relationships – with friends, romantic and sexual partners, group and community memberships, and family relationships (Jones and Carpenter, 1986).

Shy people also indicate that they receive fewer social provisions (e.g., nurturance, reassurance, support) from their relationships (Jones and Carpenter, 1986), and report being more dissatisfied with their social lives (Neto, 1993). Furthermore, shy people tend to believe that they are less liked and accepted by other people than people who are not shy (Jones and Carpenter, 1986; Leary, Kowalski and Campbell, 1988; Pozo, Carver, Wellens and Scheier, 1991). Thus, shyness appears to be associated not only with fewer interactions and relationships but also with a sense that one's needs for interpersonal acceptance and connection are unfulfilled. Clearly, shy people feel that their social lives are inadequate in some way. The question, then, is why shyness is associated with an impoverished interpersonal life.

Shyness as an impediment to social acceptance

Given the correlational nature of virtually all research on shyness, we cannot equivocally say whether shyness is an antecedent or a consequence of lowered social acceptance. Our hunch is that it is both, so we will describe how shyness may both lead to and result from a low level of social acceptance.

Shyness may undermine the formation and maintenance of social relationships in at least three ways. Shyness may:

- limit people's opportunities for social contact that are necessary for the development of satisfying relationships;
- be associated with behavioural patterns that do not facilitate acceptance and intimacy;
- convey impressions of the individual that are not optimal in terms of attracting other people's attention and interest.

Opportunities

First, shyness lowers people's opportunities to develop relationships with other people. When people feel shy, they tend to avoid social encounters, thus limiting their contact with potential friends and romantic partners. As noted earlier, people who score high on measures of shyness and social anxiety have fewer social interactions per day, attend fewer social events, and date less frequently than those who are low in shyness. Furthermore, when shy people do venture into social gatherings, they are less likely to initiate conversations with other people and they spend less time at the event. (Asendorpf and Wilpers, 1998; Dodge, Heimberg, Nyman and O'Brien, 1987; Himadi, Arkowitz, Hinton and Perl 1980; Twentyman and McFall, 1975; Watson and Friend, 1969).

Research on communication apprehension – a close cousin of shyness (communication apprehension and shyness correlate .60; McCroskey and Richmond, 1982) – shows that college students who are high in communication apprehension choose living arrangements in places that require less interaction with other people than less apprehensive students (McCroskey and Leppard, 1975). Given that one's proximity and sheer exposure to other people is an important influence on the development of friendships, shy students may thus set themselves up for fewer friendships (Festinger, Schachter and Back, 1950; Monge and Kirste, 1980).

Interpersonal style

Second, even when shy people interact with other people, their characteristic interpersonal style may work against forming friendships and other relationships. A large number of studies show that, compared to less shy individuals, shy people speak a lower percentage of the time in conversations, take longer to respond to what others say, have more difficulty in articulating their thoughts, allow more silences to develop, are less likely to break silences that occur, and are simply more inhibited (Asendorpf, 1989; Borkovec, Fleischmann and Caputo, 1973; Cheek and Buss, 1981; Mandel and Shraugher, 1980; Natale, Entin and Jaffe, 1979; Pilkonis, 1977a; Prisbell, 1991). This shy interpersonal style may thwart efforts to be accepted because merely talking with other people promotes liking (Insko and Wilson, 1977). People find it difficult to like people who don't talk to them.

In addition, shy people have particular difficulty in talking about themselves. Not only do they disclose less about themselves than people who are not shy (which, in itself, is not always a bad thing), but the information they reveal tends to be more superficial (DePaulo, Epstein and LeMay, 1990; Leary, Knight and Johnson, 1987; Snell, 1989). Because a certain amount of self-disclosure is a prerequisite to the formation of interpersonal relationships, shy people's relationships may not move along as quickly as those of less shy people. If the depth of disclosure is not appropriate to the interaction and does not escalate appropriately over time, relationships are unlikely to develop (Altman and Taylor, 1973; Archer and Cook, 1986).

Impressions

Third, a shy interpersonal style may lead other people to form less than optimal impressions of an individual. Shy people are by no means disliked; in fact, their quietness is often perceived positively (as we discuss later in the chapter). However, being overly inhibited and reserved is unlikely to make particularly positive impressions on other people. Evidence suggests that shy people have somewhat poorer interpersonal skills than less shy people. For example, they are less skilled at initiating and guiding conversations, and have more difficulty conveying their feelings and attitudes to other people (Bruch, Rivet, Heimberg, Hunt and McIntosh, 1999; Miller, 1995). Shy individuals also have difficulty in showing warmth to and empathy with other people and view themselves as having poorer interaction management skills (Prisbell, 1991). Even among children, those who are quiet, inhibited, and less talkative are perceived by their peers as less socially competent and less desirable as friends (Evans, 1993). Importantly, however, this effect may be confined to cultures that value extraverted interpersonal styles (cf. Chen, Rubin and Boshu, 1995).

Summary

Shyness may be an impediment to social acceptance and relationship development because it is associated with fewer opportunities to meet and get to know other people, and the interpersonal style of the shy person is not optimal for establishing relationships and showing oneself to be a desirable relational partner. To stress a point made earlier, nothing in the literature suggests that shy people are disliked. Rather, their behaviour simply stymies the development of relationships and does not foster the same degree of social acceptance as the behaviour of less shy individuals.

The quest for social acceptance

Importantly, shy people's lower frequency of social interaction is not attributable to the fact that they do not desire social relationships or are not motivated to be accepted by other people. On the contrary, shy people appear to be particularly motivated to be liked and accepted, and highly concerned about the possibility of rejection.

One of the strongest predictors of shyness (and social anxiety) is a high desire for social approval and fear of disapproval. Scores on measures of shyness and social anxiety correlate highly with both approval motivation and fear of negative evaluation (Jackson, Towson and Narduzzi, 1997; Jones, Briggs and Smith, 1986; Leary and Kowalski, 1993; Pilkonis, 1977b; Watson and Friend, 1969). Shyness also correlates positively with the degree to which people desire social acceptance and fear rejection (Leary, Kelly, Cottrell and Schreindorfer, 2000; Miller, 1995).

In our view, a high desire for social acceptance predicts shyness because real, imagined and potential rejection naturally causes anxiety (Baumeister and Tice, 1990), and the more one desires to be accepted, the more one is threatened by potential rejection. Human beings appear to be equipped with mechanisms that monitor the social environment for cues that indicate potential rejection, and these mechanisms induce negative affect when such cues are detected (Leary, Koch and Hechenbleikner, in press). These negative feelings alert the individual to the potential threat and motivate behaviours to avoid or eliminate it (Baumeister and Tice, 1990; Leary, in press).

As noted earlier, evidence suggests that the proximal cause of social anxiety is the belief that other people will not form the kinds of impressions of the individual that he or she desires to make. According to self-presentation theory, people experience social anxiety when they are motivated to make certain desired impressions on other individuals, but hold a low subjective probability of being able to do so (Schlenker and Leary, 1982). Tying social anxiety to the human quest for social acceptance helps to explain why self-presentational concerns induce anxiety. Typically, it is not concern about being perceived as one desires that evokes social anxiety and inhibition, but rather concern that the impressions that one is making will lead other people to devalue or reject the individual.

One of the primary reasons why people desire to convey certain impressions of themselves to other people is that they wish to be accepted or to avoid rejection (Leary, 1995; Leary, in press). By showing themselves to be a certain kind of person with particular attributes, motives, attitudes, feelings, and so on, people hope to increase the degree to which other people will value having relationships with them. As a result, people who are motivated to be accepted try to be perceived and evaluated in particular ways. Thus, people who have a high need for social acceptance tend to have a greater fear of negative evaluation and a greater desire to be perceived positively (Leary, Kelly, Cottrell and Schreindorfer, 2000). Their high level of impression motivation sets these people up to experience social anxiety because they are more chronically motivated to make desired impressions on other people. This way of thinking about shyness extends self-presentation theory and provides the missing piece of the puzzle. Although it is true that shyness and social anxiety occur when people become concerned about others' impressions of them, the primary basis for that concern is a desire for social acceptance. Self-presentational concerns cause social anxiety only to the degree that those concerns are related to concerns with being valued as a relational partner (Leary, in press).

We speculate that shyness is more common among people in modern societies than it was for people of earlier times (or for people in tribal cultures today) because those in industrialized countries are subject to a constantly shifting array of relationships and group memberships. In the ancestral environment, people were likely to live among the same relatively small group of individuals all of their lives. Even as late as the nineteenth century, most Americans spent their lives in the same general location and long-distance moves were infrequent. When everybody knows you (and, in many cases, has known you for a very long time), you give little thought to social acceptance or self-presentation on a daily basis. If everyone already knows everything about you, there is little sense in trying to make new impressions. Of course, occasional opportunities for self-presentation arise, as when people find that they have done something to lead others to form undesired impressions of them, but typically self-presentational concerns are minimal in long-term, stable groups (Moreland and Levine, 1989).

In contrast, people in modern societies are subject to constantly changing friendships and relational partners. People move a great deal (often away from their families of origin), go away to school, change jobs, become members of numerous formal and informal groups, do business with strangers (as opposed, for example, to doing business with the familiar denizens of a small town), travel to distant locations for meetings, have many short- and long-term romantic relationships, and so on. Because their reputation in others' eyes is rarely firmly established, people have reasons to be concerned with how they are being perceived by other interactants in each new encounter. When one's social acceptance is more tenuous, social anxiety and shyness are more likely to arise.

Summary

The self-presentational theory can fruitfully be extended by tracing social anxiety to people's desire to be accepted and avoid rejection. Self-presentational concerns evoke social anxiety primarily to the extent to which people are motivated to manage their impressions in order to foster or maintain relationships with other people. People who are highly motivated to be accepted or avoid rejection are thus predisposed to be shy.

Acceptance-facilitating aspects of shyness

Thus far, we have painted a rather bleak picture of shyness, suggesting that people who are shy typically have greater difficulty in satisfying the human need for social connection than people who are less shy. However, this pessimistic view overlooks the fact that shyness can sometimes ward off social rejection, and, in fact, may be a tactic for lowering the likelihood of rejection in difficult interpersonal situations.

Positive features of shyness

Gough and Thorne (1986) pointed out that shyness has positive connotations that have been overlooked by most behavioural researchers. For example, shy people are often perceived as modest, self-controlled, and discreet, and not as aggressive, bossy, egotistical, and loud. Thus, however else they may be perceived, shy people usually avoid being perceived as egotistical, arrogant, or overbearing, impressions that generally create negative reactions (Leary, Bednarski, Hammon and Duncan, 1997).

Whether a particular individual's shyness is perceived positively or negatively depends a great deal on how it is manifested in a particular social encounter. People differ in how they behave when shy, as well as in the kinds of impressions that other people form of them. Although shyness, by definition, involves anxiety and inhibition, whether these features of shyness make a good or a bad impression depends on how they are viewed.

Consider two equally shy individuals who are exceptionally uncomfortable in the same social encounter. Person A's distress is palpable. She looks uncomfortable and unhappy, and her self-consciousness makes her appear preoccupied and self-absorbed. She contributes nothing whatsoever to the interaction, standing silently by while other people converse. Finally, she leaves awkwardly and prematurely. Person B, in contrast, also contributes little of substance to the conversation, yet conveys an impression of friendly interest in what others are saying by smiling, nodding, and back-channelling (making sounds, such as 'uh-huh' and 'hmm' to indicate that she is listening). Although decidedly uncomfortable, she remains in the encounter until an appropriate opportunity to leave arises.

The first individual would be likely to make an unfavourable impression involving inferences of poor social skill, neuroticism, and lack of interest in others. People would not be likely to engage this individual during the encounter, convey much acceptance, or seek out her company in the future. In contrast, because most people are quite happy to have an attentive, interested audience, Person B may make a mildly favourable impression despite the fact that she has done no more than be a good listener. She is likely to be invited to future interactions and may feel that other people like and accept her.

Gough and Thorne's (1986) research showed that positive features of shyness, such as modesty and tact, bore little relationship to others' evaluations of the shy individual one way or the other, but that negative features of shyness, such as anxiety and awkwardness, were negatively correlated with the degree to which the person was liked by other people. Their data suggested that the effect of shyness on other people's reactions depends on the degree to which the person appears anxious, timid, and awkward. One clinical implication of this finding is that shy people might be taught ways to convey impressions of friendly, albeit quiet, interest even though they feel anxious and inhibited.

The interpersonal implications of shyness are likely to vary as a function of cultural norms and values. In American society, lively, extraverted, gregarious styles of interaction are often preferred over subdued, introverted, inhibited styles, but such is not the case in all cultures. In China, for example, quiet, unassertive behaviour is valued more highly (Pearson, 1991; Shenkar and Ronen, 1987). Along these lines, it is informative that Chinese children who were very shy and inhibited were more accepted by their peers than children who were average in shyness. Furthermore, the shy-inhibited children were more likely to be considered for roles of honour and leadership (Chen *et al.*, 1995).

Strategic aspects of shyness

Several theorists have maintained that the quiet, inhibited, unassuming behaviour of people who are shy is partly an interpersonal strategy that helps them make the best out of a difficult social situation. Most often this strategy has been characterized as a 'protective self-presentational style' (Arkin, 1981).

When people feel reasonably confident that an interpersonal encounter will go well and that others will form minimally acceptable impressions of them, they tend to adopt an acquisitive self-presentational style that seems designed to foster and maintain relatively positive impressions in other people's eyes (Arkin, 1981). The most robust finding in the self-presentation literature is that, except in unusual circumstances, people generally desire to make favourable impressions on other people (Jones and Pittman, 1982; Leary, 1995). Thus, they try to be perceived in socially desirable ways – as likeable, competent, and honest, for example – and are oriented towards gaining social approval. In certain circumstances, however, people shift to a protective orientation in which their primary goal involves avoiding social disapproval rather than obtaining approval (Arkin, 1981; Shepperd and Arkin, 1990). In these situations, people appear to forgo making positive impressions in favour of avoiding negative ones.

From our perspective, such a strategy makes a great deal of sense. When people are concerned about the impressions others are forming of them because they are worried about being devalued or rejected, minimizing one's involvement in a social encounter may reduce the chances of doing or saying the wrong thing – something that will lead to unfavourable reactions. By being quiet, unassuming, and undisclosing, people may not make a particularly favourable impression, but they are unlikely to make a blatantly negative impression either (Leary and Kowalski, 1995). (As the old saying goes, 'Better to remain silent and be thought a fool rather than to speak up and dispel all doubt'.) Thus, by behaving in a shy manner, people may reduce the likelihood that they will be rejected and, as noted earlier, possibly gain points for being quietly attentive.

Many pieces of evidence support the idea that people do, in fact, adopt a protective self-presentational style when they feel socially anxious and that dispositionally shy people tend to use such a style much of the time (for reviews, see Arkin, 1981; Arkin, Lake and Baumgardner, 1986; Leary and Kowalski, 1995; Schlenker and Leary, 1985; Shepperd and Arkin, 1990). For example, simply avoiding social interactions in which one expects to be socially anxious serves a protective function by eliminating opportunities to make unfavourable impressions and incur rejection. Furthermore, when in social encounters, interacting minimally avoids opening oneself up to controversy or criticism. The attentive, agreeable, acquiescent behaviours of shy people give others no reason to dislike or reject them. This perspective is buttressed even further by the fact that people with relatively low self-esteem – who, like shy people, doubt that others accept them as much as they wish – also seem to behave in ways that avoid disapproval (Baumeister, Tice and Hutton, 1989).

Gilbert and Trower (1990) have proposed that the inhibited behaviour that characterizes shy and socially anxious people sometimes arises from concerns with social dominance rather than acceptance. In their view, withdrawn, submissive, conciliatory behaviour is often a defensive reaction against the possibility of incurring the hostility of superior or higher-ranking individuals. The deferential, nonassertive behaviours of shy people serve the same function as the submissive, appeasing behaviours seen among the lower status members of many other primate species. Although we agree with Gilbert and Trower's (1990) analysis in many respects, the inhibited behaviour associated with concerns with social acceptance and the deferential behaviour associated with being of low rank are likely to have evolved for different reasons (a point with which Gilbert and Trower concur) and are likely to be controlled by different systems (Tooby and Cosmides, 1992). Furthermore, even when people act shy in interactions with dominant or high status individuals, we believe that their primary concern is typically rejection rather than dominance. People are typically worried about their superiors rejecting them, not about aggression or about being one-down.

Summary

Although shyness generally has negative connotations (Gough and Thorne, 1986), certain features of shyness may be beneficial to the shy person. As long as shy people do not appear exceptionally anxious, awkward, or socially inept, they may be able to foster the impression of being pleasant, modest, and interested in other people. They may not be the life of the party, but they will not be viewed as arrogant, overbearing, or self-centred. The inhibition that is the bane of many shy people may, in fact, serve a very important function, lowering their chances of making a bona fide negative impression in difficult interpersonal encounters.

Conclusions

Without denying that self-presentational concerns are the proximal cause of social anxiety and shyness, deeper inspection suggests that the fundamental, underlying concern of shy people involves social acceptance and rejection. As we have seen, human beings have a basic need to be valued and accepted by other people. When concerns with social acceptance and rejection make them worry about how they are being perceived by other people, people feel socially anxious and usually become quiet and inhibited.

Research showing that shy people rely heavily on a protective self-presentational style suggests that their predominant concern involves avoiding rejection rather than seeking acceptance. Although these motives are admittedly difficult to disentangle, the evidence strongly suggests that concerns with rejection dominate shy people's interpersonal perspectives (Arkin, 1981; Leary and Kowalski, 1995). Importantly, people who are oriented towards avoiding rejection feel and behave in a decidedly different fashion from those who are focused on being accepted (Arkin, 1981; Baumeister *et al.*, 1989), and somewhat paradoxically, they may end up making a worse impression than people who are trying to be accepted (Schreindorfer and Leary, 1996). Such is the plight of shy people who, though worried about being rejected, may undermine their own cause by being excessively careful in their approach to social encounters.

Note

1 Of course, shyness is also tied to temperamental factors, many of which appear to be inherited, but these are viewed chiefly as biological substrates that predispose people to be particularly reactive to anxiety-producing situations or to a tendency towards social inhibition (Kagan, Reznick and Snidman, 1988).

References

Altman, I. and Taylor, D. (1973) *Social Penetration: The Development of Interpersonal Relations*, New York: Holt, Rinehart, and Winston.

Archer, R.L. and Cook, C.E. (1986) 'Personalistic self-disclosure and attraction: basis for relationship or scarce resource', *Social Psychology Quarterly*, 49: 268–72.

Arkin, R.M. (1981) 'Self-presentation styles', in J.T. Tedeschi (ed.) *Impression Management Theory and Social Psychological Research* (pp. 311–33), New York: Academic Press.

Arkin, R.M., Lake, E.A. and Baumgardner, A.H. (1986) 'Shyness and self-presentation', in W.H. Jones, J.M. Cheek and S.R. Briggs (eds) *Shyness: Perspectives on Research and Treatment* (pp. 189–203), New York: Plenum.

Asendorpf, J.B. (1989) 'Shyness as a final common pathway for two different kinds of inhibition', *Journal of Personality and Social Psychology*, 57: 481–92.

Asendorpf, J.B. and Wilpers, S. (1998) 'Personality effects on social relationships', *Journal of Personality and Social Psychology*, 74: 1531–44.

Baumeister, R.F. and Leary, M.R. (1995) 'The need to belong: desire for interpersonal attachments as a fundamental human motivation', *Psychological Bulletin*, 117: 497–529.

Baumeister, R.F. and Tice, D.M. (1990) 'Anxiety and social exclusion', *Journal of Social and Clinical Psychology*, 9: 165–95.

Baumeister, R.F., Tice, D.M. and Hutton, D.G. (1989) 'Self-presentational motivations and personality differences in self-esteem', *Journal of Personality*, 57: 547–79.

Borkovec, T.D., Fleischmann, D J. and Caputo, J.A. (1973) 'The measurement of anxiety in an analogue social situation', *Journal of Consulting and Clinical Psychology*, 44: 157–61.

Bruch, M.A., Rivet, K.M., Heimberg, R.G., Hunt, A. and McIntosh, B. (1999) 'Shyness and sociotropy: additive and interactive relations in predicting interpersonal concerns', *Journal of Personality*, 67: 373–406.

Cheek, J.M. and Busch, C.M. (1981) 'The influence of shyness on loneliness in a new situation', *Personality and Social Psychology Bulletin*, 7: 572–7.

Cheek, J.M. and Buss, A.H. (1981) 'Shyness and sociability', *Journal of Personality and Social Psychology*, 41: 330–9.

Chen, X., Rubin, K.H. and Boshu, L. (1995) 'Social and school adjustment of shy and aggressive children in China', *Development and Psychopathology*, 7: 337–49.

DePaulo, B.M., Epstein, J.A. and LeMay, C S. (1990) 'Responses of the socially anxious to the prospect of interpersonal evaluation', *Journal of Personality*, 58: 623–40.

Dodge, C.S., Heimberg, R.G., Nyman, D. and O'Brien, G.T. (1987) 'Daily heterosocial interactions of high and low socially anxious college students: a diary study', *Behavior Therapy*, 18: 90–6.

Evans, M.A. (1993) 'Communicative competence as a dimension of shyness', in K.H. Rubin and J.B Asendorpf (eds) *Social Withdrawal, Inhibition, and Shyness in Childhood* (pp. 189–213), Hillsdale, NJ: Lawrence Erlbaum.

Festinger, L., Schachter, S. and Back, K. (1950) *Social Pressures in Informal Groups: A Study of Human Factors in Housing*, New York: Harper and Bros.

Gilbert, P. and Trower, P. (1990) 'The evolution and manifestation of social anxiety', in W.R. Crozier (ed.) *Shyness and Embarrassment: Perspectives from Social Psychology* (pp. 144–77), Cambridge: Cambridge University Press.

Gough, H.G. and Thorne, A. (1986) 'Positive, negative, and balanced shyness', in W.H. Jones, J.M. Cheek and S.R. Briggs (eds) *Shyness: Perspectives on Research and Treatment* (pp. 205–25), New York: Plenum.

Himadi, W., Arkowitz, H., Hinton, R. and Perl, J. (1980) 'Minimal dating and its relationship to other social problems and general adjustment', *Behavior Therapy*, 11: 345–52.

Insko, C.A. and Wilson, M. (1977) 'Interpersonal attraction as a function of social interaction', *Journal of Personality and Social Psychology*, 11: 41–50.

Jackson, T., Towson, S. and Narduzzi, K. (1997) 'Predictors of shyness: a test of variables associated with self-presentational models', *Social Behavior and Personality*, 25: 149–54.

Jones, E.E. and Pittman, T.S. (1982) 'Toward a general theory of strategic self-presentation', in J. Suls (ed.) *Psychological Perspectives on the Self* (Vol. 1, pp. 231–62), Hillsdale, NJ: Erlbaum.

Jones, W.H., Briggs, S.R. and Smith, T.G. (1986) 'Shyness: conceptualization and measurement', *Journal of Personality and Social Psychology*, 51: 629–39.

Jones, W.H. and Carpenter, B.N. (1986) 'Shyness, social behavior, and relationships', in W.H. Jones, J.M. Cheek and S.R. Briggs (eds) *Shyness: Perspectives on Research and Treatment* (pp. 227–38), New York: Plenum.

Jones, W.H., Freemon, J.E. and Goswick, R.A. (1981) 'The persistence of loneliness: self and other determinants', *Journal of Personality*, 49: 27–48.

Kagan, J., Reznick, J.S., and Snidman, N. (1988) 'Biological bases of childhood shyness', *Science*, 240: 167–71.

Leary, M.R. (1986) 'Affective and behavioral components of shyness: implications for theory, measurement, and research', in W.H. Jones, J.M. Cheek and S.R. Briggs (eds) *Shyness: Perspectives on Research and Treatment* (pp. 27–38), New York: Plenum.

Leary, M.R. (1995) *Self-presentation: Impression Management and Interpersonal Behavior*, Boulder, CO: Westview Press.

Leary, M.R. (in press) 'Social anxiety as an early warning system: a refinement and extension of the self-presentational theory of social anxiety', in S.G. Hofman and P.M. DiBartolo (eds) *Social Phobia and Social Anxiety: An Integration*, New York: Allyn & Bacon.

Leary, M.R., Bednarski, R., Hammon, D. and Duncan, T. (1977) 'Blowhards, snobs, and narcissists: interpersonal reactions to excessive egotism', in R.M. Kowalski (ed.) *Aversive Interpersonal Behaviors* (pp. 111–31), New York: Plenum.

Leary, M.R. and Dobbins, S.E. (1983) 'Social anxiety, sexual behavior, and contraceptive use', *Journal of Personality and Social Psychology*, 45: 1347–54.

Leary, M.R., Kelly, K., Cottrell, S. and Schreindorfer, L. (2000) 'Individual differences in the need to belong', Manuscript in preparation, Wake Forest University, Winston-Salem, NC.

Leary, M.R., Knight, P.D. and Johnson, K.A. (1987) 'Social anxiety and dyadic conversation: a verbal response analysis', *Journal of Social and Clinical Psychology*, 5: 34–50.

Leary, M.R., Koch, E.J. and Hechenbleikner, N.R. (in press) 'Emotional responses to interpersonal rejection', in M.R. Leary (ed.) *Interpersonal Rejection*, New York: Oxford University Press.

Leary, M.R. and Kowalski, R.M. (1993) 'The interaction anxiousness scale: construct and criterion-related validity', *Journal of Personality Assessment*, 61: 136–46.

Leary, M.R. and Kowalski, R.M. (1995) *Social Anxiety*, New York: Guilford.

Leary, M.R., Kowalski, R.M. and Campbell, C. (1988) 'Self-presentational concerns and social anxiety: the role of generalized impression expectancies', *Journal of Research in Personality*, 22: 308–21.

Leary, M.R. and Schlenker, B.R. (1981) 'The social psychology of shyness: a self-presentational model', in J.T. Tedeschi (ed.) *Impression Management Theory and Social Psychological Research* (pp. 335–58), New York: Academic Press.

Mandel, N.M. and Shrauger, J.S. (1980) 'The effects of self-evaluative statements of heterosexual approach in shy and non-shy males', *Cognitive Therapy and Research*, 4: 369–81.

McCroskey, J.C. and Leppard, T. (1975) 'The effects of communication apprehension on nonverbal behavior', Paper presented at the meeting of the Eastern Communication Association, New York.

McCroskey, J.C. and Richmond, V.P. (1982) 'Communication apprehension and shyness: conceptual and operational distinctions', *Central States Speech Journal*, 33: 458–68.

Miller, R.S. (1995) 'On the nature of embarrassability: shyness, social evaluation, and social skill', *Journal of Personality*, 63: 315–39.

Monge, P.T. and Kirste, K.K. (1980) 'Measuring proximity in human organization', *Social Psychology Quarterly*, 43: 110–35.

Moreland, R.L. and Levine, J.M. (1989) 'Newcomers and oldtimers in small groups', in P. Paulus (ed.) *Psychology of Group Influence* (Vol. 2, pp. 143–86). Hillsdale, NJ: Erlbaum.

Natale, M., Entin, E. and Jaffe, J. (1979) 'Vocal interruptions in dyadic communication as a function of speech and social anxiety', *Journal of Personality and Social Psychology*, 37: 865–78.

Neto, F. (1992) 'Loneliness among Portuguese adolescents', *Social Behavior and Personality*, 20: 15–22.

Neto, F. (1993) 'The satisfaction with life scale: psychometric properties in an adolescent sample', *Journal of Youth and Adolescence*, 22: 125–33.

Pearson, V. (1991) 'Western theory, Eastern practice: social group work in Hong Kong', *Social Work with Groups*, 14: 45–58.

Pilkonis, P.A. (1977a) 'The behavioral consequences of shyness', *Journal of Personality*, 45: 596–611.

Pilkonis, P.A. (1977b) 'Shyness, public and private, and its relationship to other measures of social behavior', *Journal of Personality*, 45: 585–95.

Pozo, C., Carver, C.S., Wellens, A.R. and Scheier, M.F. (1991) 'Social anxiety and social perception: construing others' reactions to the self', *Personality and Social Psychology Bulletin*, 17: 355–62.

Prisbell, M. (1991) 'Shyness and self-reported competence', *Communication Research Reports*, 8: 141–8.

Schreindorfer, L. and Leary, M. (1996) 'Seeking acceptance versus avoiding rejection: differential effects on emotion and behavior', Paper presented at the meeting of the Southeastern Psychological Association, Norfolk, VA.

Schlenker, B.R. and Leary, M.R. (1982) 'Social anxiety and self-presentation: a conceptualization and model', Psychological Bulletin, 92, 641–69.

Schlenker, B.R. and Leary, M.R. (1985) 'Social anxiety and communication about the self', Journal of Language and Social Psychology, 4: 171–92.

Shenkar, O. and Ronen, S. (1987) 'The cultural context of negotiations: the implications of Chinese interpersonal norms', Journal of Applied Behavioral Science, 3: 263–75.

Shepperd, J.A. and Arkin, R.M. (1990) 'Shyness and self-presentation', in W.R. Crozier (ed.) Shyness and Embarrassment: Perspectives from Social Psychology (pp. 286–314), Cambridge: Cambridge University Press.

Snell, W.E., Jr. (1989) 'Willingness to self-disclose to female and male friends as a function of social anxiety and gender', Personality and Social Psychology Bulletin, 15: 113–25.

Tooby, J., and Cosmides, L. (1992) 'The psychological foundations of culture', in J.H. Barkow, L. Cosmides and J. Tooby (eds) The Adapted Mind (pp. 19–136), New York: Oxford University Press.

Turner, S.M., Beidel, D.C. and Townsley, R.M. (1990) 'Social phobia: relationship to shyness', Behaviour Research and Therapy, 28: 497–505.

Twentyman, C.T. and McFall, R.M. (1975) 'Behavioral training of social skills in shy males', Journal of Consulting and Clinical Psychology, 43: 384–95.

Watson, D. and Friend, R. (1969) 'Measurement of social-evaluative anxiety', Journal of Consulting and Clinical Psychology, 33: 448–57.

Zimbardo, P.G. (1977) Shyness, New York: Jove.

10 Blushing, social anxiety and exposure

W. Ray Crozier

> Her state of vivid happiness this summer was markedly different. If I caught her eye, she blushed and sparkled all over, guessing that I was remembering our joint secret.
>
> (Gaskell, *Cousin Phillis*, p. 291).

In surveys, 53 per cent of shy individuals reported that they blush when they are shy (Zimbardo *et al.*, 1974), and 58 per cent of an unselected sample reported that they blush when embarrassed (Parrott and Smith, 1991). Blushing is an expression of shame (Keltner and Harker, 1998) and a presenting problem in social phobia (Scholing and Emmelkamp, 1993). It is ubiquitous but it is difficult to understand in psychological or psychophysiological terms.

A welcome increase in research in recent years has been stimulated and facilitated by significant theoretical and methodological developments. Particularly important are the extension of the self-presentation model of social anxiety to the analysis of blushing (Leary *et al.*, 1992), the construction of a reliable self-report scale to assess individual differences in blushing propensity (Leary and Meadows, 1991), and advances in measuring the blush and associated physiological changes. These measurements include skin blood flow (Drummond, 1997), facial temperature, and colour changes in the cheek and ears by means of photoelectric probes (Shearn *et al.*, 1990; Mulkens *et al.*, 1997).

Despite these advances many issues are unresolved. It is not known whether the common sense notion of the blush corresponds to more than one kind of reddening of the skin and fails to discriminate between different types of blush, each perhaps with its own cause. A blush can be accompanied by different facial expressions, such as smiling, frowning, pressing the lips together, and averting the gaze (whether this is avoidance of eye contact or an ambivalent looking and looking away). This implies that the blush coincides with different emotional states. Blushing is commonly discussed in terms of the 'self-conscious' emotions of embarrassment, shame, shyness, coyness, bashfulness and modesty. However, the nature of its relationships with these is uncertain, and there is controversy, for example as to whether the blush is a symptom of shyness or is restricted to embarrassment. Buss (1980: 129) describes blushing as the 'hallmark' of embarrassment but it is possible to be embarrassed without blushing. However, research has yet to establish the circumstances in which the blush is elicited, with or without embarrassment.

One step towards the resolution of these issues is to undertake a detailed examination of the kinds of situation that elicit a blush, and this is the focus of this chapter. It reviews the application of theoretical positions to analysis of situations that elicit blushing. It considers one set of circumstances that leads to a blush but which has hitherto received little attention, the notion that blushing involves exposure of 'secret' aspects of the self. The chapter outlines a 'rule' that summarizes this pattern and discusses some of its implications.

Situations that elicit a blush

Classification schemes

There have been attempts to classify the situations where blushing occurs. A review by Leary *et al.* (1992) concludes that blushing is elicited by four classes of situation: threats to public identity; praise and positive attention; scrutiny; accusations of blushing. Threats to public identity include violation of norms; inept performances, loss of control and behaving out-of-role, circumstances that typically give rise to embarrassment. People blush when they are singled out for praise, compliments or thanks. Conspicuousness is a cause of blushing such that people will colour just because they are the centre of attention, for example, giving a speech or arriving late at a public meeting. Finally, being told that you are blushing can induce it, and awareness of your own blushing can intensify the reaction.

There is empirical support for this classification. Factor analysis of the Leary and Meadows blushing-propensity scale yields three factors (Bögels *et al.*, 1996). Items with highest loadings on the first factor refer to being the centre of attention and 'looking stupid or incompetent in front of others'. Items in the second factor refer to interacting with an attractive person and conversing about a personal topic. The third factor has items referring to accusation of blushing and thinking of beginning to blush. Additional kinds of empirical evidence confirm that blushing occurs in these kinds of situations. For example, singing in front of an audience or listening along with other people to a recording of one's own singing performance is likely to produce changes in skin colour and temperature (Drummond, 1989, 1997; Shearn *et al.*, 1990; Mulkens *et al.*, 1997).

Theories of blushing

Theories of blushing incorporate explanations of the kinds of situation that elicit it. Working within the self-presentation framework, Leary *et al.* (1992: 453) propose that blushing is a response to undesired social attention and argue that this provides a more parsimonious account of the situations that elicit it than do explanations in terms of either shame or embarrassment. For example, they argue that it explains blushing that occurs in the absence of embarrassment in that unwanted attention without a self-presentational predicament produces blushing but not embarrassment. Conversely, a predicament without undesired attention produces embarrassment without a blush.

Castelfranchi and Poggi (1990) argue that the blush is functional, an act of appeasement or submission, intended to inhibit the aggression of another. Its involuntary nature augments its effectiveness as a signal, since it cannot be feigned. They write (ibid.: 240) that those who blush, 'are somehow saying that they know, care about, and fear others' evaluations and that they share those values deeply. They also communicate their sorrow over any possible faults or inadequacies on their part, thus performing an acknowledgement, a confession, and an apology aimed at inhibiting others' aggression or avoiding social ostracism.' Keltner and Harker (1998: 80) argue that the display of shame (which includes blushing as well as frowning, gaze aversion and downward head movement) is expressed in a distinct display similar to submissive and appeasement-related behaviour.

In the theory of affects developed by Tomkins (1963) shame is an auxiliary affect (auxiliary because it is produced by the incomplete reduction of one of two primary affects, interest or joy). It is expressed by lowering of the head, averting the eyes and blushing. Despite the central role that the face plays in his theory, Tomkins has surprisingly little to say about the blush and he shares with other theorists uncertainty about its role. He regards it as a 'response auxiliary to the shame complex' since it increases the visibility of the face whereas the 'shame response proper' reduces facial communication (ibid.: 120–1). However, he is not explicit about the grounds for deciding that the blush is auxiliary and not the proper response. It is not clear that this goes beyond re-statement of the paradox that blushing attracts attention to the self when it is least wanted. Hiding and shame have often been connected in the literature, in terms of theoretical perspectives (e.g., Lazarus, 1991) and interpretations of expressive movements and gestures such as gaze aversion and covering the face with a hand. This raises the question why shame is associated with colouring that results in the face being more visible. Although the theory does not lend itself readily to predictions (as opposed to post hoc interpretation) it implies that blushing is more likely when levels of interest and enjoyment are high but something 'shaming' interrupts positive affect. This can be illustrated by a woman's recollection of an occasion when she blushed (case 2A, Table 10.1). Her affect presumably was positive (being at a lively party with her boyfriend, in a state of sexual excitement) until it was suddenly interrupted by others drawing her attention to something untoward in her appearance.

A distinctive feature of these explanations is their insistence that blushing is not synonymous with embarrassment. Tomkins and Castelfranchi and Poggi regard blushing as an expression of shame and shyness as well as embarrassment. Leary *et al.* (1992) argue that one can be embarrassed without blushing and blush without embarrassment. This raises the question of the precise circumstances necessary to elicit a blush.

This chapter considers a class of situations that elicit blushing. It proposes that many instances adhere to the following rule. If event X brings into the open, or threatens to bring into the open, topic Y, and Y is something that the individual wishes to keep hidden or believes ought to be kept hidden, then X will elicit a blush. It proposes that the blush is a reaction to the exposure and has not evolved to have a communicative function. Also, rather than provoke a blush, unwanted attention can follow from heightened colour in the face.

Blushing and exposure

This thesis originated in an empirical investigation (Crozier, 1998), a content analysis of two episodes of shame in Elizabeth Gaskell's novel, *North and South*. In each episode, a fictional character experiences what Castelfranchi and Poggi (1990) would describe as 'shame before the other'. She acknowledges that her behaviour would be regarded as unacceptable for a woman of her social position, and thus she feels shame. Nevertheless she knows that she is blameless and has nothing to be ashamed of (there is no 'shame before the self'). Content analysis of the relevant portions of text showed that the character blushes whenever any conversation alludes to the precipitating event even when the other parties to the conversation are ignorant of the event. A similar pattern is found in another of Mrs Gaskell's novels, *Ruth*. The eponymous heroine has given birth to an illegitimate son and has been abandoned by the father. She is encouraged by friends to keep the circumstances of the birth a secret and to claim to be a widow. Thereafter, references, however oblique, to her marital status or to the age of her child cause her to blush.

These examples suggest a pattern. A conversation refers to a topic that ought to be hidden or that is a secret for at least one of the participants. Whether the reference is direct or indirect, an allusion to or an implication of what is being said, it is sufficient to elicit a blush. Many of the topics that ought to be kept from exposure are 'taboo'. In our culture, this includes reference to sexual matters, to genitals[1] and certain other body parts, to the clothing that covers them and to body functions such as menstruation, defecation, belching and flatulence. The range of topics that ought not to be aired is influenced by social considerations such as status, gender and age.

Matters that 'polite society' or 'respectable people' consider unmentionable will be discussed without shame by those who do not share these values. Other topics are personal and relate to the individual's circumstances.

In all cases the significant element is exposure, which implies more than simple visibility or conspicuousness. Exposure is making visible what is hidden, not what simply goes unnoticed. It is also clear that the self has to be connected in some way with the topic. If you do not share the value that a topic is taboo you will not blush at its mention. (As a corollary, blushing provides evidence that you accept it is taboo and this tells something about the kind of person you are as, of course, does a failure to blush). A further implication of this formulation is that one does not have to commit a moral transgression in order to blush; an allusion in a conversation to someone else's transgression might suffice. The topic need not reflect badly on the self.

Blushing is not simply a matter of physical exposure or mention of topics that are taboo in the sense that there is general agreement that they ought not to be mentioned. It can be elicited by the airing of topics that are personal and idiosyncratic. For example, in his novel, *Dan Leno and the Limehouse Golem*, Ackroyd (1994: 75) describes a conversation between two of the characters; Dan asks Lizzie if she has a 'neat hand', referring to her handwriting, and immediately blushes as he remembers that she is sensitive about her large, ugly hands. This example illustrates that the person who blushes is not necessarily the one to whom attention is drawn. Of course, Dan has made a faux pas and blushes when he realizes this and we would not dispute that he is embarrassed (or ashamed) by what he has done. However, the issue is not whether he is embarrassed but why these circumstances cause him to blush.

In another literary example, Updike presents a conversation where a man blushes when his wife's scornful remark reveals that she has uncovered his stratagem of deflecting attention from his own flirtatious behaviour by accusing *her* of flirting (Updike, 1980: 23–4). In this case, it is the exposure of the blusher's motive that elicits the reaction. A non-literary example provided by Lewis (1995: 212) also shares the characteristic of exposing a psychological state: A dental hygienist blushed when the patient asked her which of his teeth was her favourite. 'Quite by accident, I had discovered her secret. She told me she was not ashamed at having a favourite tooth – just at being uncovered.' In the first case, the individual's ploy has been unmasked, leaving him exposed and foolish; in the second the hygienist is explicit that the exposure of her thinking has discomfited her, not the content of her thoughts.

In each of these examples, the blush contributes to the person's predicament. In other circumstances it can create the predicament. For example, a woman is pregnant and wants to keep the news to herself. However, she blushes when the topic of conversation turns to a friend who is known to be pregnant, with the result that everyone guesses her secret. It is not unusual for a blush to provide an unwanted signal to others but this is an aspect that has received little attention from contemporary theories, which emphasize the benefits to the blusher of his or her response (Castelfranchi and Poggi, 1990). Furthermore, it is not the woman's conspicuousness that makes her blush (the prototypical blushing situation) but the blush that brings unwanted attention.

In all of these cases, an individual blushes because a topic has been broached, one that he or she wishes to keep hidden. In other circumstances, more than one person will blush, the person(s) exposed and those who bring this about. We illustrate this with two examples. A teenager enters her bedroom, which is being used by her cousin while he is staying with her family, to surprise him wearing only a towel. She flees and when they next meet, they both blush. A man waiting for his wife in a department store accidentally makes eye contact with another customer while she is examining some control underwear, and they both blush and look away. It is readily understood that everyone involved in these episodes is embarrassed by the breach of privacy and that it is incumbent on the person responsible to signal that the intrusion was accidental and apologize, and a blush can do this effectively. However, the subsequent recollection of these incidents or relating them to someone else can be sufficient to produce a blush. People can also blush when none of them is to blame, for example when a sexually explicit scene appears on screen while they are watching television together.

In order to investigate in a more systematic way the potential role of exposure in instances of blushing and to gain insight into their relative frequency of occurrence, three studies involving content analysis of blushing incidents were conducted. The first is an analysis of references to blushing found in a work of fiction. The other two studies elicit recollections of instances of blushing from samples of students. Space does not permit detailed consideration of these studies and our selection of examples is intended to be illustrative rather than to test specific hypotheses. Nevertheless, we think they are instructive.

Studies of circumstances eliciting blushing

Study 1

The first study identified all references to blushing in the novel *The Last September* by the Anglo-Irish writer, Elizabeth Bowen, first published in 1929. The book was systematically searched for any reference to blushing. Fourteen references were found, nine mentioned blush or blushing, two going pink, two going crimson, and one colouring of the ears. Two of the fourteen were descriptions by one character of another character's blush (in each case, a woman reporting on a man). Of the remaining twelve, a woman blushed in eight and a man in four. Eleven instances took place within conversations and three in a social gathering where many were present.

The predominant theme is that a blush is produced by an allusion to a romantic relationship that is not explicit or that is secret. This is found in eight episodes, and two others mention engagement and an amorous relationship. In another episode a woman blushes when she refers to a taboo topic (a sexual assault). There is one example of a blush when the character is simply the centre of attention but a closer reading suggests that he is blushing because he is singing a sentimental song in the presence of the woman to whom he is (secretly) attached. He only blushes when he becomes conscious of the romantic theme of the song.

One episode provides a good illustration of the structure specified in the rule. Lois hears her mother and another woman reach the conclusion that a rumour that Lois's friend Livvy is secretly engaged to be married is untrue. However, Lois knows it to be true, and blushes. Her reaction immediately makes the two older women suspicious, but eventually they interpret it as the response of (the unmarried) Lois to the mention of marriage, in effect reflecting their own intuitive application of the 'rule'. Exposure is not restricted to mention of romantic attachments. In another episode Lois and her brother are gossiping about a couple who are guests at their house. Lois blushes when he suggests that the couple might be in the adjoining room and in a position to overhear the conversation.

The incidents described in the novel are similar to those in Mrs Gaskell's novels written some sixty years previously. We decided to augment this analysis of a literary text by eliciting recollections of actual blushing incidents.

Study 2

The second study analyses replies to a postal questionnaire requesting participants to describe in their own words an incident of blushing they can recall. They were asked to 'think of an actual incident in which you blushed. Take a few moments to recall as many details of the incident as you can'. They were asked to write in detail what caused them to blush, what they were thinking and feeling at the time, how long the blushing lasted, and what caused it to change or subside. Twenty-five questionnaires were posted to students – these were almost all women, reflecting the proportion of women studying the particular course – and fifteen were returned (by thirteen women and two men). One man provided descriptions of two separate occasions, yielding a total of sixteen incidents for analysis.

In order to summarize the range of incidents that were recalled the responses were coded according to the categories in the taxonomy of situations produced by Leary *et al.* (1992): threats to public identity, receiving praise or compliments, being conspicuous and being accused of blushing. The responses were also coded in terms of whether there was an explicit reference to a sexual theme such as sexual activity, amorous relationships, being attracted to someone or being complimented on one's appearance.

The predominant theme was *threats to identity*, evident in eleven responses, four of these having a sexual theme. *Receiving praise or compliments* was mentioned in two responses, one having a sexual theme. Mention of *being accused of blushing* was not present. However, reference to an audience and to being looked at was evident in all the categories and was explicitly mentioned in twelve of the sixteen responses. These include receiving a prize in front of a large audience, speaking up in front of the class and being caught staring at someone of the other sex (there are two instances of this).

Our primary interest is in whether respondents produced examples that fit the rule that is the focus of this chapter. One response (number 2A in Table 10.1) is an unambiguous example of exposure with an explicit sexual theme: the young woman's appearance 'gives away' what she and her boyfriend have been doing. It is noteworthy that subsequent mentions of this incident cause her to blush: 'when I stopped being the centre of attention, I felt better. But they still mention it now and again and I get embarrassed and probably blush.' Other responses summarized in Table 10.1 lend themselves to interpretation in terms of attention that is drawn to the self because of something that the blusher would have preferred to keep hidden because he or she has done something foolish, incompetent or inappropriate. This can be the incompetence of the driver (2B) or the worker in the supermarket (2C) or the student's stomach rumbling (2D). In example 2E the young man's

Table 10.1 Selected instances of blushing in Study 2

2A When in a party at a friend's house, I returned downstairs with my boyfriend and everyone noticed that I had put my T-shirt back on inside out.

2B Made a hash of parking the car when two male council workers were sat in their lorry waiting for something. The space was big enough but I misjudged it.

2C I made a huge mistake regarding a customer's bill. There was a long queue and the customer I was serving and the others waiting to be served were getting very impatient. I was blushing because I didn't know what to do next and I was getting more and more flustered.

2D It happened during a tutorial when I did not know my group so well. The incident was my stomach rumbling in a painfully quiet room where there was already somewhat of an atmosphere.

2E Before I was seeing my present girlfriend, I saw her in the street and looked at her. I didn't think she could see me looking, but she could – our eyes met, and I was forced to look away. I blushed quite heavily – I could feel the heat in my face.

looking gives it away that he is attracted to the woman whom he sees in the street. He goes on to describe himself as embarrassed and says he 'desperately wanted to be *out* of the situation' (emphasis in original).

The pattern of response differs in Studies 1 and 2. The novel provides detailed descriptions of conversations where the mental equilibrium of one person is disturbed by a reference, direct or indirect, to a topic, typically of a sexual nature, that is brought into the open. The blush has little consequence for the social encounter, it seems like a 'leakage' of feeling. When actual incidents are elicited (Study 2) participants recall vivid examples, usually where a large number of people were present and the events leading up to the blush have an impact on the social encounter. In twelve of these cases, respondents explicitly stated that they experienced embarrassment. In the light of the different pattern of responses it was decided to undertake a second questionnaire study, this time focusing on situations where a blush was elicited by something that was said. This was intended to approximate the kinds of episode included in the novel.

Study 3

A questionnaire was distributed to an opportunity sample of students inviting them to recall an occasion where something that was said made them blush. It was completed by forty-seven students, all but one female, a gender bias representative of the course taken by the students. Respondents were asked to describe the situation, state why they thought they blushed, rate the intensity of the blush and report on how many people of each gender were present. Responses were coded into the same categories as those in Study 2.

The incidents tended to be relatively recent, with 43 per cent having occurred within the past week and 75 per cent within the past month. Despite the emphasis on occasions where something was said, conversations within small groups were not common. Five or more people were present in 50 per cent of incidents and twelve people or more in 25 per cent of incidents. The large majority (75 per cent) took place in mixed company.

The predominant theme was *threats to identity*, present in twenty-three responses (49 per cent of the total), nine of these having a sexual theme. *Receiving praise or compliments* was mentioned in sixteen responses (34 per cent), six having a sexual theme. Being *conspicuous* was evident in seven responses (15 per cent), none referring to a sexual theme. There were no examples of *being accused of blushing*. One response could not be classified. The major difference between Studies 2 and 3 is the increase in Study 3 of examples of being praised or complimented.

There were a number of instances of exposure of a secret or something the person would have preferred not to be disclosed. Table 10.2 presents some examples. In example 3A a taboo topic is raised in conversation. In 3B the person does not want details of her personal life known. In 3C what is exposed is something the individual has done and which she did not want the other

Table 10.2 Selected instances of blushing in Study 3

	Incident recalled	Why do you think this made you blush?
3A	Flatmates talking about hearing other flatmates having sex	Because it's embarrassing
3B	Something personal was told to a lecturer by a friend	I was embarrassed that he knew about my personal life
3C	My friend was told that an embarrassing photo of me was shown at work	I was embarrassed that she knew how I'd posed in the photo
3D	That I fancied a particular bloke	Because I didn't know anybody else had realised this
3E	Friends talking in a pub about having sex in the park	I did it, once

person to know. In 3D it is the revelation of the woman's attraction to someone else, an attraction that she thought she had kept hidden, that elicits the blush. In 3E, there is a risk that the blush provides an unwanted signal to others, and will give the person away.

The questionnaire constructed for this study asked respondents to state why they thought they had blushed. Further insight into blushing could be achieved by coding these reasons into categories. Four categories were formed and the responses coded. It was not possible to devise mutually exclusive categories since some responses mentioned more than one facet, for example, being looked at and feeling embarrassed. Nevertheless, the majority of reasons could be coded into a single category. The first includes references to exposure, to being found out or the truth of whatever was said, for example, 'because I didn't know that anyone else had realized this', 'because I felt it was true', 'direct reference to a stage in my life I like to forget', 'the comments came very close to the mark'. There were ten instances of this category, 19 per cent of the total number of reasons coded. The second category includes references to being the centre of attention and being looked at (nineteen instances/36 per cent). The third category includes references to feeling embarrassed, stupid and foolish (twelve instances/23 per cent). The fourth category includes references to uncertainty how to behave and being surprised (ten instances/19 per cent). Two responses did not fit into any of the categories.

In summary, the questionnaire elicited a number of examples that fit the pattern identified in this chapter. Something is said that exposes or threatens to expose something the individual would prefer be hidden. This includes taboo topics as well as more personal matters including actions that have been taken and attitudes that are held. These account for some 19 per cent of the reasons that are produced for blushing. As in Study 2, the audience is a key factor in blushing and is directly mentioned in 36 per cent of the reasons given. Furthermore the majority of instances of blushing took place when five or more people were present.

Discussion of studies

The instances taken from literature, whether these are from Bowen's novel or elsewhere, present a picture of blushing that is more focused on a sexual theme and more closely related to the exposure of a secret than is found in the two empirical studies. Recalled incidents are dominated by the theme of threats to identity. This is the case whether respondents are free to report on any kind of incident or are asked to focus on something that has been said.

The pattern of results is influenced by the method of eliciting examples. When people are asked to recall incidents they tend to produce vivid, memorable examples. Vividness in the case of a social phenomenon such as blushing tends to be something that happens in front of other people or that makes a substantial impact on a social encounter. Miller (1996) argues that there may be a similar bias in recollections of embarrassing incidents and recommends the use of diary methods to try to overcome this. The literary examples are subtler and the events have a slighter social impact. The authors tend to refer to the blush when describing the psychological state of the character. Inspection of the context shows that blushing often occurs when there is an encounter between young people of opposite sex where something is said or done that has an implication of sexual interest or attractiveness. Nevertheless, it would be wrong to argue that references to exposure of a secret of a sexual nature are essentially a literary device. Examples are found in non-literary sources and are elicited in the questionnaire studies reported here.

Some implications

Superficially the notion of exposure is similar to that of conspicuousness, but it has extra meaning, a sense of something being revealed or uncovered. However, while many instances of blushing have a common pattern (whether or not they are interpreted as associated with embarrassment, shame or shyness) it remains to be seen how useful it is to extend this analysis to accommodate all cases. The person who makes a faux pas exposes his or her incompetence. People who receive a compliment have their qualities brought into the open in contradiction of conventions of modesty that they should be hidden. On the other hand, someone can be in the public eye without being conscious of this, and hence will not blush. Being conspicuous is not sufficient. We now turn to discussion of the communicative significance of the blush before considering the implications of our argument for understanding its physiology. Finally, the chapter discusses why shy people might be prone to blushing.

The blush as signal

Blushing has been analysed in terms of its function as an 'acknowledgement, a confession, and an apology' (Castelfranchi and Poggi, 1990: 240) and as an appeasement display (Keltner and Harker, 1998). It inhibits others from responding aggressively to the violation of a rule. It is also regarded as serving a remediation function, the restoration of social relationships (Halberstadt and Green, 1993). There is empirical support for the hypothesis that a display of embarrassment can deflect negative evaluation (Semin and Manstead, 1982). Leary *et al.* (1996) report that a blush can serve as a remedial device but only if it is noticed by others and interpreted as a blush and not as flushing of the face due to, say, physical exercise or alcohol. There is no doubt that a blush can serve valuable social functions by signalling that the person is appropriately embarrassed. For example, Harré (1990: 195) has argued that when people's appearance breaches standards of modesty it is not sufficient to take remedial action, they have to show embarrassment as well. If they fail to do both they risk being thought shameless. A blush is a particularly effective way of showing embarrassment because it is involuntary and hence likely to be interpreted as sincere (indeed, unblushing is given in Roget's *Thesaurus* as a synonym of shameless and brazen).

The fact that a blush serves useful social functions is not in itself reason to conclude that it is *intended* as a signal (Castelfranchi and Poggi, 1990: 240 acknowledge that it can be non-intentional and even counter-voluntary). The signal can be unwanted and a blush exposes what people want to keep hidden and creates a predicament for them that would not otherwise have occurred. Rather than offering an apology or an appeasement, the blush is an involuntary and unwelcome confession. A blush can be an unhelpful response to being teased; a young woman who blushes when a letter from her boyfriend is read aloud by a friend reinforces the tease by her evident discomfiture.

There is a parallel between a blush and expressions of fear. The pallor and trembling of fear gives it away (signals) that someone is frightened, nevertheless, there seems a sufficient explanation of these physiological changes and their contribution to preparation of the body for action, without attributing communicative functions to them. There are circumstances in which pallor or trembling can provide a useful signal, for example in appeasing a more powerful opponent. There are also situations where they are unwanted because they give fresh encouragement to an opponent or contradict the impression someone is trying to convey, for example, making it difficult for an officer to lead troops into battle. Top sportsmen and women (or business people) might be as alert to signs of fear or weakness in their opponents as most people are alert to signs of embarrassment in daily life.

From the perspective of the rule outlined here, the reading of the letter is equivalent to the circumstances of the fictional characters described by Gaskell, Bowen, or Updike. A blush is triggered by the exposure of something private; it is an involuntary response that nevertheless communicates something about the blusher. It shows recognition that it *is* an exposure. Similarly, those who blush at the mention of a taboo topic or when they hear a salacious joke acknowledge to others that this is something that ought not to be mentioned. Those who fail to blush in these circumstances reveal that they do not share this value. People who blush at a compliment show that they are modest and avoid appearing conceited or smug. Again, the involuntary nature of the blush adds credibility to judgements that are made.

Finally, a further problem with accounts in terms of a signal is the assumption that there is an actual person to be influenced by the blush. Theories that emphasize the adoption of an 'other-perspective' in embarrassment and shame propose that the other whose perspective is adopted is not necessarily an actual other who is present but an imagined audience, a 'possible detached observer of the self', as Taylor (1985) puts it. Taylor argues that even if others are present, it is not necessarily what *they* might think that causes shame.

The physiology of the blush

Research has been guided by the assumption that the blush is an expression of social anxiety. Nevertheless, psychophysiological research fails to show a consistent link between blushing and anxiety. Fear and anxiety are likely to be associated with pallor of the face rather than heightened colour, since vasoconstriction of facial capillaries results from heightened sympathetic system arousal. Nor is blushing reliably correlated with other measures of sympathetic arousal, for example, it tends to be associated with reduction rather than increase in heart rate (Keltner and Buswell, 1997) implying inhibition of sympathetic nervous system activity.[2]

Our analysis suggests that it might be less productive to focus on the link between blushing and anxiety but have greater heuristic value to consider systems involved in exposure and hiding. A balance of sympathetic and parasympathetic arousal may produce the blush. Blushing seems to occur when there is a sudden increase in alertness and readiness for action but no offensive or defensive action is immediately required. That is, equilibrium is established at a level above the baseline because parasympathetic activity increases to restrain 'fight or flight' responses. This is similar to a position argued by Schore (1998: 72) who characterizes the shame reaction as passive disengagement in order to become unseen. He opposes 'sympathetically driven "fight-flight" active coping strategies' to 'parasympathetically mediated passive coping mechanisms expressed in immobility and withdrawal associated with "giving up" ... and submission'.

In even more speculative fashion we can reflect on the reasons for the high frequency of sexual themes in accounts of blushing. Perhaps incidents with sexual implications are common simply because they are especially likely to produce embarrassment or unwanted attention among the young people who typically take part in psychological research (and who are often of most interest to novelists). Furthermore, sex tends to be a taboo topic and hence more likely to be a matter of secrecy. Alternatively blushing might be a signal of sexual interest or, more specifically, communicating awareness of being the object of sexual interest. From an evolutionary perspective the reason people blush when they are praised or complimented may be related to sexual selection, in that these draw attention to desirable qualities in a potential mate. Blushing when the object of attention even if there are no sexual connotations may be an extension of this. The tendency for women to apply rouge to their face to enhance their attractiveness may be a related phenomenon. So too may evidence that the frequency of blushing declines with age (the neurochemical receptors that control the dilation of the facial veins become less numerous with age, Mellander *et al.*, 1982). Psychoanalytic perspectives on blushing also tend to link it with sexual excitement; for example, Feldman (cited by Karch, 1971: 44) argues that women (but not men, where the picture is allegedly 'more complex') blush to 'prove their innocence and chastity, and ... to indicate sexual excitement and reveal their interest in sex'.

Shyness and blushing

Why are those who are shy prone to blush? Shy individuals believe that they lack the qualities required to interact effectively, at least in some situations. This is the approach to shyness taken by Goffman (1972: 107):

> Various kinds of recurrent encounters in a given society may share the assumption that participants have attained certain moral, mental, and physiognomic standards. The person who falls short may everywhere find himself inadvertently trapped into making implicit identity-claims which he cannot fulfil ... And, if he only imagines that he possesses a disqualifying attribute, his judgment of himself may be in error, but in the light of this, withdrawal from contact is reasonable.

Since the costs of revealing failure to reach these standards are so high, shy people will strive to keep this fact (as they see it) hidden from others. This hiding is evident in their reticence, hesitation in making spontaneous contributions, reluctance to assert or commit themselves, and the evasions involved in 'niceness', conformity and attitude neutrality. Shy people believe that the evaluations of others are particularly important and that these are likely to be negative. As numerous theorists have pointed out, the shy adopt self-protective strategies (Shepperd and Arkin, 1990) or have recourse to 'safety behaviours' (Clark and Wells, 1995; Wells, this volume, Chapter 12) to keep these failings hidden. When the risk of being 'found out' is high, so too is the likelihood of blushing.

Concluding remarks

It is argued here that many cases of blushing occur when an event exposes or threatens to expose something that the blusher would prefer to keep hidden. In many of these cases the blush has the undesired effect of giving away the secret.

Perhaps this is a special case of blushing that can be explained by existing theories of embarrassment or unwanted attention. This chapter argues for the value of studying in detail what it is about being the centre of attention that produces a blush. Research into blushing might be more productive if it set aside assumptions about the primacy of social anxiety and focused instead on the role of exposure.

Acknowledgements

I am grateful to Val Rees for her help with Study 3 and to anonymous participants in Studies 2 and 3. I have made minor changes to the examples to ensure confidentiality.

Notes

1 The word pudenda, referring to the external genital organs, is from the Latin *pudenda*, the gerundive of *pudere*, meaning things to be ashamed of. The less common English word pudency – meaning modesty, bashfulness and shamefacedness – also derives from *pudere*, to be or make ashamed.

2 On the other hand, there is evidence that blushing is mediated to some extent by sympathetic activity via beta-adrenergic receptors in the facial vein (Mellander *et al.*, 1982). Drummond (1997) examined the effects of blocking these receptors in blood vessels by means of the local administration of an antagonistic drug and found that this had a small but significant effect on participants' blushing in an embarrassing situation.

References

Ackroyd, P. (1994) *Dan Leno and the Limehouse Golem*, London: Sinclair-Stevenson.

Bögels, S.M., Alberts, M. and de Jong, P.J. (1996) 'Self-consciousness, self-focused attention, blushing propensity and fear of blushing', *Personality and Individual Differences*, 21: 573–81.

Bowen, E. (1998) *The Last September*, London: Vintage. (1929 edition, London: Constable & Co.).

Buss, A.H. (1980) *Self-consciousness and Social Anxiety*, San Francisco: Freeman.

Castelfranchi, C. and Poggi, I. (1990) 'Blushing as a discourse: was Darwin wrong?' in W.R. Crozier (ed.) *Shyness and Embarrassment: Perspectives from Social Psychology* (pp. 230–51), New York: Cambridge University Press.

Clark, D.M. and Wells, A. (1995) 'A cognitive model of social phobia', in R. Heimberg, M. Liebowitz, D.A. Hope, and F.R. Schneier (eds) *Social Phobia: Diagnosis, Assessment and Treatment* (pp. 69–93), New York: Guilford Press.

Crozier, W.R. (1998) 'Self-consciousness in shame: the role of the "other"', *Journal for the Theory of Social Behaviour*, 28: 273–86.

Drummond, P.D. (1989) 'Mechanism of emotional blushing', in N.W. Bond and D.A.T. Siddle (eds) *Psychobiology: Issues and Applications* (pp. 363–70) Amsterdam: North-Holland.

Drummond, P.D. (1997) 'The effect of adrenergic blockade on blushing and facial flushing', *Psychophysiology*, 34: 163–8.

Gaskell, E. (1986) *Cranford/Cousin Phillis*, London: Penguin (*Cousin Phillis* first published 1864).

Goffman, E. (1972) *Interaction Ritual*, Harmondsworth, Middlesex: Penguin.

Halberstadt, A.G. and Green, L.R. (1993) 'Social attention and placation theories of blushing', *Motivation and Emotion*, 17: 53–64.

Harré, R. (1990) 'Embarrassment: a conceptual analysis', in W.R. Crozier (ed.) *Shyness and Embarrassment: Perspectives from Social Psychology* (pp. 181–204), New York: Cambridge University Press.

Karch, F.E. (1971) 'Blushing', *Psychoanalytic Review*, 58: 37–50.

Keltner, D. and Buswell, B.N. (1997) 'Embarrassment: its distinct form and appeasement functions', *Psychological Bulletin*, 122: 250–70.

Keltner, D., and L.A. Harker (1998) 'The forms and functions of the nonverbal signal of shame', in P. Gilbert and B. Andrews (eds) *Shame* (pp. 78–98) New York: Oxford University Press.

Lazarus, R.S. (1991) *Emotion and Adaptation*, New York: Oxford University Press.

Leary, M.R., Britt, T.W., Cutlip, W.D. and Templeton, J.L. (1992) 'Social blushing', *Psychological Bulletin*, 107: 446–60.

Leary, M.R., Landel, J.L. and Patton, K.M. (1996) 'The motivated expression of embarrassment following a self-presentational predicament', *Journal of Personality*, 64: 619–36.

Leary, M.R. and Meadows, S. (1991) 'Predictors, elicitors, and concomitants of social blushing', *Journal of Personality and Social Psychology*, 60: 254–62.

Lewis, M. (1995) 'Embarrassment: the emotion of self-exposure and evaluation', in J.P. Tangney and K.W. Fischer (eds) *Self-conscious Emotions: The Psychology of Shame, Guilt, Pride and Embarrassment* (pp.199–218), New York: Guilford Press.

Mellander, S., Andersson, P.-O., Afzelius, L.-E. and Hellstrand, P. (1982) 'Neural beta-adrenergic dilation of the facial vein in man: possible mechanisms in emotional blushing', *Acta Physiologica Scandinavica*, 114: 393–9.

Miller, R.S. (1996) *Embarrassment: Poise and Peril in Everyday Life*, New York: Guilford Press.

Mulkens, S., De Jong, P.J. and Bögels, S.M. (1997) 'High blushing propensity: fearful preoccupation or facial coloration?', *Personality and Individual Differences*, 22: 817–24.

Parrott, W.G. and Smith, S.F. (1991) 'Embarrassment: actual vs. typical cases, classical vs. prototypical representations', *Cognition and Emotion*, 5: 467–88.

Scholing, A. and Emmelkamp, P.M. (1993) 'Cognitive and behavioural treatments of fear of blushing, sweating or trembling', *Behaviour Research and Therapy*, 31: 155–70.

Schore, A. (1998) 'Early shame experiences and infant brain development', in P. Gilbert and B. Andrews (eds) *Shame* (pp. 57–77), New York: Oxford University Press.

Semin, G.R. and Manstead, A.S.R. (1982) 'The social implications of embarrassment displays and restitution behavior', *European Journal of Social Psychology*, 12: 367–77.

Shearn, D., Bergman, E., Hill, K., Abel, A. and Hinds, L. (1990) 'Facial coloration and temperature responses in blushing', *Psychophysiology*, 27: 687–93.

Shepperd, J.A. and Arkin, R.M. (1990) 'Shyness and self-presentation', in W.R. Crozier (ed.) *Shyness and Embarrassment: Perspectives from Social Psychology* (pp. 286–314), New York: Cambridge University Press.

Taylor, G. (1985) *Pride, Shame, and Guilt: Emotions of Self-assessment*, Oxford: Clarendon Press.

Tomkins, S.S. (1963) *Affect, Imagery, Consciousness. Vol. 2: The Negative Affects*, New York: Springer.

Updike, J. (1980) *Your Lover Just Called*, Harmondsworth, Middlesex: Penguin.

Zimbardo, P.G., Pilkonis, P.A. and Norwood, R.M. (1974) *The Silent Prison of Shyness*, Office of Naval Research Technical Report Z-17, Stanford University.

11 What shy individuals do to cope with their shyness

A content analysis

Bernardo J. Carducci

Introduction

Within the last 20 years, the contemporary literature on shyness represents a steady progression characterized by an increasing level of theoretical, methodological, and clinical sophistication. Early investigations in the study of shyness took a clinical approach by emphasizing psychoanalytical explanations of shyness (cf. Hampton, 1927; Lewinsky, 1941). The impetus for a more empirical and systematic study of shyness was provided in the mid-1970s by Zimbardo and his colleagues with the development of the Stanford Survey on Shyness as part of the Stanford Shyness Project (cf. Zimbardo, 1986). Zimbardo and his colleagues investigated the self-reported degree of, and personal experiences with, shyness using the survey method primarily with adult samples (cf. Zimbardo, 1977, 1986; Zimbardo, Pilkonis and Norwood, 1974, 1975).

Early experimental research attempting to investigate the construct validity of shyness as conceptualized by Zimbardo, his colleagues, and others used specific questions from the Stanford Survey on Shyness (Zimbardo, Pilkonis and Norwood, 1974) or Shyness Scale (Cheek and Buss, 1981) to select groups of individuals who were then exposed to various experimental conditions. These early experimental studies provided evidence supporting the construct validity of shyness by utilizing actual or anticipated interactions with other individuals and the assessment of various verbal and non-verbal responses and behavioural and cognitive measures in controlled laboratory settings (Brodt and Zimbardo, 1981; Carducci and Webber, 1979; Cheek and Buss, 1981; Pilkonis, 1977a, 1977b).

Since these initial surveys and laboratory studies, the systematic study of shyness has developed a substantial body of research that has expanded our knowledge with regard to such general issues as clarifying the definition of shyness (cf. Cheek and Melchior, 1990; Bruch, Gorsky, Collins and Berger, 1989; Leary and Kowalski, 1995), the nature of the behavioural, affective, and cognitive components of shyness, and the relationship of shyness to other personality concepts and processes (cf. Carducci, 1999a, 2000; Carducci and Zimbardo, 1995; Cheek, 1989; Cheek and Buss, 1981; Cheek and

Krasnoperova, 1999; Cheek and Melchior, 1990; Henderson and Zimbardo, 1998; Jones, Cheek and Briggs, 1986). In addition to these general developments in the study of shyness, more specific developments have occurred in such areas as the identification and validity of strategies for measuring shyness (cf. Briggs and Smith, 1986; Jones, Briggs and Smith, 1986; Leary, 1990), the developmental aspects of shyness (cf. Beidel and Turner, 1998; Rubin and Asendorpf, 1993), the biological bases of shyness (cf. Kagan, 1994; Reznick, 1989; see Kagan, this volume, Chapter 2), and the implementation and assessment of therapeutic techniques for the treatment of shyness (cf. Henderson and Zimbardo, 1998).

While much has been gained through the use of the psychometric approach to investigating shyness and the study of shyness in college students, this approach lacks a certain degree of ecological validity and has been the source of some debate among shyness researchers. A principal argument in this debate is the extent to which this approach used most frequently by researchers to study the conceptualization, impact, and treatment of shyness reflects the actual nature of how shyness is experienced by shy individuals in their everyday life (Carducci *et al.*, 1998; Harris, 1984a, 1984b; Cheek and Watson, 1989). In an attempt to address this issue, Cheek and Watson (1989) performed a content analysis of the written responses of shy individuals and found evidence to suggest that shy individuals tend to utilize a three-component definition of shyness that is consistent with affective-cognitive behaviour conceptualization of shyness typically used by shyness researchers when conceptualizing shyness for the purpose of conducting research and providing treatment (cf. Buss, 1984; Carducci, 1999a; Cheek and Melchior, 1985; Henderson, 1994). To examine further how shy individuals conceptualize their shyness, Carducci and his colleagues have also investigated, through the content analysis of extended written comments, what shy individuals believe to be the cause of their shyness (Carducci *et al.*, 2000) and how shyness has affected various aspects of their lives (Carducci, 2000; Carducci *et al.*, 1998).

In an attempt to extend previous research seeking to understand how shy individuals experience their shyness, this chapter discusses a programme of study investigating the extended written responses of shy individuals describing what they say they do to deal with their shyness. Since survey research indicates that 78 per cent of shy individuals believe that their shyness could be overcome and 87 per cent express a willingness to do something about it (Carducci and Clark, 1993), a more complete understanding of what shy individuals say they actually do to deal with their shyness has both theoretical and practical implications (e.g., it can help mental health professionals provide support to shy individuals seeking assistance).

The extended written responses

Because of the uniqueness of the data discussed in this chapter, a brief description of the nature of the written responses is in order. The extended written comments examined here are based on 158 self-labelled shy individuals (sixty-eight males and eighty-seven females, with three respondents failing to indicate gender, ranging in age from 12 to 63) who completed a shyness survey appearing in the November/December 1995 issue of *Psychology Today* (Carducci and Zimbardo, 1995). The respondents, who represented a variety of educational levels and ethnic backgrounds, were randomly selected from a larger sample of over 800 respondents who returned the surveys. To help increase the validity of the written statements, all of the participants were assured of confidentiality of their responses.

The 1995 *Psychology Today* Survey on Shyness (Carducci and Zimbardo, 1995) consisted of ten fixed-format items and five open-ended questions. Examples of the fixed-format questions include: 'Do you consider yourself to be a shy person?' (yes; no), 'How often do you experience (or have you experienced) feelings of shyness?' (every day; almost every day; often, nearly every other day; once or twice a week; occasionally, less than once a week; rarely, once a month or less), and 'Do you think your shyness can be overcome?' (yes; no; uncertain). The open-ended questions requested the participants to describe what factors contributed to their shyness, how their shyness was expressed, problems their shyness caused, what they had tried to do to overcome shyness, and anything else they would like to report about their shyness.

The written responses to the open-ended question discussing what the shy individuals did to deal with their shyness were examined by four independent raters, each of whom was assigned to read the written responses of forty of the respondents within a one-week period. (Two surveys were discarded because of incomplete information.) After reading the extended written responses, the raters were asked to provide brief summary descriptions (e.g., 'went to parties' or 'drank to relax') of the extended statements provided by the respondents. (Samples of these extended written statements are provided within this chapter.) All of the brief statements were read aloud to the four raters simultaneously. As each summary description was presented to the raters, they discussed with which other descriptions it seemed most similar. The organization of the brief descriptions yielded ten distinctively different categories of self-selected strategies the shy individuals used to deal with their shyness. The remainder of this chapter is a discussion of these ten categories.

Analysis of self-selected strategies

Presented in this section is a summary of the most frequent self-selected strategies shy individuals report employing to deal with their shyness.

Overall analysis

The content analysis of the surveys revealed ten common self-selected strategies listed by the respondents for overcoming shyness. These ten strategies are listed in Table 11.1. Overall, 91.2 per cent of the respondents tried at least one strategy to overcome their shyness, 40 per cent tried two strategies, and 15 per cent tried as many as three strategies while 8.2 per cent stated they had tried nothing and 0.6 per cent did not indicate a response.

Strategy-by-strategy analysis

The strategy-by-strategy analysis presented in this section describes the ten self-selected strategies identified in the content analysis of the extended written statements provided by the shy respondents when describing what they did to deal with their shyness. Within the discussion of each self-selected strategy is a sample of personal statements from the shy individuals describing their efforts. These statements serve to illustrate the characteristic features of each strategy.

Forced extraversion

Clearly, the most frequently self-selected strategy employed by shy individuals to deal with their shyness was a strategy defined as 'forced extraversion'. This strategy was mentioned by 66.5 per cent of the shy individuals. Forced extraversion is characterized by the shy individuals

Table 11.1 A frequency and chronological analysis of self-selected strategies to overcome shyness*

| Self-selected strategy | Total | Ordinal position | | |
		1st	2nd	3rd
Forced extraversion	66.5	44.9	40.3	30.4
Self-induced cognitive extraversion	26.0	15.2	14.5	26.1
Educational extraversion	15.2	9.5	6.5	21.7
Sought professional help	14.6	8.2	11.3	8.7
Liquid extraversion	12.7	6.3	12.9	8.7
Other strategies	9.5	4.4	9.7	0.0
Stated 'did nothing'	8.2	8.2	0.0	0.0
Physical activity/exercise	2.5	1.9	0.0	4.3
Modify physical appearance	2.5	0.6	4.8	0.0
No responses given	0.6	0.6	0.0	0.0
Total number of respondents	**158**	**158**	**62**	**23**

* Response frequencies given in percentages based on the number of respondents.

forcing themselves to go to public places where they would be in the presence of other individuals. Shy individuals indicated that they went to parties, bars, dances, the mall, and/or took classes in an attempt to place themselves in the proximity of others.

While such a strategy has merits, shy individuals seem to fall short in their efforts. More specifically, after showing up, shy individuals expected others to do all the work: to approach them, start conversations, and keep the conversation going; they expected others to draw them out of their shyness. Comments reflecting this strategy include:

> I have tried to overcome my shyness by being around new people as much as possible and getting involved in the conversation, however, after a few seconds I become quiet. I have a problem keeping the conversation flowing.

> [I] say 'the Hell with it' to myself and force myself to do or say something.

> I have tried to get more involved socially, realizing that the next person could be just as shy.

As a strategy for dealing with shyness, simply showing up is not enough. Not only is it ineffective and unfair (expecting others to do the work), it concedes control of interactions to others; the shy let others choose them. It also exemplifies the mistaken expectations that shy people often have about social life. Hand-in-hand with the expectation that others will approach them is their sense of perfectionism. The shy believe that anything they may say has to come out perfect, sterling, supremely witty, as if everyday life is some kind of situation comedy. They believe that everybody is watching and judging them – a case of the narcissism of the shy (Cheek and Krasnoperova, 1999). Thus, under such self-imposed pressure, maybe just showing up is the best shy people feel that they can do.

Self-induced cognitive extraversion

The second most popular strategy selected by shy individuals to deal with their shyness was a strategy defined as 'cognitive extraversion'. This strategy was reported by 26 per cent of the shy individuals. Self-induced cognitive extraversion is characterized by the shy individuals creating a set of cognitions that reflects self-affirming statements and attempts to minimize the perceived threats of social situations; it involves shy individuals trying to change the way they think about their shyness and about other people. A sample of the comments reflecting this strategy includes:

> I have tried to convince myself that what other people think shouldn't bother me. I have been trying to completely change my mindset and outlook on other people.

> Talking to myself, running a movie in my head of the right thing to do in a certain situation. This only works in situations that are not entirely overwhelming. What else can I say? I hate it.

While the importance of the cognitive component of shyness is well documented (cf. Carducci, 1999a; Leary and Kowalski, 1995), simply trying to talk or think themselves into not being shy is not enough. Shy individuals must also know how to respond appropriately when in the presence of others (cf. Henderson, 1994).

Educational extraversion

The third most frequently employed strategy utilized by shy individuals to deal with their shyness was a strategy defined as 'educational extraversion'. This strategy was reported by 15.2 per cent of the shy individuals. Educational extraversion is characterized by shy individuals seeking to gain information and educating themselves about their shyness in an attempt to overcome it. To gain such information, shy individuals reported reading self-help books and attending seminars and workshops. A sample of the comments reflecting this strategy include:

> To overcome my shyness I have tried reading books on improving self-confidence, self-esteem, and ways of communicating.

> I have taken workshops – assertiveness, persuasion, art appreciation and joined support groups in the hope I will learn to feel more comfortable going over to a person after a session and saying hello.

> I have read many, if not all self-help books on the subject of shyness and related topics, bought self-help tapes, etc. They're all good at explaining the many different aspects of shyness and social anxiety but have little when it comes to treatments (effective or specific).

Obtaining knowledge about the nature and dynamics of shyness through self-help books and seminars can help shy individuals make more informed decisions about how to control their shyness, provided such information is based on sound research. The only limitation with the self-selection of this strategy is that not enough shy individuals seem to be utilizing it.

Sought professional help

The fourth most frequently employed strategy utilized by shy individuals to deal with their shyness was a strategy labelled as 'sought professional help'. This strategy was reported by 14.6 per cent of the shy individuals. The seeking of professional help is characterized by shy individuals participating in an assortment of treatment programmes guided by a variety of mental health professionals to overcome their shyness, including one-on-one therapy, group therapy, self-esteem enhancement workshops, stress-management seminars, assertiveness training classes, Toastmasters, and prescription medications. A sample of the comments reflecting this strategy include:

> I got involved in therapy and a twelve-step program two years ago and my life improved.

> I've been in psychotherapy for two years. It has helped me a lot, but I still have a long way to go to becoming the fearless extrovert I would like to be.

> I've joined a couple of social anxiety phobia groups which were of some help.

As the statements reflect, such actions seem to help. However, the principal limitation associated with this strategy is that not enough shy individuals seem to be utilizing it.

Liquid extraversion

The fifth most frequently employed strategy utilized by shy individuals to deal with their shyness was one classified as 'liquid extraversion'. This strategy was reported by 12.7 per cent of the shy individuals. Liquid extraversion is characterized by shy individuals utilizing an assortment of non-prescription drugs and alcohol as a social lubricant in an attempt to reduce the tension and anxiety associated with what they perceived as threatening social situations. A sample of the comments reflecting this strategy include:

> In social situations, I will use alcohol moderately to relax and be less self-conscious and more outgoing.

> Since I'm in college now, most of the social functions involve alcohol. I admit I use it as a social lubricant. If there is a social function with a large group of people that I'm uncomfortable with, I will not go unless there is alcohol.

Liquid extraversion poses the great danger of over-consumption of alcohol. Indeed, additional research (Carducci and McLeish, 2000) has noted that 11 per cent of shy individuals surveyed were labelled 'shy alcoholics'. These shy individuals say that drinking gives them courage and drowns out their arousal. Under the influence of alcohol they can pay less attention to themselves and more to other people. But shy alcoholics indicate they do not like having to drink to perform better; they feel uneasy and lack confidence in their true selves. They begin to believe that people will like them only when they are outgoing, not as they really are. A sample of the comments reflecting this tendency include:

> I do like drinking with my friends, but I notice that I tend to indulge myself in alcohol to feel more loose and more talkative when it comes to meeting my boyfriend's friends. But then when I see them sober, I feel like a loser because they just saw me the other night as a happy talkative drunk.

> As a teenager, I started to use drugs. Although they made it possible for me to talk more, they were still never able to make me overcome my phobia about dancing. When the drugs wore off, it was back into my shell.

> I drink when possible at social gatherings to ease tension and loosen lips. This, however, seems to make the problem worse the following day.

In addition to the personal concerns for the shy, the notion of the shy alcoholic raises some professional issues as well. A concern is that almost as many shy individuals elect to deal with their shyness by self-medicating as those who seek professional help. Secondly, it reflects the belief that if you have to drink to be social, whether you are shy or not, you have a problem with alcohol that needs to be addressed (cf. Conners, Maisto and Derman, 1994; Stacy, Wildaman and Marlatt, 1990). Both of these concerns suggest that mental health professionals dealing with shy individuals should pay special attention to the possible presence of alcohol-related problems. A sample of comments reflecting this issue include:

> To overcome shyness I'd drink and take tranquilizers and have overdosed as a result.

> My problem created by my shyness is alcoholism and drug abuse and loneliness.

All of these personal and professional concerns have implications for the treatment of shy problem drinkers. More specifically, one of the most pervasive programmes for problem drinkers, Alcoholics Anonymous (AA), works squarely against shy people. Whereas the shy are slow to warm up, AA asks people to stand up right away, to be highly visible, and to disclose highly personal information immediately. The inconsistencies between the affective tendencies of shy individuals and the procedures of AA suggest that there exists the possibility of developing a form of an AA for the shy. Such a programme should take into consideration the nature and dynamics of shyness (cf. Carducci, 2000). For example, a meeting might begin by having a leader speak for the first 45 minutes, while the shy warm up, followed by a break, in which the leader is available to answer questions. This then paves the way for a general question-and-answer period.

Residual strategies

In addition to the five major strategies identified, there were five others that were each used by 10 per cent or fewer of the shy individuals. Because of the low rate of frequency, these strategies are presented collectively in this section in their descending order of utilization. An 'other strategies' category, containing 9.5 per cent of the respondents, included an assortment of strategies that did not fit into any of the other categories. As seen by the sample of the statements from this category, the range of the strategies is considerable:

> If I'm in an isolated situation with a strange female, I'll usually tell a quick joke about the surroundings.

> I have tried being humorous and smiling often and laughing often.

> To learn to be more secure through religion.

A 'did nothing' category was identified that accommodated 8.2 per cent of the respondents. In this category, the shy individuals stated that they had taken no action to deal with their shyness, either because they did not know what to do or felt that taking action was futile. Sentiments from this category include:

> Nothing, just carried on!

> I have done nothing to overcome my shyness. I will live with my shyness now that I am retired. *It's too late to change.*

> I have done nothing to overcome my shyness. I do participate when asked in whatever capacity I can as long as I am asked.

> Don't know what to do ... P.S. Please help me Mr Carducci.

A category labelled 'physical activity/exercise' contained 2.5 per cent of the respondents. In this category, the shy individuals stated that they had engaged in a variety of activities to deal with their shyness. A sample of comments from this category includes:

> I've tried to get more confidence by exercising. It makes me feel better about myself.

> I've tried to jog 4–5 miles in the morning every day. It seems to lower my blood pressure.

An underlying feature of this strategy is that the individuals seem to be exercising for constructive reasons: to be healthy and feel better about themselves, and not necessarily to make themselves more attractive to others.

Another category utilized by 2.5 per cent of the respondents was identified as 'modify physical appearance'. The most common strategy shy individuals seem to utilize to modify their physical appearance was to lose weight. A sample of the comments from this category includes:

> My shyness was exacerbated by the fact that I was overweight and have a stuttering problem. I have since lost 92 pounds. My shyness has subsided somewhat since the weight loss but it is still a big hindrance.

> A few years ago, in an attempt to develop a dating relationship with a woman at work, I made a sustained effort to lose weight and work out. It was effective. I trimmed down and developed a physique that I was almost proud of and my self-confidence increased. However, the coworker reconciled with her husband and our relationship cooled. I regained the weight, and feel worse than ever.

An underlying feature of this strategy is the individuals seem to be losing the weight to make themselves more attractive to others, not necessarily to be healthier. And, as indicated by the comments, weight loss alone did not necessarily resolve the concerns the individuals had with their shyness. In addition to trying to lose weight, other strategies by which individuals attempted to modify their appearance to deal with their shyness included working out/body building, attempting to dress in a manner others would find attractive, trying a new hair style, changing hair colour, getting tattoos, and body piercing.

Finally, 0.6 per cent of the respondents were classified into a 'no response given' category because they failed to give any type of response to the query regarding what they did to deal with their shyness.

Chronological analysis

Since 40 per cent of the respondents tried two strategies and 15 per cent tried as many as three strategies, a chronological analysis was performed to determine the order in which the respondents tried the self-selected strategies to overcome their shyness. The ordinal position of the self-selected strategies is presented in Table 11.1. Self-induced extraversion was the most frequently selected first, second, and third strategy. Self-induced cognitive modification was the second most frequently selected first, second, and third strategy. Seeking professional help and self-medication formed another cluster of two strategies tried second, while reading self-help books or attending seminars was a frequently appearing third strategy.

Treatment implications

While self-induced extraversion and cognitive modification were strategies frequently selected by shy individuals to help overcome their shyness, the effectiveness of these strategies seems to be limited. More specifically, individuals who used these strategies tended to report that even though they could talk themselves into going out (i.e., self-induced cognition extraversion) and/or force themselves to be in proximity to others (i.e., forced extraversion), they felt anxious and self-conscious and unable to perform in a socially appropriate manner. These shy individuals indicated that this state of heightened anxiety and self-consciousness interfered with their ability to think and speak clearly during these episodes of self-induced extraversion.

In response to this negative outcome, most shy individuals did not elect to pursue other strategies, which suggests that they either continued to employ the same self-defeating strategies or gave up. However, those individuals who elected to pursue additional strategies sought professional help, and/or utilized self-help books or workshops to increase their ability to interact more successfully with others in those self-induced social situations. Nevertheless, it should be noted that a similar number of shy individuals resorted to the use of drugs and alcohol as a solution to reducing inhibitions and anxiety.

These patterns of results have important implications for the development of specific programmes to treat different dimensions of shyness (cf. Pilkonis, 1986). More specifically, rather than just forcing themselves to go into social situations without the necessary social skills and, thus, experiencing anxiety and disappointment, shy individuals should be advised to select first those strategies that will provide them with the requisite affective state and cognitive and social skills necessary to perform successfully in social situations before placing themselves in proximity to others (cf. Henderson, 1994; Oakman *et al.*, Chapter 13, and Wells, this volume, Chapter 12). Thus, reading self-help books and attending shyness seminars or seeking therapy should be strategies tried *before* the use of self-induced extraversion, not after.

Further insight into the process by which shy individuals self-select strategies to overcome their shyness might also be gained by considering the motivational nature underlying their decisions. The tendency of shy individuals to self-select strategies that place them in the social proximity to others may reflect the strong desire shy individuals have to be with others (cf. Cheek and Buss, 1981). Unfortunately, this strong desire to be with others probably outweighs the need to delay social gratification and demonstrate the necessary degree of patience these shy individuals will require in order to gain the requisite knowledge and skills when they seek professional help or utilize self-help books and workshops. Based on research involving affective states and the self-regulation of social interaction (cf. Baumeister, Heatherton and Tice, 1994), a consideration of such motivational issues should be incorporated as part of the self-selection strategies employed by shy individuals to overcome their shyness

Because some shy individuals elected to seek professional advice as a self-selected strategy to overcome their shyness, a comment about the nature of the specific professional help is also in order. For those individuals who experience their shyness in the form of increased anxiety, these requisite skills are most likely to be obtained through professional help involving biofeedback and other forms of relaxation training (cf. Pilkonis, 1986; Schneier and Welkowitz, 1996). For those individuals who experience shyness related to a lack of social skills, these requisite skills are more likely to be obtained through professional help involving group therapy and other forms of social support where developing social skills and learning to receive feedback from others in a social setting are emphasized (cf. Carducci, 1999b; Henderson, 1994; Pilkonis, 1986; Schneier and Welkowitz, 1996). Thus, shy individuals who wish to overcome their shyness should first select strategies that provide them with the necessary skills and knowledge to perform successfully in social situations before engaging in the process of self-induced extraversion and cognitive modification. To help in this regard, future research should attempt to clarify the relationship between the cognitive and motivational determinants of the self-selected strategies to overcome shyness, as well as to identify those treatment programmes designed to supplement the efforts by shy individuals to cope with their shyness.

Conclusions

While the stereotypical view of shy individuals is one of passivity and inactivity, a totally different picture appears when investigating what shy people do to deal with their shyness. The shy put a lot of effort into their attempts to overcome their shyness. While they may have the right intentions, the strategies they self-select seem limited in their effectiveness, due to their incomplete nature and/or restrictive use, and they are sometimes even counterproductive. Occasionally these self-selected strategies can be potentially dangerous (e.g., substance abuse). Understanding the process by which shy individuals make decisions to deal with their shyness has theoretical, personal, and professional implications. More specifically, the present analysis complements previous research by helping to provide a link between what shy individuals do in response to how they experience their shyness and the areas of life where shyness has created the most difficulties for them. Shy individuals are presented with feedback regarding the strengths and limitations of their self-selected strategies. Finally, mental health professionals can use such information to anticipate the nature of the difficulties shy individuals may experience when seeking assistance and develop programmes of support to meet these difficulties.

Author's note

Preparation of this manuscript was supported by release time for research granted to the author by the Indiana University Southeast Office of Academic Affairs. The author wishes to thank Carol R. Marion, David Lynch, Melissa M. Docsh, and Amanda L. Boley for providing assistance with this research. Portions of this chapter were presented at the International Conference on Shyness and Self-consciousness, Cardiff, Wales, July 1997.

References

Baumeister, R.F., Heatherton, T.F. and Tice, D.M. (1994) *Losing Control: How and Why People Fail at Self-regulation*, San Diego, CA: Academic Press.

Beidel, D.C. and Turner, S.M. (1998) *Shy Children, Phobic Adults: Nature and Treatment of Social Phobia*, Washington, D.C.: American Psychological Association.

Briggs, S.R. and Smith, T.G. (1986) 'The measurement of shyness', in W.H. Jones, J.M. Cheek and S.R. Briggs (eds) *Shyness: Perspectives on Research and Treatment* (pp. 47–60), New York: Plenum Press.

Brodt, S.E. and Zimbardo, P.G. (1981) 'Modifying shyness-related social behavior through symptom misattribution', *Journal of Personality and Social Psychology*, 41: 437–49.

Bruch, M.A., Gorsky, J.M., Collins, T.M. and Berger, P.A. (1989) 'Shyness and sociability reexamined: a multicomponent analysis', *Journal of Personality and Social Psychology*, 57: 904–15.

Buss, A.H. (1984) 'A conception of shyness', in J.A. Daly and J.C. McCroskey (eds) *Avoiding Communication: Shyness, Reticence, and Communication Apprehension* (pp. 39–49), Beverly Hills, CA: Sage.

Carducci, B.J. (1999a) *Shyness: A Bold New Approach*, New York: HarperCollins.

Carducci, B.J. (1999b) *The Pocket Guide to Making Successful Small Talk: How to Talk to Anyone, Anytime, Anywhere about Anything*, New Albany, IN: Pocket Guide Publishing.

Carducci, B.J. (2000) 'Shyness: the new solution', *Psychology Today*, 33: 38–40, 42–5, and 78.

Carducci, B.J. and Clark, D.L. (1993) *The Personal and Situational Pervasiveness of Shyness: A Replication and Extension of the Stanford Survey on Shyness 20 Years Later*

(IUS Tech. Report), New Albany, IN: Indiana University Southeast Shyness Research Institute.

Carducci, B.J., Henderson, D., Henderson, M., Walisser, A.M., Brown, A., Mayfield, D. and McLeish, A.C. (2000) *Why shy?: A Content Analysis of Self-perceived Causes of Shyness* (SRI Tech. Report), New Albany, IN: Indiana University Southeast Shyness Research Institute.

Carducci, B.J. and McLeish, A.C. (2000) *The Shy Alcoholic: Cognitive Correlates of Shy Subtype* (SRI Tech. Report), New Albany, IN: Indiana University Southeast Shyness Research Institute.

Carducci, B.J., Ragains, K.D., Kee, K.L., Johnson, M.R. and Duncan, H.R. (1998, August) 'Identifying the pains and problems of shyness: a context analysis', Poster presentation at the annual meeting of the American Psychological Association, San Francisco, CA.

Carducci, B.J. and Webber, A. (1979) 'Shyness as a determinant of interpersonal distance', *Psychological Reports*, 44: 1075–8.

Carducci, B.J. and Zimbardo, P.G. (1995, Nov./Dec.) 'Are you shy?', *Psychology Today*, 34–41, 64, 66, 68, 70, 78, and 82.

Cheek, J.M. (1989) *Conquering Shyness: The Battle Anyone Can Win*, New York: Dell Publishing.

Cheek, J.M. and Buss, A.H. (1981) 'Shyness and sociability', *Journal of Personality and Social Psychology*, 41: 330–9.

Cheek, J.M. and Krasnoperova, E.N. (1999) 'Varieties of shyness in adolescence and adulthood', in L.A. Schmidt and J. Schulkin (eds) *Extreme Fear, Shyness, and Social Phobia: Origins, Biological Mechanisms, and Clinical Outcomes* (pp. 224–50), New York: Oxford University Press.

Cheek, J.M. and Melchior, L.A. (1985, August) 'Measuring the three components of shyness', in M.H. Davis and S.L. Fanzio (co-chairs), *Emotions, Personality, and Well-being II*. Symposium conducted at the annual meeting of the American Psychological Association, Los Angles.

Cheek, J.M. and Melchior, L.A. (1990) 'Shyness, self-esteem, and self-consciousness', in H. Leitenberg (ed.) *Handbook of Social Anxiety and Evaluation Anxiety* (pp. 47–82), New York: Plenum Press.

Cheek, J.M. and Watson, A.K. (1989) 'The definition of shyness: psychological imperialism or construct validity', *Journal of Social Behavior and Personality*, 4: 85–95.

Conners, G.J., Maisto, S.A. and Derman, K.H. (1994) 'Alcohol-related expectancies and their implications to treatment', in R.R. Watson (ed.) *Drug and Alcohol Abuse Reviews: Vol. 3. Alcohol Abuse Treatments* (pp. 203–31), Totowa, NJ: Human Press.

Hampton, F.A. (1927) 'Shyness', *Journal of Neurology and Psychopathology*, 8: 124–31.

Harris, P.R. (1984a) 'Shyness and psychological imperialism: on the dangers of ignoring the ordinary language roots of the terms we deal with', *European Journal of Social Psychology*, 14: 169–81.

Harris, P.R. (1984b) 'The hidden face of shyness: a message from the shy for researchers and practitioners', *Human Relations*, 37: 1079–93.

Henderson, L. (1994) *Social Fitness Training: A Treatment Manual for Shyness and Social Phobia*, Palo Alto, CA: Shyness Institute.

Henderson, L. and Zimbardo, P.G. (1998) 'Shyness', *Encyclopedia of Mental Health* (Vol. 3, pp. 497–509), San Diego, CA: Academic Press.

Jones, W.H., Briggs, S.R. and Smith, T.G. (1986) 'Shyness: conceptualization and measurement', *Journal of Personality and Social Psychology*, 51: 629–39.

Jones, W.H., Cheek, J.M. and Briggs, S.R. (eds) (1986) *Shyness: Perspectives on Research and Treatment*, New York: Plenum Press.

Kagan, J. (1994) *Galen's Prophecy: Temperament in Human Nature*, New York: Westview Press.

Leary, M.R. (1990) 'Social anxiety, shyness, and related constructs', in J.P. Robinson, P.R. Shaver and L.S. Wrightsman (eds) *Measures of Personality and Social Attitudes: Vol. 1 of Measures of Social Psychological Attitudes* (pp. 161–194), San Diego, CA: Academic Press.

Leary, M.R. and Kowalski, R.M. (1995) *Social Anxiety*, New York: Guilford Press.

Lewinsky, H. (1941) 'The nature of shyness', *British Journal of Psychology*, 32: 105–13.

Pilkonis, P.A. (1977a) 'The behavioral consequences of shyness', *Journal of Personality*, 45: 596–611.

Pilkonis, P.A. (1977b) 'Shyness, public and private, and its relationship to other measures of social behavior', *Journal of Personality*, 45: 585–95.

Pilkonis, P.A. (1986) 'Short-term group psychotherapy for shyness', in W.H. Jones, J.M. Cheek and S.R. Briggs (eds) *Shyness: Perspectives on Research and Treatment* (pp. 375–85), New York: Plenum.

Reznick, J.S. (ed.) (1989) *Perspectives on Behavioral Inhibition*, Chicago: University of Chicago Press.

Rubin, K.H. and Asendorpf, J.B. (eds) (1993) *Social Withdrawal, Inhibition, and Shyness in Childhood*, Hillsdale, NJ: Erlbaum.

Schneier, F. and Welkowitz, L. (1996) *The Hidden Faces of Shyness: Understanding and Overcoming Social Anxiety*, New York: Avon Books.

Stacy, A.W., Wildaman, K.F. and Marlatt, G.A. (1990) 'Expectancy models of alcohol use', *Journal of Personality and Social Psychology*, 58: 918–28.

Zimbardo, P.G. (1977) *Shyness: What it is, What to do about it*, Reading, MA: Addison-Wesley.

Zimbardo, P.G. (1986) 'The Stanford Shyness Project', in W.H. Jones, J.M. Cheek and S.R. Briggs (eds) *Shyness: Perspectives on Research and Treatment* (pp. 17–25), New York: Plenum Press.

Zimbardo, P.G., Pilkonis, P.A. and Norwood, R.M. (1974) *The silent prison of shyness* (ONR Tech. Rep. Z-17), Stanford, CA: Stanford University Press.

Zimbardo, P.G., Pilkonis, P.A. and Norwood, R.M. (1975) 'The social disease called shyness', *Psychology Today*, 8: 68–72.

12 Modifying social anxiety

A cognitive approach

Adrian Wells

While this chapter focuses on social phobia – a disruptive form of social anxiety – less disruptive forms of social anxiety are a common personal experience. Most people would expect to feel some anxiety prior to an important job interview or before a first romantic date. The feelings of apprehension and anxiety in these situations are very similar to those experienced by people with social phobia.

Social phobia is characterized by a fear of performance or social evaluative situations. The affected individual fears behaving in a way that will lead to humiliation or being negatively evaluated by others. Two sub-types of social phobia are identified in DSM-III-R and DSM-IV (American Psychiatric Association, 1987; 1994). The generalized sub-type is characterized by a fear of most social situations. However, more specific forms of social phobia can be identified in which the individual experiences fear in a particular situation: for example, using public lavatories. Exposure to feared social situations almost invariably provokes anxiety in social phobia, and the person realizes that the fear is excessive. The experience of social anxiety is often accompanied by physical symptoms, such as sweating, trembling, and blushing. These symptoms are in many cases a cause of embarrassment and fear, in so much that individuals are worried that other people will notice a symptom of anxiety and this will lead to criticism, negative evaluation, or loss of status. In some cases, socially phobic individuals fear that they will perform in an embarrassing way by making a mistake, speaking strangely, or behaving in a way that will attract attention and lead to negative evaluation.

Social phobia has overlapping features with avoidant personality disorder as defined in DSM-III-R and DSM-IV. The overlap is particularly evident with generalized sub-types of social phobia. Holt, Heimberg and Hope (1992) have suggested that avoidant personality disorder is severe generalized social phobia. Individuals with avoidant personality are preoccupied with being criticized or rejected in social situations. Situations such as promotion at work are avoided because the new responsibilities may result in criticism from co-workers. These individuals avoid making friends unless they are certain of being liked and accepted without criticism. However, a feature of avoidant personality disorder that is somewhat different from social phobia is the tendency to exaggerate the potential dangers of ordinary situations.

Cognitive behavioural treatment

Treatment approaches to social phobia have consisted of anxiety management therapies (Butler *et al.*, 1984), social skills training (e.g. Marzillier, Lambert and Kellet, 1976; Trower, Yardley, Bryant and Shaw, 1978), exposure (e.g. Emmelkamp, Mersch, Vissia and van der Helm, 1985) and combined treatments involving exposure and cognitive therapy. Cognitive therapy has been based on Rational Emotive Therapy (e.g. Emmelkamp *et al.*, 1985), or cognitive therapy based on Beck's general schema theory (e.g. DiGiuseppe, McGowan, Sutton-Simon and Gardner, 1990). Cognitive behavioural treatments have used combinations of techniques that teach individuals coping skills, restructure negative thoughts, and introduce exposure-based exercises, on an individual or group treatment basis. Heimberg and colleagues have developed and evaluated a cognitive behavioural group therapy of social phobia (Heimberg and Juster, 1994; Heimberg, Saltzman, Holt and Blendell, 1993; Heimberg, Liebowitz, Hope *et al.*, 1998).

In a meta-analysis of 42 treatment outcome trials of cognitive behavioural treatments for social phobia, Taylor (1996) demonstrated that only cognitive therapy plus exposure yielded a significantly larger effect-size than placebo. Exposure alone, social skills training, and cognitive restructuring alone, did not show a significantly larger effect size than placebo. In each instance of treatment, effect sizes increased from post-treatment to three-month follow-up. However, there is emerging evidence that gains increase or are maintained over longer-term follow-up evaluations. In particular, Heimberg, Saltzman, Holt and Blendell (1993) report that patients receiving cognitive behavioural group therapy continue to do well at 4.5 to 6.25 years follow-up.

Although cognitive behavioural therapy is an effective treatment for social phobia, some patients fail to respond and the degree of cognitive change in existing cognitive behavioural treatments is small. The weak effect of treatment on negative cognitions such as Fear of Negative Evaluation (FNE) is likely to result from an underdeveloped understanding of cognitive mechanisms underlying social phobia. There is a need to develop treatments that modify the underlying mechanisms that contribute to a maintenance of distorted cognitions in social phobia. Recently, Clark and Wells (1995) have advanced such a model. In the remainder of this chapter the model is described and specific strategies for cognitive modification are discussed.

A cognitive model of social phobia

In developing their model of social phobia, Clark and Wells have drawn on clinical experience, cognitive theory (e.g. Beck, 1976; Heimberg and Barlow, 1988) and on recent theoretical developments in conceptualising information processing in emotional disorder that emphasize self-referent processing (Wells and Matthews, 1994; 1996).

The model is presented diagrammatically in Figure 12.1. The central aspect of the model (perceived social danger, processing of the self, safety behaviours, and somatic and cognitive symptoms), concern the processes that occur during exposure to feared social situations. We will consider these processes first. When entering feared social situations, the person with social phobia becomes concerned about his/her ability to present a favourable impression. This concern is apparent as negative automatic thoughts representing fears of showing signs of anxiety or performing in a way that will be humiliating or embarrassing. Such automatic thoughts are accompanied by a shift in the direction of attention. The socially anxious individual becomes self-focused and begins to process an impression of how s/he thinks s/he appears to others. This impression often occurs as a mental image from an 'observer perspective' in which the individual can see the self as if from someone else's vantage point. In this image, anxiety symptoms and inadequacies are highly conspicuous. The impression may also occur as a 'felt

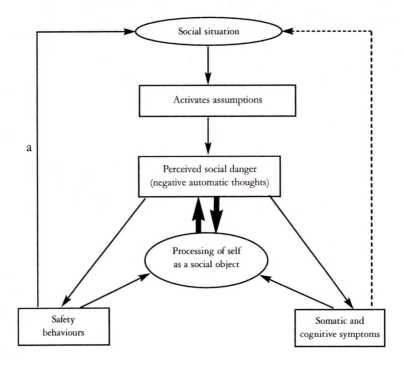

Figure 12.1 A cognitive model of social anxiety

Source: Reproduced from Wells, A. (1997), *Cognitive Therapy of Anxiety Disorders: A Practice Manual and Conceptual Guide*, Chichester, Sussex, Wiley, p. 169 with the permission of John Wiley & Sons Limited

sense' in which the person assumes that particular anxiety symptoms 'look as bad as they feel'. Interoceptive information is an important source of data influencing the content of the self-image. For example, a patient fearful of making formal presentations at work had an impression of himself in which his voice quavered, and fear was written on his face in the form of wide startled eyes and a deeply furrowed brow. In fact, the patient did not resemble this self-image even when he was 90 per cent anxious, although he was convinced that this was the way he actually appeared.

When the person with social phobia appraises the social situation as dangerous, particular safety behaviours are used in order to avert feared catastrophes, conceal anxiety, and prevent embarrassment or humiliation. Safety behaviours may include complete avoidance of the feared social situation, but when this is not possible they consist of more subtle forms of in-situation behaviour. Such behaviours are problematic in four ways. First, some safety behaviours exacerbate or maintain self-consciousness and this is depicted by the bi-directional arrows between safety behaviours and processing of the self in Figure 12.1. Second, safety behaviours support an attributional bias in which the non-occurrence of social catastrophe can be attributed to use of the safety behaviour. Thus, safety behaviours prevent unambiguous disconfirmation of negative appraisals, and of the negative self-image. Third, some safety behaviours intensify the somatic and cognitive symptoms of anxiety. For instance, wearing additional layers of clothing in order to conceal sweating will increase the person's propensity to sweat, or cognitive rehearsal of sentences before speaking can divert attention away from processing aspects of the social environment, and can impart a cognitive load that interferes with fluent social performance. Fourth, safety behaviours may contaminate the social situation as depicted by the feedback loop labelled 'A' in Figure 12.1. Behaviours such as avoiding eye contact, avoiding self-disclosure and waiting for other people to make the first move in a social situation can lead others to think that the person with social anxiety is disinterested in them or is aloof and unfriendly. There is a paradox here, since the social phobic assumes that others will see him/her as overly anxious, when in fact others may be more likely to perceive the person with social phobia as unfriendly or aloof.

Examples of negative automatic thoughts, self-processing and safety behaviours are presented in Table 12.1.

Assumptions and beliefs

Three types of underlying belief have been identified in the Clark and Wells model. These beliefs are thought to contribute to the cyclical processes that maintain social phobia as depicted in Figure 12.1. The three types are:

- unrealistic rules for social performance (e.g. 'I must never show signs of anxiety');

Table 12.1 Examples of negative automatic thoughts, self-processing
and safety behaviours from three social phobic patients

Negative automatic thoughts	Self-processing	Safety behaviours
I'll look anxious Everyone will look at me	Self conscious: image of self with a tight mouth, bright red face, and blank face.	Keep smiling, avoid self-disclosure, wear cool clothes, hide face with hand, avoid eye contact.
I'll sweat – people will think I'm abnormal	Self-conscious: image of face with rivers of sweat rolling down it, hair looking soaked.	Sip cold drinks, hold handkerchief, wipe forehead, wear cool clothes, leave situation, sit by open window.
I won't know what to say.	Self conscious: impression of own voice as weak and stilted; image of self looking like the 'village idiot'.	Plan what to say, mentally rehearse sentences, try to talk fluently, monitor voice, try to look interested, avoid self-disclosure, look away from people.

- conditional assumptions (e.g. 'If I don't have something to say everyone will think I'm pathetic');
- unconditional beliefs (e.g. 'I'm boring; I'm stupid; I'm weird').

Unrealistic rules are vulnerable to being broken by circumstance, at which point the individual may become self-absorbed and is likely to appraise the self negatively. Conditional assumptions represent exaggerated self–other negative contingencies that contain distortions such as overgeneralization or dichotomous reasoning. Unconditional beliefs in social phobia consist of negative self-concepts in a social domain and are accepted as 'truths' about the self when activated. There may be individual differences in the accessibility of such beliefs, when chronically accessible, individuals with social anxiety are likely also to have low self-esteem.

Anticipatory and post-event processing

While the model depicted in Figure 12.1 focuses primarily on the in-situation mechanisms maintaining social phobia, two other features of the model are important. In anticipation of an anxiety-provoking situation, the person with social phobia typically worries about the forthcoming situation. This takes the form of negative thoughts about what will happen in the situation and may consist of plans of how to cope. Such mental planning or preparation can be viewed as a safety behaviour with the attendant problems as outlined above. A problem with anticipatory processing is that it is invariably negative and it primes the individual for dysfunctional self-focused processing prior to entering the social situation. The individual is often in a state of chronic readiness for maladaptive self-processing prior to entering the feared social situation. Thus, the stage is set for a diminished ability to engage in other types of attentional processing capable of disconfirming negative beliefs.

On leaving the social situation, negative self-relevant processing does not necessarily cease. Individuals with social phobia have a tendency to go over aspects of the social situation in the form of a mental post mortem. Since attention was dominated by self-processing in the social situation, the post-mortem is based predominantly on how the individual felt, and on the distorted impression of the self. This bias in processing contributes to the maintenance of a negative impression of the self and of social performance. There is little information available in the post mortem capable of disconfirming the individual's social fears.

Empirical support for the model

Evidence from several sources is consistent with key features of the model:

1 Data from individuals with social phobia and high socially anxious subjects show that these individuals report heightened self-focused attention, (Fenigstein, Scheier and Buss, 1975; Hope and Heimberg, 1988).

2 High socially anxious subjects negatively appraise their own social performance (Rapee and Lim, 1992; Stopa and Clark, 1993).

3 Social phobics overestimate how anxious they appear to others (McEwan and Devins, 1983).

4 Compared to low socially anxious subjects, high socially anxious subjects have poorer memory for the details of a recent social interaction (Kimble and Zehr, 1982; Daly, Vangelisti and Lawrence, 1989; Hope, Heimberg and Klein, 1990).

5 Social phobics show an observer perspective in images of recent anxiety provoking social situations, and a field perspective for non-social situations (Wells, Clark and Ahmad, 1998). Evidence suggests that the observer perspective is relatively specific to disorders involving social anxiety (Wells and Papageorgiou, 1999). In addition, it appears that observer perspective images occur spontaneously in social phobia (Hackmann, Suraway and Clark, 1998).

6 Post-event processing (post mortem) is greater in high socially anxious individuals than low socially anxious individuals, and such thoughts are intrusive (Rachman, Grüter-Andrews and Shafran, in press).

A cognitive therapy approach

In the model outlined above, a number of processes lead to the persistence of social anxiety. Treatment based on the model (Wells and Clark, 1995) consists of a range of interlocking strategies designed to modify the cognitive and behavioural factors involved in the maintenance of social anxiety. The main components of this treatment are described in this section and for a detailed account the interested reader should consult Wells (1997).

In order to potentiate cognitive-affective change, a particular treatment sequence is specified. Initially, an idiosyncratic case formulation is derived based on the cognitive model. Socialization in the model is accomplished through verbal methods and behavioural experiments. Behavioural experiments are used early in treatment not only to socialize the patient but to commence modification of attention and behaviours that could otherwise retard cognitive-emotional change. In particular, initial socialization experiments are intended to configure the patient's cognitive system in a way that maximizes disconfirmatory processing. To this end, specific practice is given in dropping safety behaviours and shifting to external focused attention during exposure to feared social situations. If attention remains self-focused, and/or the individual continues to engage in safety behaviours during exposure to social threat, it is less likely that the individual will process information capable of modifying the negative appraisals and beliefs underlying anxiety. Following this stage of treatment, therapy then focuses on modifying the negative self-image using videotape and audio-tape feedback. Later sessions of treatment focus on testing specific predictions based on the individual's negative appraisals, and finally on modifying underlying assumptions and beliefs about social performance and the self as a social object. Each of these stages of treatment will briefly be described in turn.

Deriving a case formulation

An idiosyncratic version of the model should be generated by reviewing a recent episode in which the individual felt socially anxious. This is reviewed in fine detail and each component of the model is elicited. This task is complicated when individuals are highly avoidant and have difficulty recalling a recent situation in which they felt anxious. In these circumstances, it is helpful to discuss the thoughts and feelings occurring in the initial therapeutic sessions. Alternatively, when social situations are highly specific, a Behavioural Assessment Test (BAT) should be run involving exposure to an analogue or real social situation. This process enables the patient and therapist to activate and elicit 'hot' cognitions. Construction of a case formulation depends on eliciting information concerning:

- initial negative automatic thoughts just prior to or on exposure to the social situation;
- anxiety symptoms;
- safety behaviours intended to avert feared catastrophes and/or conceal symptoms;
- the contents of self-consciousness.

A high degree of detail is required in each of these domains since subsequent interventions are based on manipulating specific safety behaviours and testing the details of the individual's negative self-image.

The following are examples of the types of questions that are useful for eliciting components of the situational case formulation.

Negative automatic thoughts (about feared social catastrophe)

- Just before, or on entering the situation, did you have any negative thoughts?
- What did you think might happen?
- What is the worst that could happen?
- Were you worried what other people might think of you?
- What were you worried about?

Anxiety symptoms

- When you began to feel anxious, what symptoms did you notice?
- What were the physical symptoms?
- Did you have any mental symptoms such as difficulty concentrating or poor memory?

Safety behaviours

- When you felt anxious and thought ('Negative Automatic Thought'), did you do anything to prevent that from happening? What did you do?
- Did you do anything to conceal or hide your symptoms? What was that?
- Did you do anything to try and create a good impression? What did you do?
- How does (safety behaviour) prevent (feared catastrophe) from happening? (e.g. 'How does rehearsing sentences in your mind prevent people thinking you are foolish'?)

Self-processing

- When you were in the social situation, how self-conscious did you feel?
- What were you most self-conscious of?

- Did you have an impression of how you think you looked?
- What did you look like?
- If I could have seen you in that situation, what would I have seen?
- How would anxiety be apparent in your behaviour or in the way you looked?

A case formulation based on an interview consisting of these types of questions is presented in Figure 12.2.

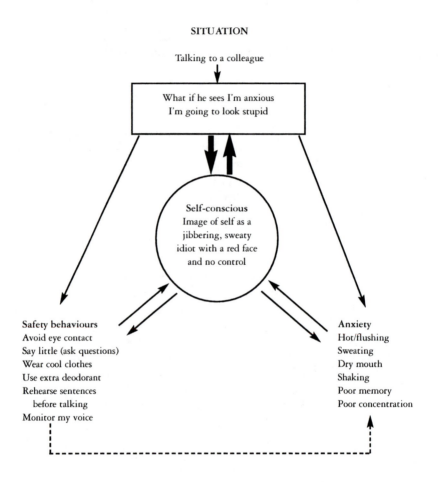

Figure 12.2 An idiosyncratic social anxiety case conceptualization

Socialization and cognitive-behavioural preparation

The next step in treatment consists of socialization to the model and involves illustrating links between thoughts, feelings, and emotion. To accomplish this, therapist and patient review the idiosyncratic case formulation. The therapist uses a Socratic dialogue and guided discovery with the aim of enabling the patient to understand how negative thoughts, safety behaviours and self-consciousness interact in maintaining social anxiety. This is followed by a socialization experiment, which also provides cognitive preparation for subsequent exposure exercises. The experiment consists of an increased and decreased safety behaviours manipulation. Decreasing of safety behaviours is combined with shifting attention towards the external environment. In this experiment, patients are exposed to real or analogue social situations for a brief period (e.g. five minutes), and asked to increase the intensity and range of safety behaviours used. Exposure is then repeated whilst the individual stops engaging in safety behaviours and shifts to external focused attention on other people in the environment. The degree of anxiety, self-consciousness, and specific predictions concerning the consequences of dropping safety behaviours are tested. For instance, one patient who was fearful of making formal presentations in front of a group was asked to talk about himself for five minutes in front of four of the therapist's colleagues. He did this while increasing safety behaviours and then was asked to repeat the exercise while abandoning his safety behaviours and shifting to external attention. He was asked to predict what would happen if he dropped his safety behaviours. He predicted that he would appear more anxious and be unable to speak. Contrary to his prediction, on dropping his safety behaviours and shifting to external focused attention, the patient was able to discover that his symptoms actually improved and he began to feel less self-conscious. In this instance, the increased and decreased safety behaviours manipulation was used to socialise in the model (i.e. illustrate the unhelpful role of self-attention and safety behaviours) while also presenting an initial challenge to a negative prediction. At this stage of treatment, homework assignments typically consist of exposure to specific situations while practising the abandonment of safety behaviours plus external focused attention.

Video feedback

Once the patient is socialized to the model and preliminary attentional and safety-behaviours manipulations have been implemented in conjunction with exposure, attention is turned to modifying the individual's distorted self-image. Video feedback provides an effective technique for correcting the patient's distorted self-image and beliefs about how visible anxiety symptoms are to other people. However, this procedure should be implemented in a particular way to avoid some potential difficulties. A difficulty with video feedback is that watching oneself on video often increases self-consciousness and feelings of embarrassment, and leads to negative self-evaluation. These are the type of responses that therapy aims to counteract, but which also interfere with processing of the actual observable self depicted. Thus, there is a danger that the patient, when exposed to video feedback, will not accurately process the videotaped image from an external and objective standpoint. In some cases, an individual may confuse feeling uncomfortable while watching the video with the idea that he or she must look uncomfortable in the video itself. A further potential problem is that an individual may notice an aspect of his/her performance that was not previously a focus of concern, but which subsequently becomes such a focus.

The video feedback procedure has been designed in a particular way to overcome these problems. Patients are encouraged to review in fine detail and operationalize in concrete observable terms the nature of observable symptoms and inadequacies in performance. A complete list of such responses should be constructed. For example, in operationalizing these responses, a patient concerned about having a furrowed brow was asked to instruct the therapist to model this type of response so that its conspicuousness could be clearly identified. Similarly, a patient fearful of blushing was shown different coloured cards and asked to identify the colour of her own blush. Moreover, the extent of the area affected was clearly identified and quantified. This process of operationalization and detailed analysis can be thought of as constructing and running a 'mental video' against which the actual video is compared. Following this initial phase, patients are asked to watch the video as if from another person's perspective and the therapist checks the conspicuousness of each of the symptoms on the video against those in the mental video. This procedure may have to be repeated with fine adjustments in order fully to modify the patient's distorted self-image. In order to implement video feedback the patient should be videotaped while engaging in a feared social activity. Typically, we have a video running throughout treatment, and we usually use the video of the increased/decreased safety-behaviours manipulation for feedback purposes. It is important to ensure that the patient actually felt anxious during the videotaped exercise that will be used. If this is not the case the discrepancy between the video-image and the self-image can be attributed to a lack of anxiety.

Challenging specific fears

Verbal and behavioural reattribution methods are used in therapy to modify specific fears and predictions. Verbal methods include reviewing the evidence that supports negative automatic thoughts. This evidence usually stems from self-appraisal rather than from objective events and this conclusion can be sought through guided discovery. In some cases tangible evidence does exist and the goodness of this evidence is then collaboratively reviewed with the aim of questioning its validity, reframing its meaning, or considering strategies for changing problematic situations. The predominant thinking errors evident in negative automatic thoughts, such as mind-reading (e.g. 'she thinks I'm boring'), catastrophizing (e.g. 'I'll completely lose it and look stupid'), and personalization (e.g. 'he is not talking to me, he must think I'm stupid') can be identified and used to weaken the validity of negative appraisals.

Although verbal reattribution procedures are useful for weakening belief in negative appraisals and for presenting a mental set emphasizing cognitive reattribution, behavioural experiments provide an indispensable means of testing specific appraisals and beliefs. These experiments provide a way of testing the reactions of others in social situations, and are based on strategies that are intended to interrogate the environment. The P-E-T-S protocol (Wells, 1997) offers a blueprint for implementing behavioural experiments in cognitive therapy of anxiety. In this blueprint, behavioural experiments consist of a phase of Preparation, Exposure, Testing of predictions and Summarizing of the results in terms of the cognitive formulation. Preparation consists of identifying key idiosyncratic negative thoughts or beliefs, and the behaviours (e.g. avoidance, safety behaviours) that prevent disconfirmation of appraisals. In social phobia, thoughts often consist of concerns about negative evaluation by others. It is necessary, therefore, to devise a strategy for assessing the thoughts that other people may have. This may be done by:

1 Making predictions about specific observable behaviours that would be logically derived from particular appraisals (e.g. if someone thinks you are boring, how will that person behave towards you. What will you see?)
2 Using probe questions that seek to determine what people noticed and what they thought in an actual situation.

Following identification of a means of assessing reactions and thoughts, experiments consist of exposure to feared situations while the individual behaves in a manner that is intended to test the appraisal or prediction. This behaviour forms the test phase of the behavioural experiment. Examples of such tests include deliberately focusing on other people to determine their reactions; and deliberately showing signs of anxiety or failed performance in order to examine how others really react. As we have seen, early in treatment behavioural experiments consist of exposure to situations plus the abandonment of safety behaviours, in which the abandonment of safety behaviours is a disconfirmatory manoeuvre or test of predictions. Finally, the results of behavioural experiments are interpreted and summarized in terms of the cognitive model and belief in negative thoughts or predictions is reassessed in the light of the experimental results. To enhance compliance with experimental procedures of this kind, behavioural experiments are undertaken in the therapy session and are guided by the therapist. Experiments can then be repeated for homework, in order further to challenge negative predictions and belief in negative thoughts. Compliance with experiments can be facilitated by the therapist performing experiments while being observed by the patient. For instance, a patient treated recently was fearful of drinking in public, fearing that he would shake uncontrollably, spill his drink, and this would lead everyone to stare at him. In order to test this out, the patient and therapist set aside time in a therapy session to visit a local tea-room. The patient was not willing deliberately to shake and spill some of his drink (the test component of the behavioural experiment) and so the therapist executed this experiment while the patient observed the reactions of others. The experiment consisted of deliberately shaking and spilling some tea into a saucer while carrying it to a table to be seated. The patient was surprised to notice that no one paid a significant amount of attention to the therapist, despite the fact that the cup and saucer were audibly rattling as the therapist deliberately trembled.

In summary, behavioural experiments involve exposure to feared situations and the manipulation of behaviours that permit a direct test of negative thoughts. Avoidance of situations provides a marker for behavioural experiments that should be used to test idiosyncratic thoughts and predictions underlying avoidance. Exposure of this kind constitutes a central feature of cognitive therapy based on the model. Much of the mid- to late therapy sessions are devoted to specific experimental tests of thoughts and beliefs involving exposure-based manipulations.

Bandwidth manoeuvres

It is common for people with social anxiety to restrict their social behaviour in social situations. Some individuals have led restricted social lives for many years and operate within the confines of restricted behavioural repertoires. For example, a patient may refrain from making complaints in public, refrain from asking for direction from strangers, or may remain quiet in group situations and try to blend into the background. While this apparent timidity or shyness is likely to be a reflection of safety behaviours, over an extended period these behaviours lead to a confined social experience. Bandwidth manoeuvres are intended to increase the range of behaviours that the patient believes are acceptable. Typically, this involves engaging in behaviours that are considered to be socially 'dangerous' so that the individual can discover that a wide range of behaviours are acceptable and do not lead to irretrievable loss of self-worth or loss of face. The deliberate commission of unacceptable behaviours (e.g. acting restlessly in a waiting room) allows the individual to discover that it is not necessary continuously to monitor and control behaviour and blend into the background. Procedures of this kind can be seen as an extension of behavioural experiments. Aside from using them to challenge specific idiosyncratic appraisals and beliefs they can also be used for the acquisition of knowledge concerning what is acceptable and safe behaviour in a social context.

Modifying assumptions and beliefs

The strategies already reviewed for challenging predictions and negative thoughts can also be used to challenge assumptions and beliefs. Negative self-appraisals elicited and modified early in treatment will often be direct reflections of underlying beliefs and assumptions. Conditional assumption can be treated in the same manner as predictions, and unrealistic rules for social performance may be conceptualized as factors underlying narrow bandwidth behaviours and are thus amenable to test by behavioural experiments and bandwidth widening strategies.

Core beliefs concerning the social self (e.g. 'I'm foolish, I'm boring, I'm unlikeable'), appear to vary in their persistence. These types of beliefs should be conceptualized as vulnerability markers for the development of subsequent problems. Core beliefs are often held as unquestioned and oversimplified constructions of the self and others in a social domain. Because they are simplified and unquestioned, a preliminary strategy for weakening these beliefs consists of defining the constructs represented in them and questioning the evidence for the belief. A particular sequence of strategies for belief modification of this kind (Wells, 1997) is as follows:

- Carefully define the central dysfunctional concept. For instance, if a patient believes 'I am inadequate', it is necessary to generate a detailed definition of inadequacy. This renders a belief more tangible and facilitates a logical reanalysis.
- Generate a full range of characteristics that define or constitute inadequacy. Follow this by systematically evaluating the number of characteristics the patient actually has. The aim here is to establish that the patient has few of the defining characteristics.
- The distorted nature of the belief should be emphasized and evidence in support of the belief examined. Supporting evidence should be reinterpreted and counter-evidence collected and considered.
- A replacement self-belief should be specified which can be used as a self-statement whenever the negative belief becomes activated.
- The patient should be encouraged to behave in new ways that are capable of sustaining the replacement self-belief. A useful strategy here is the development of a new 'script' for social behaviour that increases the propensity of positive social feedback from other people.

Other common strategies for dealing with maladaptive beliefs include the positive data log in which the patient is asked to record information that is inconsistent with the old belief but consistent with the new belief. This strategy is also used for counteracting selective attention to negative experiences, and can be completed on a daily basis.

Dealing with anticipatory processing and the post mortem

During the course of treatment, strategies are used that lead to an interruption and discontinuation of anticipatory and post-event worrying. In dealing with anticipatory processing, an advantages/disadvantages analysis of this activity is undertaken. This strategy is intended to increase motivation for relinquishing anticipatory processing. Ideally, more disadvantages than advantages should be generated and emphasized. Typical disadvantages include focusing excessively on feelings and not facts, that anticipatory processing is rarely accurate, it focuses attention on negative events and is not balanced, it increases anxiety, leads to over-preparation, acts as a safety behaviour that prevents disconfirmation, and increases self-consciousness. Once the disadvantages have been established, the patient can then be asked simply to modify anticipatory processing, and a new plan for anticipatory processing that does not involve excessive rehearsal and preoccupation with negative events can be constructed and practised. For instance, a dysfunctional anticipatory processing strategy may consist of devoting many hours to repeatedly rehearsing a presentation, and trying to imagine problems that could arise and ways of dealing with them. An alternative strategy may consist of preparing a presentation and rehearsing this only twice, and engaging in some alternative activity the evening before the presentation.

The post mortem should also be subject to an advantages and disadvantages analysis. Moreover, the distorted nature of the post mortem should be emphasized. It is important to show that the individual's post mortem consists of reviewing how he or she felt in social situations and this does not necessarily accurately reflect what actually happened in those situations or how he or she was seen by others. One particular strategy consists of asking the patient to run a post mortem in the therapy session, and asking him or her to shift perspectives, to give a description of the social environment, and how other people were reacting. This shift in perspective can establish that little external social information has been encoded. Once the disadvantages and the biased nature of the post mortem are established, the patient can be simply asked to ban post mortem processing following social encounters.

Relapse prevention

Towards the end of therapy, an increasing amount of therapeutic time is devoted to issues of relapse prevention. Typically, patients are asked to write a detailed summary of the information learned during the course of treatment. This summary consists of examples of the idiosyncratic case conceptualization and an account of the mechanisms responsible for maintaining social anxiety coupled with specific strategies the individual has found useful for overcoming fear and self-consciousness.

At this stage of treatment, any remaining avoidance of social situations is indicative of underlying, unresolved fears. Residual fears and avoidance should be conceptualized and dealt with before termination of regular therapy. Following treatment, booster sessions are typically scheduled at 3 and 6 months.

Empirical evaluation of specific therapeutic strategies

Empirical support for the effectiveness of specific therapeutic components of the present treatment has emerged from a number of studies:

1 Social phobic patients show greater decrements in anxiety and negative beliefs during brief exposure to idiosyncratic feared situations when they abandon their safety behaviours compared with when they use their safety behaviours. In this study, instructions to abandon safety behaviours were presented in the context of a cognitive therapy rationale that emphasized dropping safety behaviours as a disconfirmatory strategy. In the contrasting condition, an exposure-based rationale was presented (Wells, Clark, Salkovskis, Ludgate, Hackmann and Gelder, 1995).
2 In a comparison of one session of brief exposure alone, with one session of brief exposure plus external attention focus in which patients were asked to enter an idiosyncratic feared social situation under both conditions, exposure plus external attention was significantly more effective in reducing in-situation anxiety and negative beliefs. This condition was also superior in shifting patients away from an observer perspective to a field perspective in post-exposure images of the anxiety-provoking social situation (Wells and Papageorgiou, 1998).
3 Cognitive preparation involving clear operationalization of conspicuous symptoms, in conjunction with video feedback, is more effective than video feedback alone in modifying the distorted self-image of individuals with social phobia (Harvey, Clark, Ehlers and Rapee, in press).

Efficacy of treatment

To date, two studies have been conducted investigating the effectiveness of the new treatment. In a pilot evaluation by Clark and Wells, (reported by Clark, 1999), fifteen patients with social phobia were treated with individual cognitive therapy. Almost all of these patients had generalized social phobia. Significant improvements were observed on all specific social anxiety measures and on general measures. Of particular note, patients' change in Fear of Negative Evaluation was such that at follow-up the average score fell within the range of the general population mean. Thus, initial indications are that cognitive changes following this treatment are greater than for existing interventions. In a large-scale follow-up randomized trial, Clark and colleagues have demonstrated that the treatment is superior to a pharmacological intervention (Fluoxetine) plus exposure, and placebo plus exposure at post-treatment (at the time of writing, follow-up data are not yet fully available).

Brief treatment

While preliminary indications are that the new treatment is effective, a course of treatment consists of up to sixteen individual sessions. With greater clinical experience in delivering the treatment and on the basis of empirical studies that have explored the consequences of specific therapeutic strategies, Wells and Papageorgiou (in press) have devised a brief form of this new treatment. In a single case series, six consecutively referred patients meeting DSM-IV criteria for social phobia received a mean of 5.5 treatment sessions (1-hour duration each). The number of treatment sessions ranged from four to eight. Self-ratings of self-consciousness were used as a treatment termination criterion. Treatment was terminated when patients' self-consciousness ratings for the preceding week reached a level of 1 on a 0–8 rating scale, and this level could not be attributed to increased social avoidance. This criterion was selected as self-focused attention is viewed as a general marker for maladaptive beliefs and processes in emotional disorders (Wells and Matthews, 1994) and it is linked to the maintenance of anxiety in the Clark and Wells model of social phobia.

Brief cognitive therapy differed from full cognitive therapy in several respects. Particular components of the full treatment were either enhanced, abbreviated or omitted. Brief treatment focused more on modifying excessive self-focused attention and providing detailed instructions to ban and postpone worry in the form of anticipatory and post-event processing. Moreover, at least two *in vivo* behavioural experiments, aimed at disconfirming negative beliefs and thoughts, were implemented in each treatment session. These experiments adhered strictly to the P-E-T-S protocol as outlined by Wells (1997) for facilitating optimal change. Consistent with full cognitive therapy, the brief treatment incorporated video feedback methods. The results showed that brief treatment was highly effective and patients showed a 57 per cent improvement in dysfunctional cognitions as measured by the Fear of Negative Evaluation questionnaire. Gains on all measures were maintained at three and six months follow-up. Figure 12.3 shows mean social phobia scores for these patients at pre- and post-treatments and at six-month follow-up. This treatment was delivered by a trained cognitive therapist under close supervision, and the results need replicating; however, it appears that abbreviated forms of the treatment can be highly effective.

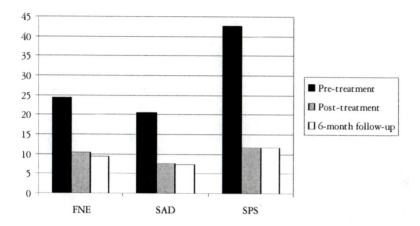

FNE refers to Fear of Negative Evaluation and SAD to Social Avoidance and Distress (Watson and Friend, 1969); SPS refers to Social Phobia Scale (Mattick and Clarke, 1989)

Figure 12.3 Mean social phobia ratings at pre- and post-treatment and at follow-up after brief treatment

Summary and conclusions

As cognitive models have become more specific and sophisticated in describing the interplay of mechanisms that maintain disorders, the content of cognitive therapy treatments has been refined. The perspective adopted here does not assume that individuals with social anxiety have a deficit in social skills. The model predicts that socially anxious individuals experience difficulty in social situations and manifest inhibition in behaviour as a consequence of cognitive interference produced by self-focused processing and particular safety behaviours. The fear of negative evaluation experienced by people with social anxiety is influenced by the individual's negative self-processing which occurs as an image or 'felt sense' depicting appearance. In treatment, modification of negative beliefs and appraisals is based predominantly around strategies that manipulate the individual's coping behaviours and attentional processes in a way that leads to disconfirmation of maladaptive social self-knowledge. An early aim of treatment is to increase the flow of corrective information that the individual can use to revise negative appraisals and beliefs. This is achieved by reorienting attention and by combining exposure with manipulations of attention and safety behaviours in the form of experimental tests of predictions and appraisals.

The extent to which the model presented here and the treatment can be applied to cases of shyness remains to be established. Some commentators have argued that shyness is not synonymous with social anxiety (e.g. Buss,

1980; Leary, 1983), but shyness may be seen as a sub-type of social anxiety. Leary (1986) defines shyness as 'combining both social anxiety and inhibited (e.g. withdrawn, reticent) behaviour, resulting from the prospect or presence of interpersonal evaluation'. It is conceivable that the inhibition thought to characterize shyness may well be accounted for by mechanisms presented in the present model. For instance, inhibition may be the observed objective consequence of engaging in particular safety behaviours such as avoiding self-disclosure, saying little, or avoiding eye contact as a means of concealing anxiety and averting appraised catastrophes. Similarly, inhibition may result from the adherence to rigid rules for social performance or be a product of excessive self-focused processing that interferes with more spontaneous engagement with social situations.

References

American Psychiatric Association (1987) *Diagnostic and Statistical Manual of Mental Disorders* (3rd edn, revised), Washington, DC: American Psychiatric Association.

American Psychiatric Association (1994) *Diagnostic and Statistical Manual of Mental Disorders* (4th edn.), Washington, DC: American Psychiatric Association.

Beck, A.T. (1976) *Cognitive Therapy and the Emotional Disorders*, New York: International Universities Press.

Buss, A.H. (1980) *Self-consciousness and Social Anxiety*, San Francisco, CA: Freeman.

Butler, G., Cullington, A., Munby, M., Amies, P. and Gelder, M.(1984) 'Exposure and anxiety management in the treatment of social phobia', *Journal of Consulting and Clinical Psychology*, 52: 642–50.

Clark, D.M. (1999) 'Anxiety disorders: why they persist and how to treat them', *Behaviour Research and Therapy*, 37: 5–27 (Special issue).

Clark, D.M. and Wells, A. (1995) 'A cognitive model of social phobia', in R.G. Heimberg, M. Liewbowitz, D.A. Hope and F.R. Scheier (eds) *Social Phobia: Diagnosis, Assessment and Treatment* (pp. 69–93), New York: Guilford Press.

Daly, J.A., Vangelisti, A.I. and Lawrence, S.G. (1989) 'Self-focused attention and public speaking anxiety', *Personality and Individual Differences*, 10: 903–13.

DiGiuseppe, R., McGowan, L., Sutton-Simon, K. and Gardner, F. (1990) 'A comparative outcome study of four cognitive therapies in the treatment of social anxiety', *Journal of Rational-Emotive and Cognitive-Behaviour Therapy*, 8: 129–46.

Emmelkamp, P.M.G., Mersch, P.P., Vissia, E. and van der Helm, M. (1985) 'Social phobia: a comparative evaluation of cognitive and behavioural interventions', *Behaviour Research and Therapy*, 23: 365–9.

Fenigstein, A., Scheier, M.F. and Buss, A.H. (1975) 'Public and private self-consciousness: assessment and theory', *Journal of Consulting and Clinical Psychology*, 43: 522–7.

Hackmann, A., Suraway, C. and Clark, D.M. (1998) 'Seeing yourself through others' eyes: a study of spontaneously occurring images in social phobia', *Behavioural and Cognitive Psychotherapy*, 26: 3–12.

Harvey, A.G., Clark, D.M., Ehlers, A. and Rapee, R.M. (in press) 'Social anxiety and self-impression: cognitive preparation enhances the beneficial effects of video feedback following a stressful task', *Behaviour Research and Therapy*.

Heimberg, R.G. and Barlow, D.H. (1988) 'Psychosocial treatment for social phobia', *Psychosomatics*, 29: 27–37.

Heimberg, R.G. and Juster, H.R. (1994) 'Treatment of social phobia in cognitive-behavioural groups', *Journal of Clinical Psychiatry*, 55: 38–46.

Heimberg, R.G., Liebowitz, M., Hope, D.A., *et al.* (1998) 'Cognitive behavioral group therapy vs phenelzine therapy for social phobia', *Archives of General Psychiatry*, 55: 1133–41.

Heimberg, R.G., Saltzman, D.G., Holt, C.S. and Blendell, K.A. (1993) 'Cognitive behavioral group treatments for social phobia: effectiveness at five-year follow-up', *Cognitive Therapy and Research*, 14: 1–23.

Holt, C.S., Heimberg, R.G. and Hope, D.A. (1992) 'Avoidant personality disorder and the generalised sub-type of social phobia', *Journal of Abnormal Psychology*, 101: 318–25.

Hope, D.A. and Heimberg, R.G. (1988) 'Public and private self-consciousness and social anxiety', *Journal of Personality Assessment*, 52: 629–39.

Hope, D.A., Heimberg, R.G. and Klein, J.F. (1990) 'Social anxiety and the result of interpersonal feedback', *Journal of Cognitive Psychotherapy*, 4: 185–95.

Kimble, C.E. and Zehr, H.D. (1982) 'Self-consciousness, information load, self-presentation and memory in a social situation', *Journal of Social Psychology*, 118: 39–46.

Leary, M.R. (1983) *Understanding Social Anxiety: Social, Personality, and Clinical Perspectives*, Beverly Hills, CA: Sage.

Leary, M.R. (1986) 'Affective and behavioural components of shyness: implications for theory, measurement and research', in W.H. Jones, J.M. Check and S.R. Briggs (eds) *Shyness: Perspectives on Research and Treatment* (pp. 27–38), New York: Plenum Press.

Marzillier, J.S., Lambert, C. and Kellet, J. (1976) 'A controlled evaluation of social skills training for socially inadequate psychiatric patients', *Behaviour Research and Therapy*, 14: 225–38.

Mattick, R.P. and Clarke, J.C. (1989) 'Development and validation of measures of social interaction anxiety', Unpublished manuscript.

McEwan, K.L. and Devins, G.M. (1983) 'Is increased arousal in social phobia noticed by others?' *Journal of Abnormal Psychology*, 92: 417–21.

Rachman, S., Grüter-Andrew, J. and Shafran, R. (in press) 'Post-event processing in social anxiety', *Behaviour Research and Therapy*.

Rapee, R.M. and Lim, L. (1992) 'Discrepancy between self and observer ratings of performance in social phobics', *Journal of Abnormal Psychology*, 181: 728–31.

Stopa, L. and Clark, D.M. (1993) 'Cognitive processes in social phobia', *Behaviour Research and Therapy*, 31: 255–67.

Taylor, S. (1996) 'Meta-analysis of cognitive-behavioural treatments for social phobia', *Journal of Behavior Therapy and Experimental Psychiatry*, 27: 1–9.

Trower, P., Yardley, K., Bryant, B. and Shaw, P. (1978) 'The treatment of social failure: a comparison of anxiety reduction and skills acquisition procedures on two social problems', *Behaviour Modification*, 2: 41–60.

Watson, D. and Friend, R. (1969) 'Measurement of social-evaluative anxiety', *Journal of Consulting and Clinical Psychology*, 33: 448–57.

Wells, A. (1997) *Cognitive Therapy of Anxiety Disorders: A Practice Manual and Conceptual Guide*, Chichester, Sussex: Wiley.

Wells, A. and Clark, D.M. (1995) *Cognitive Therapy of Social Phobia: A Treatment Manual*, Oxford University Press.

Wells, A., Clark, D.M. and Ahmad, S. (1998) 'How do I look with my mind's eye: perspective taking in social phobic imagery', *Behaviour Research and Therapy*, 36: 631–4.

Wells, A., Clark, D.M., Salkovskis, P., Ludgate, J., Hackmann, A. and Gelder, M. (1995) 'Social phobia: the role of in-situation safety behaviours in maintaining anxiety and negative beliefs', *Behavior Therapy*, 26: 153–61.

Wells, A. and Matthews, G. (1994) *Attention and Emotion: A Clinical Perspective*, Hove, Sussex: Erlbaum.

Wells, A. and Matthews, G. (1996) 'Modelling cognitive in emotional disorder: the S-REF Model', *Behaviour Research and Therapy*, 34: 881–8.

Wells, A. and Papageorgiou, C. (1998) 'Social phobia: effects of external attention on anxiety, negative beliefs, and perspective taking', *Behavior Therapy*, 29: 357–70.

Wells, A. and Papageorgiou, C. (1999) 'The observer perspective: biased imagery in social phobia, agoraphobia, and blood/injury phobia', *Behaviour Research and Therapy*, 37: 653–8.

Wells, A. and Papageorgiou, C. (in press) 'Brief cognitive therapy of social phobia: a single case series', *Behaviour Research and Therapy*.

13 Challenges in the treatment of generalized social phobia

Why our treatments work, and why they don't work better

Jonathan M. Oakman, Peter Farvolden,
Michael Van Ameringen and Catherine Mancini

This chapter may seem like a bit of an oddity; it is a chapter about challenges in the treatment of generalized social phobia (GSP) that appears in a book about shyness. In comparison with the literature on shyness and its treatment, the literature on the assessment and treatment of social phobia is very new. However, when people present for treatment because of extreme social anxiety, they receive a diagnosis of social phobia (DSM-IV) rather than a diagnosis of 'shyness'. Although there has been an unfortunate lack of communication between researchers interested in the study of shyness and those interested in the study of social phobia, excellent summaries of both the treatment of shyness and the treatment of GSP are available elsewhere (e.g. Jones, Cheek and Briggs, 1986; Heimberg, Leibowitz, Hope and Schneier, 1995). It is not our purpose to provide another review of these literatures. Rather, we would like to describe our current attempt to integrate the shyness and social phobia literature that we hope will improve our understanding and treatment of patients with social phobia.

Social phobia, or social anxiety disorder, is distinct from other anxiety disorders, including agoraphobia and specific phobias. As described in the DSM-IV (American Psychiatric Association, 1994), persons with social phobia avoid a wide variety of social and performance situations in which they are exposed to unfamiliar persons or to possible scrutiny by others. The individual with social phobia fears that he or she will do something or will show anxiety symptoms that will result in humiliation or embarrassment.

Several treatments have been found to be effective in the treatment of social phobia, including pharmacotherapy and cognitive-behavioural therapy (CBT). Current practice in the psychotherapeutic treatment of generalized social phobia is dominated by CBT. However, the CBT treatment of generalized social phobia is not without controversy. Beidel and Turner (1986) and Sweet and Loizeaux (1991) have argued that there is little evidence that a focus on thoughts in treatment adds anything to a strictly behavioural orientation. Chambless and Gillis (1993), in reviewing cognitive therapy for anxiety disorders, found that 'although clearly effective with the socially phobic clinical population, CBT is not consistently superior to behavioral treatments' (p. 255). Similarly, Taylor's (1996) meta-analytic review also reveals roughly equivalent effect sizes for cognitive therapy (.63 at endpoint, .96 at three-month follow-up), behaviour therapy (.82 at endpoint, .93 at three-month follow-up), and CBT (1.06 at endpoint, 1.08 at three-month follow-up) in the treatment of social phobia. Finally, although cognitive-behavioural treatment for social phobia can be very effective (Heimberg and Juster, 1995; Taylor, 1996), it is unfortunately unavailable to many patients except in large urban areas or academic centres. As a result, pharmacotherapy is often the most practical treatment option for most patients with social phobia.

Current practice in the pharmacological treatment of generalized social phobia is dominated by the use of SSRI medications. There is also evidence that MAOIs are effective, although their use is circumscribed due to an undesirable side effect profile. There is limited evidence that benzodiazepines, gabapentin, buproprion, and clonidine may also be effective (Van Ameringen, Mancini, Farvolden and Oakman, 1999; Van Ameringen, Mancini, Oakman and Farvolden, 1999). Although effective medications target a range of neurotransmitter systems to differing extents, the most effective medications target the serotonin system.

Although the effectiveness of the various treatments of generalized social phobia is encouraging, it is disappointing that we know so little about *why* the treatments work. If generalized social phobia is a condition of serotonin dysregulation, the SSRI medications should *cure* it, not merely improve it. Likewise, there is a formidable body of empirical evidence indicating that people with social phobia differ from normal controls in their cognitive functioning (Elting and Hope, 1995; Foa *et al.*, 1996; Wells, this volume, Chapter 12). If fear of negative evaluation is the central concern of GSP, as Turner, Beidel and Townsley (1990) have argued, then interventions targeting evaluation concerns (cognitions) ought to be of primary importance in treatment. However, neither pharmacological nor psychotherapeutic interventions offer cures; most treatment results in improved functioning, but a substantial minority of people with generalized social phobia experience little or no improvement.

We (among others) are currently trying to understand the efficacy of treatments for social phobia and why standard treatments work for many patients but not for others. Our developing model attempts to explain the clinical phenomenology and mixed treatment response of generalized social phobia in terms of what is known about the neurobiology of social phobia.

The neuropsychology of fear

The recent resurgence in interest in understanding the neuropsychology of fear has been heralded as a 'paradigm shift' by Hyman (1998) and popularized by LeDoux's (1996) bestselling book *The Emotional Brain*. This work may inform our understanding of the mechanism of action and efficacy of current treatments of social phobia.

According to LeDoux (1996, 1998) the 'fear circuit' prominently involves the transmission to the amygdala of fear-relevant information via four main routes, three of which are of special relevance. The first route proceeds from the sensory thalamus to the amygdala. The existence of a route which bypasses the neocortex suggests that fear can be learned (and fear responses initiated) without the involvement of higher processing systems in the brain thought to be the seat of thinking and reasoning. This thalamic route is 'faster' than the cortical route, but is capable of less fine distinctions. Lesions in the thalamic route interfere with fear conditioning (associating a stimulus with an aversive consequence). The second route to the amygdala is from the hippocampus to the amygdala, and allows for the instantiation of fear on the basis of context, and the consideration of context when processing fear cues. Finally, LeDoux (1996) argues that the medial prefrontal cortex connects to the amygdala allowing for the process of extinction through prefrontal inhibition of the amygdala.

One implication of this work is that there may be precious little ' thinking' involved in fear. The predominant connections are from thalamic, sensory, and hippocampal regions to the amygdala. These circuits bypass the neocortex. The amygdala then connects to the neocortex, so the cognitive and emotional experience of fear and the activation of defensive behaviour are coincident and relatively late in processing. The thinking and feeling experience of fear can then be seen more as a 'commentary' on the activation of the fear circuit than as causal in the process of fear. If this is the case then there is little opportunity for cognitive interventions to affect the triggering of the fear response.

The reduction in the fear response is apparently mediated by the medial prefrontal cortex (LeDoux, 1998). Damage to the medial prefrontal cortex prolongs the time it takes for extinction of the fear response. In behavioural terms, extinction *requires* exposure to the feared stimulus without the aversive consequent experience. Perhaps by voluntary control mediated by the medial prefrontal cortex, one may be able to mimic the process of extinction. The implication of this is that thinking may be highly relevant in the reduction of fear, even if thinking is not much *causally* involved in fear. This may provide the mechanism of action of cognitive therapy. Reliance on self-generated medial prefrontal activation and inhibition of the amygdala in order to *mimic* the natural occurrence of extinction seems, however, a poor substitute for the actual experience of the stimulus unpaired with the aversive outcome.

Is the fear circuit sufficient to account for social phobia?

While this neuropsychological fear model makes sense of (1) the modest evidence for the efficacy of cognitive techniques in the treatment of social phobia and (2) the relatively consistent evidence for the efficacy of exposure or combined exposure and cognitive therapy, it may not be sufficient to explain treatment response in social phobia.

Both shyness and social phobia seem to be multi-component constructs. While factor analytic studies of shyness measures usually produce findings of one predominant source of variance (e.g. Jones, Briggs and Smith, 1986), many researchers continue to use multi-component descriptions of shyness (e.g. Cheek and Melchoir, 1990). Furthermore, there is much evidence for making a distinction between early developing fearful shyness (quite possibly related to behavioural inhibition) and self-conscious shyness (e.g. Asendorpf, 1989, 1990, 1993; Buss, 1986; Buss and Plomin, 1984). Self-conscious shyness becomes less related to behavioural inhibition as development proceeds, and is additive with fearful shyness in predicting adult inhibition.

Behavioural inhibition refers to fear of the novel or unfamiliar, which may legitimately represent a threat, and for which defensive behaviour (escape, freezing, etc.) may be appropriate. Behavioural inhibition is thought to be related to amygdala excitability (Kagan, Reznick and Snidman, 1988; see Kagan, this volume, Chapter 2) and may well be explained by the fear conditioning model outlined by LeDoux (1996). In contrast, self-conscious shyness refers to a metacognitive concern about how one appears to others. It is something of a stretch to call this a 'fear' rather than a source of anxiety, as the negative opinions of others do not imply immediate harm for which defensive behaviour might be helpful. Therapeutic interventions may demonstrate differential efficacy for the two kinds of shyness. For example, exposure-based CBT might work well for treating fearful shyness, which may in turn be based on the fear circuit described by LeDoux (1996). Self-conscious shyness, however, is a metacognitive concern that may be better approached via cognitive interventions.

Social phobia is also a heterogeneous condition (Rapee, 1995). Some patients report predominant fears in only one social situation (usually public speaking), some report central performance fears (such as eating, drinking, or writing in public), while others fear social interactions, especially with strangers, members of the opposite sex, or authority figures. Some of these social fears may be best explained by a fear conditioning model (LeDoux, 1996). However, other social fears may require a different explanatory model with different implications for treatment.

The ethological relevance of social fear

Trower, Gilbert and Sherling (1990) propose an ethological model of social anxiety that may provide an explanatory framework for the diversity of social fears, and in particular for self-conscious shyness. Following Gilbert (1989), they propose a human defence system composed of three separate systems: the antipredator system, the territorial breeding system, and the group living (agonic) system. The antipredator system is a defence system based on preparedness theory (Seligman, 1971) that has evolved to defend the organism against typical predators. Defects in the antipredator system are likely to be responsible for animal phobias and panic disorder. The territorial breeding system manages distance and proximity for highly territorial animals that do not live in groups. This system allows otherwise solitary animals to meet and breed when they would normally either attack each other or flee. Trower, Gilbert, and Sherling (1990: 17) suggest that this system may form the basis for stranger fears.

More important for humans are the systems that have evolved to allow members of a species to live in groups. The agonic system replaces the territorial breeding system for group-living animals such as apes, monkeys, and humans. The system largely guides dominance and submission, allowing a member of the species to lose a dominance challenge and submit to the dominant member without being forced to relocate. Members of a species can signal non-threat (submission) to each other, and thereby inhibit the dominant member from attacking. Submission is common in primates. Cues for submission include gaze avoidance, crouching, care eliciting, and behaviours that are related to courtship repertoires.

Beyond defensive systems, Trower, Gilbert and Sherling (1990) describe three safety systems: the individual safety system, the attachment system, and the hedonic system. The individual safety system responds to cues of physical safety, and the attachment system maintains the relationship between adult and young and prevents adults from harming or cannibalizing their young. The third safety system is of most interest for our discussion because the hedonic system regulates mutual social interaction and allows for the co-ordination of group behaviour. In contrast to agonic regulation of group behaviour, the hedonic system regulates group relationships via inclusion and affiliation. Behaviours in primates such as hugging, kissing, lip smacking, and other forms of greetings would be part of this behavioural repertoire.

Much 'self-conscious' or 'social-evaluative' social anxiety would be related to the action of the agonic and hedonic systems.[1] Feeling 'lesser than' or 'inferior to' others is commonly reported by people with social phobia who describe feeling angry or challenged, and seem curiously sensitive or hostile in response to the innocuous social overtures of others. Similarly, gaze aversion is commonly reported by people with GSP, and may be related to the basic process of signalling threat or non-threat to other members of a dominance hierarchy. These fears may have their origin in the agonic system.

In contrast, many socially anxious people fear rejection, and are overly acquiescent to the wishes of others. They may worry excessively about being negatively evaluated by others, being disliked, or excluded. These fears could be seen more as hedonic fears – they concern inclusion or affiliation, and seem less oriented to status.

The interpersonal circumplex and social phobia

At the risk of oversimplifying, we could think of the agonic and hedonic social systems as being oriented to two dimensions of social behaviour. The agonic system is concerned with social dominance and submission, while the hedonic system is related to affiliation. These two processes have been studied extensively by personality psychologists under the framework of the interpersonal circumplex.

There are several versions of the interpersonal circumplex (e.g. Kiesler, 1983; Leary, 1957; Wiggins, 1982). Each model posits two main dimensions, one anchored by poles commonly entitled hostile and warm, and the other anchored by poles commonly entitled dominant and submissive (e.g. Figure 13.1).

Although we know of no studies describing GSP in terms of the interpersonal circumplex space, there have been several studies examining Avoidant Personality Disorder (APD) in interpersonal terms. Although GSP and APD are diagnosed separately and appear on different axes of the DSM-IV system, Avoidant Personality Disorder (APD) is highly related to

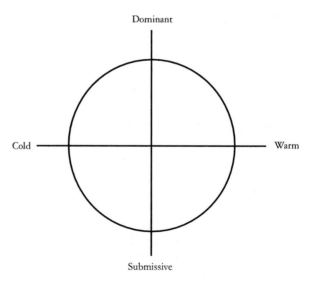

Figure 13.1 The interpersonal circumplex

DSM-IV GSP; the two diagnoses share many defining features. Several researchers (Herbert, Hope and Bellack, 1992; Turner *et al.*, 1986; Turner, Beidel and Townsley, 1992) have argued that APD subsumes GSP, and that the two diagnoses are primarily discriminable on the basis of severity – APD is characterized by more severe social anxiety and poorer social skills.

Soldz *et al.* (1993) examined the interpersonal circumplex location of 102 consecutive personality disorder admissions. They found that APD was located in the cold submissive quadrant, along a diagonal aptly entitled 'socially avoidant'. To the extent that the goal of therapy with people with GSP is to improve interpersonal relatedness, the goal of therapy would be to move them on both dimensions; they would need to become more dominant and also interpersonally warmer.

Casting these findings in the ethological framework of Trower, Gilbert and Sherling (1990), it would seem that people with GSP see themselves as submissive and others as dominant (the agonic system) and feel unlikeable and may dislike others (the hedonic system). The implications of an interpersonal circumplex description of GSP are quite interesting. There are two rules of interpersonal complementarity: (1) submissive behaviour draws dominant behaviour from others; (2) cold behaviour draws cold behaviour from others. According to these rules of complementarity, the interpersonal world of a person with GSP would be populated with cold, dominant people because the interpersonal style of being cold and submissive would draw cold and dominant responses. The social world would inescapably appear to be a pecking order, where most other people would be seen as in a dominant position.

Neuropsychological substrate of dominance and affiliation

Little is known about the neuropsychology of social dominance in humans. However, considerable research has been conducted on social dominance in infrahuman species. We will confine our brief review to studies of primates as they are the closest to us phylogenetically, and different systems guiding social behaviour are likely to have evolved in more advanced animals (Trower, Gilbert and Sherling, 1990). Much of the work on social dominance in primates implicates the role of the neurotransmitter serotonin.

Serotonin in social phobia

Raleigh *et al.* (1991) report a compelling study of the role of serotonin in social dominance in male vervet monkeys. Twelve social groups were studied, each containing three males. Once each group had established a dominance hierarchy, the researchers removed the dominant male from the group. They simultaneously randomly treated one of the remaining males with tryptophan or fluoxetine (Prozac) to increase available serotonin in that monkey, while the other monkey received a drug that decreased serotonin (fenfluramine or cyproheptadine). The monkeys treated with tryptophan or fluoxetine became dominant in all instances. Medication was then discontinued, and the original male was reintroduced to the group. In all instances the original male became dominant again. The dominant male was again removed, and this time the formerly submissive male was treated with fluoxetine or tryptophan to increase serotonin levels, while the formerly dominant male was treated with fenfluramine or cyproheptadine to reduce serotonin levels. In all cases, the animal treated with fluoxetine or tryptophan became dominant.

Interestingly, the mechanism of social dominance in vervet monkeys apparently involves an increase in affiliative behaviour (Raleigh *et al.*, 1980; Raleigh *et al.*, 1985). In the vervet monkey, at least, social dominance is at least in part a function of affiliation, and would be likely to be described as a warm dominant interpersonal orientation in interpersonal circumplex terms.

Higley *et al.* (1996) studied the social behaviour of female rhesus monkeys across a baseline period and following the social stressor of an unfamiliar female being added to the group. They found that females with above average serotonin levels were more likely to attain a dominant status than those with low serotonin levels and argued that competent social behaviour in rhesus monkeys may require average or above average serotonin functioning. Similarly, Westergaard and colleagues (1999) studied female monkeys of both macaque and rhesus species and found that within each species, serotonin levels were negatively correlated with escalated aggression and positively correlated with social dominance rank.

The limited research evidence regarding the role of serotonin in social behaviour of normal adult humans bears a striking similarity to the primate work. Knutson *et al.* (1998) administered paroxetine (an SSRI medication that increases serotonin functioning) or placebo to two groups of psychiatrically healthy volunteers in a double-blind manner. They found that SSRI administration led to a decrease in negative affect (and thereby a decrease in indices of aggression or hostility), but did not alter positive affect. In addition, SSRI administration led to increases on a behavioural index of affiliation, with affiliation correlating $r = .65$ with plasma paroxetine levels.

In summary, serotonin seems related to social dominance, but not to aggression per se. Additionally, the mechanism of change in dominance status seems to require affiliation, with changes in affiliation preceding changes in dominance. Although it is tempting to think of serotonin as controlling friendly social dominance (but not aggression), there is a literature that implicates both lower and higher than normal levels of serotonin in aggressive and violent behaviour in humans (Berman and Coccaro, 1998; Cherek *et al.*, 1999; Moffitt *et al.*, 1998). These observations are somewhat inconsistent with a simple connection of serotonin to dominance. The term 'serotonin syndrome' has been used to describe the diverse collection of symptoms that can result when toxic levels of serotonin are present as the result, for example, of SSRI overdose. However, while aggressive and violent behaviour is occasionally observed as a part of serotonin syndrome, it most often is not (Gillman, 1998; Spigset, 1999). In addition, it is important to note that the behavioural effects of serotonin toxicity may be quite unlike the behavioural effects of high (but in the normal range) serotonin levels.

With this important exception in mind, the behavioural effects of the range of normal serotonin levels can be well characterized. They seem to guide social behaviour oriented to social status. In particular, dominant social status seems associated with high serotonin levels, while low serotonin levels are associated with subordinate status. Additionally, dominant social status seems to be achieved at least partly by affiliative behaviour. Figure 13.2 depicts the hypothesized dimension of serotonin functioning in interpersonal circumplex space. We propose that the dimension may be moderately correlated with both dominance and affiliation. We estimate the angle of the dimension of serotonin action with respect to dominance and affiliation to be at 50 degrees from affiliation (corresponding to a correlation of .65 with affiliation).

Although this work is quite suggestive of the role of serotonin in important social behaviour that may be related to social phobia, it is probably overly optimistic to think that such a complex disorder may simply be related to dysfunction in a single neurotransmitter system. Indeed neurotransmitter systems do not work in isolation, but instead interact with each other in sophisticated and complex ways. Although the pharmacological treatment of GSP with serotonin acting drugs has demonstrated good results, these drugs

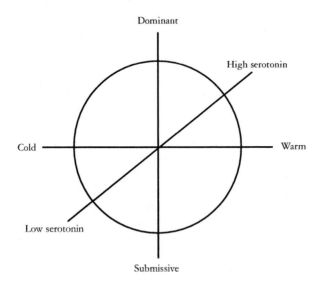

Figure 13.2 The hypothesized effects of serotonin functioning in interpersonal circumplex space

are not completely effective in the majority of cases. It is unlikely that serotonin is the whole story in the neurochemistry of GSP; there may be other neurotransmitter systems involved. One leading candidate for the role of 'best supporting actor' in the neurochemistry of GSP is dopamine.

Dopamine in social phobia

It is interesting that social anxiety disorder is the only anxiety disorder in which there is some evidence of dopaminergic dysfunction. Despite some inconsistent findings regarding the role of dopamine in social phobia (Tancer et al., 1994), recent results of a SPECT study using a specific ligand for the dopamine transporter site revealed reduced binding of dopamine in the basal ganglia of patients with social phobia (Tiihonen et al., 1997). This result suggests the importance of regional alterations in dopaminergic function in social phobia (Nutt et al., 1998; Stein, 1998). Similarly, Schneier et al. (2000) report a SPECT study showing reduced D_2 receptor (a dopamine receptor) binding potential in patients with social phobia. These results are quite interesting given the evidence that social status in monkeys as determined by agonistic interactions is reflected in dopamine D_2 striatal differences (Grant et al., 1998). Grant et al. (1998) interpret this result as a demonstration of the behavioural and physiological consequences of the stress of low social rank.

It is possible that there is a relatively non-specific effect of stress in producing dysregulation in dopaminergic functioning. However, the ascending dopamine system has also been found to play an important role in reward and motivation. For example, Contreras-Vidal and Schultz (1999) have proposed a neural network model of dopamine and prefrontal cortex guidance of reward-related learning of approach behaviour. This model attempts to account for the dopamine responses to novelty, generalization, and discrimination of appetitive and aversive stimuli. Similarly, Koob (1996) has proposed that the function of the mesolimbic dopamine system is to allow or actually release species-specific approach responses. Based on a series of studies of the effects of lesions, receptor blocking, electrical self-stimulation, and drugs of abuse, Schultz (1998) has also suggested that mid-brain dopamine systems are involved in processing reward information and learning approach behaviour. There is a large body of evidence to suggest that the prefrontal cortex (PFC) plays a critical role in the cognitive control of behaviour, including inhibition of behaviour (Cohen et al., 1996). Both the PFC and dopamine are widely implicated in learning and decision-making (Egelman et al., 1998).

Given the abundant evidence for a role for dopamine in responses to novelty, generalization, discrimination of appetitive and aversive stimuli, and the control of approach behaviour, it seems at least possible that dopamine has a role in general systems guiding behavioural approach. Depue et al. (1994) conducted a dopamine D_2 receptor agonist challenge in psychiatrically healthy volunteers. They found that the degree of reactivity in central dopamine activity was strongly related to positive emotionality (r = .75 to r = .90, and when corrected for unreliability, approaching unity), but was unrelated to other personality traits. Positive emotionality is often called extraversion, and was used in this study as a measure of an overall behavioural approach tendency. This finding suggests that the dopamine system may be centrally relevant in approach motivation in humans, and may make sense both of the findings of dopamine abnormalities in social phobia and of the importance ascribed to avoidance in social phobia (in contrast with shyness).

Figure 13.3 depicts the role of dopamine functioning as almost overlapping that of serotonin in interpersonal circumplex space. The theoretical location of extraversion (and therefore dopamine functioning) in interpersonal circumplex space extends at 45 degrees through the warm-dominant quadrant (McCrae and Costa, 1989; Soldz *et al.*, 1993; Trapnell and Wiggins, 1990). It is interesting to note that the extension into the cold-submissive quadrant accords well with findings relating dopamine levels to social dominance (e.g. Grant *et al.*, 1998).

Norepinephrine and neuroticism in social phobia

Soldz *et al.* (1993) argue strongly that the two interpersonal dimensions of warmth and dominance are insufficient to account for all of the variance in interpersonal pathology as measured by DSM-IV Axis II disorders

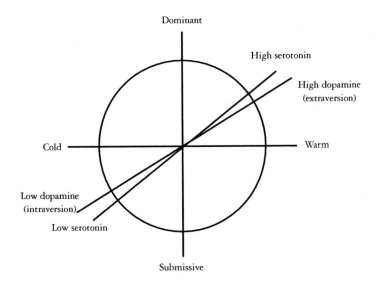

Figure 13.3 The hypothesized effects of dopamine and serononin functioning in interpersonal circumplex space

(Personality Disorders). They found that several personality disorders, in particular Dependent, Self-defeating, and Paranoid personality disorders, fell close to the origin in interpersonal circumplex space, indicating that these disorders were not well explained by the two circumplex dimensions. Soldz *et al.* (1993) argue that Neuroticism (or its opposite Emotional Stability) is what is missing from the circumplex. Neuroticism is also called negative emotionality.

There is certainly much evidence to suggest that norepinephrine plays an important, but probably non-specific role in negative affect states including depression (Ressler and Nemeroff, 1999; Schatzberg, 1998), anxiety (Rosen and Schulkin, 1998), and hostility (Suarez *et al.*, 1998). Another good candidate for explaining general anxiety or stress is Corticotropin Releasing Factor (CRF). It appears that the release of CRF is closely associated with activation of the noradrenergic system and the non-specific stress response (Koob, 1999). With respect to pathological anxiety, it is well known that some combination of genetic predisposition and biological stress may be an important determinant of a non-specific hyper-excitability to fear-inducing stimuli. Such non-specific hyper-excitability to fear-inducing stimuli is usually associated with cortisol, epinephrine, and norepinephrine (Rosen and Schulkin, 1998). The CRF–norepinephrine system guides response to non-specific stress reactions and may underlie the personality dimension of Neuroticism.

Finally, GABA is the brain's main inhibitory neurotransmitter and GABAergic pathways are widely distributed in the central nervous system in close proximity and functional relationship to the benzodiazepine receptors. It seems likely that the GABA/benzodiazepine receptor complex plays a non-specific role in the mediation of anxiety (Coplan and Lydiard, 1998). This may explain the limited evidence of the efficacy of agents that effect the GABA/benzodiazepine complex (gabapentin, benzodiazepines) in the treatment of social phobia.

Motivation as a component of the model

While the model articulated so far makes sense of the findings relating both serotonin and dopamine functioning to social phobia, and of the findings relating dopamine to behavioural approach and serotonin to social dominance, there is an apparent inconsistency inherent in the model. We have described dopamine and serotonin functioning as essentially overlapping dimensions that cut at 45 degrees through interpersonal circumplex space. However, although dopaminergic and serotonergic cells innervate many of the same areas, they are thought to provide *opposing* influences on approach and avoidance behaviour (Cloninger, 1998). In particular, dopamine is thought important in systems that guide behavioural approach, while serotonin is thought important in systems that guide avoidance. The medial prefrontal cortex is thought to be the site of the resolution of such conflicts. In order to understand this apparent paradox, we need to extend our model to include the motivational state of the person.

Gray (1982) argues that there are two primary systems that guide all behaviour: the behavioural activation (BA) system and the behavioural inhibition (BI) system. The BI system is sensitive to cues of punishment and operates to remove the organism from courses of action likely to result in punishment. The BA system is sensitive to cues for reward and operates to guide the organism towards reinforcers. As we have already discussed, dopamine is seen by many as central to approach motivation, and is likely to be central to behavioural activation (e.g. Depue *et al.*, 1994; Koob, 1996). In contrast, serotonin has been implicated in avoidance (e.g. Deakin and Graeff, 1991; Hansenne and Ansseau, 1999). Deakin and Graeff (1991) argue that there are two distinct fear systems: one that results in the experience of anxiety, the behavioural consequence of which is avoidance, and one that results in the experience of panic, the consequence of which is fight or flight. They argue that the anxiety system is primarily mediated by serotonin, and that the panic system is mediated by norepinephrine.

The overlap of serotonin and dopamine in our model can be resolved by taking the characteristic motivational state of the person into account. Reductions in avoidance or increases in reward-driven behaviour have similar behavioural outcomes in terms of the interpersonal circumplex; both lead to increases in affiliation and social dominance.

Limitations and alternatives

We acknowledge that there may be other neurotransmitters relevant to GSP. For example, the proposed model does not explain why agents that affect the tachykinins (e.g. substance P, Neurokinin A and B receptor antagonists) may prove to be effective in the treatment of social phobia. The potential role and efficacy of agents that affect the tachykinins (e.g. substance P, NK A and B receptor antagonists) is unknown. There is simply not enough information available about the mechanism of these agents, although substance P is reported to be concentrated in the amygdala near the cell bodies of both dopaminergic and noradrenergic neurons (Saria, 1999; Stahl, 1999).

In addition, we acknowledge that there are some alternatives to the formulation we are advancing here. Prominent among these is the psychobiological model of personality and personality disorders proposed by Cloninger (1998, 1986). Cloninger proposes that there are seven main factors to personality: four temperaments and three character styles. Cloninger's temperamental theory proposes temperaments of harm avoidance, novelty seeking, reward dependence, and persistence.

Cloninger's (1998, 1986) model is far more ambitious than is ours. He attempts to explain the variants of personality and personality disorders. In contrast, we confine our discussion to the heterogeneous presentation of generalized social phobia. The two models are not easily translated into each other, although one key difference is that we consider generalized social phobia to be a heterogeneous condition with dysfunction in a number of systems. In contrast, Cloninger's model would apparently consider generalized social phobia to be largely a function of harm avoidance.

Summary and implications

The challenge for current treatments of social phobia is to begin to account for the complexity of the presentation of GSP, and to begin to tailor treatment appropriately. While admittedly incomplete, we believe the model we are proposing may be a useful starting place for more refined theorizing about the interrelationships of neurotransmitter functioning, personality predispositions, and psychotherapeutic interventions.

We have developed a model of social fears that incorporates work on the fear circuit described by LeDoux (1996), and is based on neuropsychological and pharmacological evidence regarding the social dimensions of affiliation and dominance, and the personality dimension of neuroticism.

Different social fears have different developmental roots, and may be based on quite different neuropsychological systems. Early developing (fearful) shyness seems conceptually related to behavioural inhibition, and may be based on LeDoux's (1996) fear circuit. These sorts of 'social novelty' fears may be best treated with exposure-based psychotherapeutic interventions, as the role of thinking may occur relatively late in the fear appraisal and response system. We speculate that norepinephrine may be the most relevant neurotransmitter, as it is associated with general fearfulness and Kagan (1989) connects norepinephrine with behavioural inhibition. Fearful shyness and behavioural inhibition are thought to be temperamental, which may make sense of the commonly reported age of onset of GSP in very early childhood (Schneier *et al.*, 1992).

Self-conscious shyness develops later in childhood and reaches its climax in early adolescence. This kind of social fear is more clearly cognitive, being characterized by feelings of self-consciousness and concern about other's perceptions of oneself. Self-conscious shyness may be amenable to more purely cognitive interventions that target distorted assumptions about what others might be thinking.

It may also be important to distinguish concerns about dominance from concerns about affiliation. If self-conscious cognitions focus on feelings of incompetence, inferiority, or assumptions about the harsh judgement, ill will, or ridicule of others, we might suspect the person is strongly oriented to social dominance. Such a person might have difficulty with eye contact, and might have difficulty in assertive interactions such as returning purchases, refusing requests, arguing with peers, and interacting with authority figures.

Many people with GSP may have difficulty with affiliation as well as with social dominance. While current treatment strategies often intervene by attempting to reduce avoidance (Gray's BI system), it might also be effective to try to increase the incentive value of social interaction (Gray's BA system). Early learning history may well have established social interaction either as a punishing experience or as both a reinforcing and a punishing experience. The former history would be best addressed by reducing avoidance, while the latter could be equally well approached by emphasizing approach motivation.

The implications for CBT treatment of this constellation of problems are clear – the therapist might be wise to restructure distorted thoughts about winning or losing arguments, and modify the core construct that interpersonal relations are hierarchically ordered and determined by power. Behavioural experiments might include disagreeing, returning purchases, or interacting with (making requests of?) employers.

The therapeutic implications of the proposed model might be further broadened with reference to the interpersonal circumplex. Therapists would be encouraged to behave in a warm way, without being too directive (dominant) or too submissive (non-directive). The therapist's interpersonal behaviour should not be contingent on the interpersonal dominance of the client at the micro level; requests for support or reassurance should be responded to in the same way as challenges or cancellations. According to our model, it would be important to emphasize affiliation in discussions with the patient in order to sensitize them to that dimension of interpersonal behaviour. Furthermore, we might emphasize rewards of interpersonal behaviour strongly, in addition to helping the client to overcome avoidance. We might think of such a patient as only weakly reward driven, so emphasizing pleasure and having fun with others may be more important than for those who genuinely enjoy affiliation.

In contrast to interpersonal concerns that seem oriented to dominance, other people with GSP seem to express their social concerns in more affiliative terms. Some people with GSP have predominant concerns about not being liked. They worry about being excluded from groups, and are very concerned about not imposing on others. We might think of this kind of behaviour as being primarily oriented to affiliation, and characterized less by weak social reward motivation but rather by high avoidance motivation. The CBT recommendations for such cases are also clear. Distorted cognitions about acceptance and interpersonal rejection would need to be challenged, and the core construct of needing to be liked by everyone would be the indirect target of change. These patients may be keenly attuned to affiliation, and might be encouraged to attend more to interpersonal dominance. The goal would be to care less about being liked. This might help to reduce avoidance motivation, as the punishment of rejection would seem less severe. Therapists might encourage their clients to take more social risks such as expressing opinions, talking about themselves, or politely disagreeing. Changes in these sorts of dominant interpersonal behaviours would be expected to have two main interpersonal effects. First, the person would be revealing more of him or herself and would therefore be less likely to get neutral interpersonal responses. There is a risk of disapproval; however, there is also a greater chance of being strongly affirmed. Second, submissive interpersonal behaviour draws dominant interpersonal behaviour from others, while dominant interpersonal behaviour evokes a much broader range of behaviour from others. The effect of this is that the full range of interpersonal behaviour is much more apparent when one's own behaviour does not tend to draw a limited set of characteristic responses from others.

Although we are tempted to draw psychopharmacological implications from our model, available drugs are not specific enough to permit this. Ideally we would like a highly selective serotonin reuptake inhibitor, a highly selective dopamine agonist, and a highly selective norepinephrine antagonist. Such drugs do not exist. Even if they did exist, the neurotransmitter systems are not independent, so serotonin-acting drugs can have downstream effects on dopamine or norepinephrine. Drawing pharmacological implications from our model awaits further validation of the model and advances in our understanding of pharmacodynamics.

Perhaps the most generative implications of our model for psychopharmacology are theoretical rather than applied. A starting place for further research might be to track change across treatment in terms of the interpersonal circumplex. We would expect SSRI administration to have an initial impact on affiliation, and a later impact on interpersonal dominance. We might also expect the addition of a stimulant to have mild dopamine agonist effects which would increase reward motivation. Such a change should be detected in self-report or informant-report ratings of extraversion, as long as such ratings were constrained to be about recent interpersonal behaviour.

In developing this model we have tried to integrate the research literature on shyness with recent research on social phobia. We have tried to account for different kinds of social fears, the developmental evidence that different fears develop at different times, and neuropsychological evidence that different fears may be subserved by different systems. While this model is likely to be incorrect in some ways and incomplete in others, we hope it can become a starting point for more complex theorizing about social phobia and its treatment. We are currently following the treatment implications of this model to see where they lead us. We hope the reader may also find this model useful when thinking about social phobia from either an applied or a theoretical perspective.

Note

1 Here we depart from Trower, Gilbert and Sherling (1990) who consider social anxiety to be primarily a product of the agonic system, and fear of strangers to be a product of the territorial breeding system. We argue, instead that the hedonic system is highly relevant for understanding social phobia, in addition to the agonic and territorial breeding systems.

References

American Psychiatric Association (1994) *Diagnostic and Statistical Manual of Mental Disorders* (4th edn), Washington, DC: American Psychiatric Association.

Asendorpf, J.B. (1989) 'Shyness as a final common pathway for two different kinds of inhibition', *Journal of Personality and Social Psychology*, 57: 481–92.

Asendorpf, J.B. (1990) 'Development of inhibition during childhood: evidence for situational specificity and a two-factor model', *Developmental Psychology*, 26: 721–30.

Asendorpf, J.B. (1993) 'Abnormal shyness in children', *Journal of Child Psychology and Psychiatry*, 34: 1069–81.

Beidel, D.C. and Turner, S.M. (1986) 'A critique of the theoretical bases of cognitive-behavioral theories and therapy', *Clinical Psychology Review*, 6: 177–97.

Berman, B.E. and Coccaro, E.F. (1998) 'Neurobiological correlates of violence: relevance to criminal responsibility', *Behavioral Science and Law*, 16(3): 303–18.

Buss, A.H. (1986) 'Two kinds of shyness', in R. Schwarzer (ed.) *Self-related Cognitions in Anxiety and Motivation*, Hillsdale, NJ: Lawrence Erlbaum Associates.

Buss, A.H. and Plomin, R. (1984) *Temperament: Early Developing Personality Traits*, Hillsdale, NJ: Lawrence Erlbaum Associates.

Chambless, D.L. and Gillis, M.M. (1993) 'Cognitive therapy of anxiety disorders', *Journal of Consulting and Clinical Psychology*, 61: 248–60.

Cheek, J.M. and Melchior, L.A. (1990) 'Shyness, self-esteem, and self-consciousness', in H. Leitenberg (ed.) *Handbook of Social and Evaluation Anxiety* (pp. 47–82), New York: Plenum Press.

Cherek, D.R., Moeller, F.G., Khan-Dawood, F., Swann, A. and Lane, S.D. (1999) 'Prolactin response to buspirone reduced in violent compared to nonviolent parolees', *Psychopharmacology*, 142: 144–8.

Cloninger, C.R. (1986) 'A unified biosocial theory of personality and its role in the development of anxiety states', *Psychiatric Development*, 3: 167–226.

Cloninger, C.R. (1998) 'The genetics and psychobiology of the seven-factor model of personality', in K.R. Silk (ed.) *Biology of Personality Disorders* (pp. 63–92), Washington, D.C.: American Psychiatric Press.

Cohen, J.D., Braver, T.S. and O'Reilly, R.C. (1996) 'A computational approach to prefrontal cortex, cognitive control and schizophrenia: recent developments and current challenges', *Philosophical Transactions of the Royal Society of London. Series B: Biological Sciences*, 351: 1515–27.

Contreras-Vidal, J.L. and Schultz, W. (1999) 'A predictive reinforcement model of dopamine neurons for learning approach behavior', *Journal of Computational Neuroscience*, 6: 191–214.

Coplan, J.D. and Lydiard, R.B. (1998) 'Brain circuits in panic disorder', *Biological Psychiatry*, 44: 1264–76.

Deakin, J.F.W. and Graeff, F.G. (1991) '5-HT and mechanisms of defense', *Journal of Psychopharmacology*, 5: 305–15.

Depue, R.A., Luciana, M., Arbisi, P., Collins, P. and Leon, A. (1994) 'Dopamine and the structure of personality: relation of agonist-induced dopamine activity to positive emotionality', *Journal of Personality and Social Psychology*, 67: 485–98.

Egelman, D.M., Person, C. and Montague, P.R. (1998) 'A computational role for dopamine delivery in human decision-making', *Journal of Cognitive Neuroscience*, 10: 623–30.

Elting, D.T. and Hope, D.A. (1995) 'Cognitive assessment', in R.G. Heimberg, M.R. Liebowitz, D.A. Hope and F.R. Schneier (eds) *Social Phobia: Diagnosis and Treatment* (pp. 232–58), New York: The Guilford Press.

Foa, E.B., Franklin, M.E., Perry, K.J. and Herbert, J.D. (1996) 'Cognitive biases in generalized social phobia', *Journal of Abnormal Psychology*, 105: 433–9.

Gilbert, P. (1989) *Human Nature and Suffering*, Brighton: Lawrence Erlbaum.

Gillman, P.K. (1998) 'Serotonin Syndrome: History and risk', *Fundamentals of Clinical Pharmacology*, 12: 482–91.

Grant, K.A., Shively, C.A., Nader, M.A., Ehrenkaufer R.L., Line, S.W., Morton, T.E., Gage, D.H. and Mach, R.H. (1998) 'Effect of social status on striatal dopamine D2 receptor binding characteristics in cynomolgus monkeys assessed with positron emission tomography', *Synapse*, 29: 80–3.

Gray, J.A. (1982) *The Neuropsychology of Anxiety*, Oxford: Oxford University Press.

Hansenne, M. and Ansseau, M. (1999) 'Harm avoidance and serotonin', *Biological Psychiatry*, 51: 77–81.

Heimberg, R.G. and Juster, H.R. (1995) 'Cognitive-behavioral treatments: literature review', in R.G Heimberg, M.R. Liebowitz, D.A Hope and F.R. Schneier (eds) *Social Phobia: Diagnosis, Assessment, and Treatment* (pp. 261–309), New York: The Guilford Press.

Heimberg, R.G., Liebowitz, M.R., Hope, D.A. and Schneier, F.R. (eds) (1995) *Social Phobia: Diagnosis, Assessment, and Treatment*, New York: The Guilford Press.

Herbert, J.D., Hope, D.A. and Bellack, A.S. (1992) 'Validity of the distinction between generalized social phobia and avoidant personality disorder', *Journal of Abnormal Psychology*, 101: 332–9.

Higley, J.D., King, S.T. Jr., Hasert, M.F., Champoux, M., Suomi, S.J. and Linnoila, M. (1996) 'Stability of interindividual differences in serotonin function and its relationship to severe aggression and competent social behavior in rhesus macaque females', *Neuropsychopharmacology*, 14: 67–76.

Hyman, S.E. (1998) 'Brain neurocircuitry of anxiety and fear: implications for clinical research and practice', *Biological Psychiatry*, 44: 1201–3.

Jones, W.H., Briggs, S.R. and Smith, T.G. (1986) 'Shyness: conceptualization and measurement', *Journal of Personality and Social Psychology*, 51: 629–39.

Jones, W.H., Cheek, J.M. and Briggs, S.R. (eds) (1986) *Shyness: Perspectives on Research and Treatment*, New York: Plenum Press.

Kagan, J. (1989) 'The concept of behavioral inhibition to the familiar', in J.S. Reznick (ed.) *Perspectives on Behavioral Inhibition* (pp. 1–23), Chicago: University of Chicago Press.

Kagan, J., Reznick, J.S. and Snidman, N. (1988) 'Biological bases of childhood shyness', *Science*, 240: 167–71.

Kiesler, D.J. (1983) 'The 1982 interpersonal circle: a taxonomy for complementarity in human transactions', *Psychological Review*, 90: 185–214.

Knutson, B., Wolkowitz, O.M., Cole, S.W., Chan, T., Moore, E.A., Johnson, R.C., Terpstra, J., Turner, R.A. and Reus, V.I. (1998) 'Selective alteration of personality and social behavior by serotonergic intervention', *American Journal of Psychiatry*, 155: 373–9.

Koob, G.F. (1996) 'Hedonic valence, dopamine and motivation', *Molecular Psychiatry*, 1: 186–9.

Koob, G.F. (1999) 'Corticotropin-releasing factor, norepinephrine, and stress', *Biological Psychiatry*, 46: 1167–80.

Leary, T. (1957) *Interpersonal Diagnosis in Personality: A Functional Theory and Methodology for Personality Evaluation*, New York: Ronald Press.

LeDoux, J. (1996) *The Emotional Brain*, New York: Simon & Schuster.

LeDoux, J. (1998) 'Fear and the brain: where have we been, and where are we going?' *Biological Psychiatry*, 44: 1229–38.

McCrae, R.R. and Costa, P.T., Jr. (1989) 'The structure of interpersonal traits: Wiggins' circumplex and the five-factor model', *Journal of Personality and Social Psychology*, 56: 586–95.

Moffitt, T.E., Brammer, G.L., Caspi, A., Fawcett, J.P., Raleigh, M., Yuwiler, A. and Silva, P. (1998) 'Whole blood serotonin relates to violence in an epidemiological study', *Biological Psychiatry*, 43: 446–57.

Nutt, D.J., Bell, C.J. and Malizia, A.L. (1998) 'Brain mechanisms of social anxiety disorder', *Journal of Clinical Psychiatry*, 59 (Suppl 17): 4–11.

Raleigh, M.J., Brammer, G.L., McGuire, M.T. and Yuwiler, A. (1985) 'Dominant social status facilitates the behavioral effects of serotonergic agonists', *Brain Research*, 348: 274–82.

Raleigh, M.J., Brammer, G.L., Yuwiler, A., Flannery, J.W., McGuire, M.T. and Geller, E. (1980) 'Serotonergic influences on the social behavior of vervet monkeys (Cercopithecus aethiops sabaeus)', *Experimental Neurology*, 68: 322–34.

Raleigh, M.J., McGuire, M.T., Brammer, G.L., Pollack, D.B. and Yuwiler, A. (1991) 'Serotonergic mechanisms promote dominance acquisition in adult male vervet monkeys', *Brain Research*, 559: 181–90.

Rapee, R.M. (1995) 'Descriptive psychopathology of social phobia', in R.G. Heimberg, M.R. Liebowitz, D.A. Hope and F.R. Schneier (eds) *Social Phobia: Diagnosis and Treatment* (pp. 41–66), New York: The Guilford Press.

Ressler, K.J. and Nemeroff, C.B. (1999) 'Role of norepinephrine in the pathophysiology and treatment of mood disorders', *Biological Psychiatry*, 46: 1219–33.

Rosen, J.B. and Schulkin, J. (1998) 'From normal fear to pathological anxiety', *Psychological Review*, 105: 325–50.

Saria, A. (1999) 'The Tachykinin NK_1 receptor in the brain: pharmacology and putative functions', *European Journal of Pharmacology*, 375: 51–60.

Schatzberg, A.F. (1998) 'Noradrenergic versus serotonergic antidepressants: predictions of treatment response', *Journal of Clinical Psychiatry*, 59, Supplement 14: 15–18.

Schneier, F.R., Johnson, J., Hornig, C.D., Liebowitz, M.R. and Weissman, M.M. (1992) 'Social phobia: comorbidity and morbidity in an epidemiological sample', *Archives of General Psychiatry*, 49: 282–8.

Schneier, F.R., Liebowitz, M.R., Abi-Dargham, A., Zea-Ponce, Y., Lin, S.-H. and Laruelle, M. (2000) 'Low dopamine D_2 receptor binding potential in social phobia', *American Journal of Psychiatry*, 157, 457–9.

Schultz, W. (1998) 'Predictive reward signal of dopamine neurons', *Journal of Neurophysiology*, 80: 1–27.

Seligman, M.E.P. (1971) 'Phobias and preparedness', *Behavior Therapy*, 2: 307–20.

Soldz, S., Budman, S., Demby, A. and Merry, J. (1993) 'Representation of personality disorders in circumplex and five-factor space: explorations with a clinical sample', *Psychological Assessment*, 5: 41–52.

Spigset, O. (1999) 'Adverse reactions of selective serotonin reuptake inhibitors: reports from a spontaneous reporting system', *Drug Safety*, 20: 277–87.

Stahl, S.M. (1999) 'Peptides and psychiatry part 3: substance P and serendipity: novel psychotropics are a possibility', *Journal of Clinical Psychiatry*, 60: 140–1.

Stein, M.B. (1998) 'Neurobiology of social phobia', *Biological Psychiatry*, 44: 1277–85.

Suarez, E.C., Kuhn, C.M., Schanberg, S.M., Williams, R.B. and Zimmerman, E.A. (1998) 'Neuroendocrine, cardiovascular, and emotional responses of hostile men: the role of interpersonal challenge', *Psychosomatic Medicine*, 60: 78–88.

Sweet, A.A. and Loizeaux, A.L. (1991) 'Behavioral and cognitive treatment methods: a critical comparative review', *Journal of Behavioral Therapy and Experimental Psychiatry*, 22: 159–85.

Tancer, M.E., Mailman, R.B., Stein, M.B., Mason, G.A., Carson, S.W. and Golden, R.N. (1994/1995) 'Neuroendocrine responsivity to monoaminergic system probes in generalized social phobia', *Anxiety*, 1: 216–23.

Taylor, S. (1996) 'Meta-analysis of cognitive-behavioral treatments for social phobia', *Journal of Behavioral Therapy and Experimental Psychiatry*, 27: 1–9.

Tiihonen J., Kuikka, J. and Bergstrom, K. (1997) 'Dopamine reuptake site densities in patients with social phobia', *American Journal of Psychiatry*, 154: 239–42.

Trapnell, P.D. and Wiggins, J.S. (1990) 'Extension of the Interpersonal Adjective Scales to include the Big Five Dimensions of Personality', *Journal of Personality and Social Psychology*, 59: 781–90.

Trower, P., Gilbert, P. and Sherling, G. (1990) 'Social anxiety, evolution, and self-presentation: an interdisciplinary perspective', in H. Leitenberg (ed.) *Handbook of Social and Evaluation Anxiety*, 11–45, New York: Plenum Press.

Turner, S.M., Beidel, D.C. and Townsley, R.M. (1990) 'Social phobia: relationship to shyness', *Behavioral Research and Therapy*, 28: 497–505.

Turner, S.M., Beidel, D.C. and Townsley, R.M. (1992) 'Social phobia: a comparison of specific and generalized subtypes and avoidant personality disorder', *Journal of Abnormal Psychology*, 101: 326–34.

Turner, S.M., Beidel, D.C., Dancu, C.V. and Keys, D.J. (1986) 'Psychopathology of social phobia and comparison to avoidant personality disorder', *Journal of Abnormal Psychology*, 95: 389–94.

Van Ameringen, M., Mancini, C., Farvolden, P. and Oakman, J.M. (1999) 'Pharmacotherapy of social phobia: what works, what might work and what doesn't work at all', *CNS Spectrums*, 4 (11): 61–8.

Van Ameringen, M., Mancini, C., Oakman, J.M. and Farvolden, P. (1999) 'Selective serotonin reuptake inhibitors in the treatment of social phobia: the emerging gold standard', *CNS Drugs*, 11: 307–15.

Westergaard, G.C., Mehlman, P.T., Suomi, S.J. and Higley, J.D. (1999) 'CSF 5-HIAA and aggression in female macaque monkeys: species and interindividual differences', *Psychopharmacology*, 146: 440–6.

Wiggins, J.S. (1982) 'Circumplex models of interpersonal behavior in clinical psychology', in P. Kendall and J. Butcher (eds) *Handbook of Research Methods in Clinical Psychology*, 183–221, New York: Wiley.

Index